Summoning the Mountains

WITHDRAWN

pilgrimage into forty

AMY ALLEN

Summoning the Mountains: Pilgrimage Into Forty
Amy Allen

Copyright © 2012 Amy Allen. All rights reserved.

Print Edition ISBN: 9781936214839
Library of Congress Control Number: 2012943495

Quote pg. 66 from "The Miracle of Mindfulness" by Thich Nhat Hanh, Copyright © 1975, 1976 by Thich Nhat Hanh

Preface and English Translation Copyright © 1975, 1976, 1987 by Mobi Ho, Reprinted by permission of Beacon Press, Boston

Quote pg. 228 from *Mastery* by George Leonard, Reprinted with permission from Penguin Books

Quote pg. 280 from *A Season on the Appalachian Trail* by Lynn Setzer, Reprinted with permission of Menasha Ridge Press

Author photo: Charles Hodges

† indicates photograph displayed at:
www.facebook.com/SummoningtheMountains/photos_stream

Published by Saille Productions, a Wyatt-MacKenzie Imprint
saille@wyattmackenzie.com

www.amyallenbooks.com

It is solved by walking.

~Saint Augustine~

Contents

The pale line that divides wisdom from insanity grows fainter as we age, or perhaps we no longer need lines to divide the two for we have come to recognize they are one in the same. My hands beneath the pool surface glide forward, pull back, spearing the center of the black line that waves up from the bottom. How exactly does my ability to stay centered on this line relate to my ability to stay centered in my life? Musing, my mind enters the space between breaths that comes somewhere after the first few yards of each lap. I come to the pool wall, turn and push off. My hands come to center and out again, center and out, breathe in, breathe out. There is a rhythmic calm to the breast stroke that has soothed the ache in my heart all these months. Looking back from where I am now, I recognize this calm as a place of truth, a constant—that being the source of its power. Repeatedly, I have dragged my weary body and restless mind to the gym to swim laps. Wall; turn. The quest to find peace in my heart led to this place in my mind, this place of meditative calm where the rhythm of breath is timed by water and motion, blending all three into synchronistic harmony. Here I have embraced the pain of loss as I have immersed myself in the waters of emotion, pale blue water.

I have confronted my fear of losing love as I have dismantled my fear of water, one breath at a time.

Unfolding

As a 39-year-old Gemini, the mother of two teenage boys, I have toiled for the last 10 years at a thankless office job for a pittance in the shadow of corporate profit-mongering. I've been an hourly slave, whose college degree meant nothing. Any delusions of security and financial stability have faded as the cost of insurance premiums out-stripped any raise scrapped from the inner circles of power and overtime ended with recession. Following a difficult divorce, over the last two years I have instilled more changes in my life than I could have ever thought was possible, or needed, and found that I have so much more to go. A catalyst for making these changes was fear; I was afraid of living without love, afraid of still loving. This fear sent me on a personal quest. What specifically did I not have, that I thought I should have, that caused such feelings of unworthiness? I pulled out every stop in this search. I went to conferences, wrote volumes, started projects, took on community service, learned CPR, started swimming three times a week, ran a mile a day, taught classes and volunteered. When quite on a whim I learned to fly a plane, the searching stopped, and I found equilibrium again. Finally, I could see clearly. Somewhere over Transylvania County I realized I had been suffocating in responsibility ever since the children were born. As a stay-at-home mother, I was alone most of the time while Adam's job kept him out of town three or four days a week. When the children grew older, I became a full-time student and took a part-time job in addition to mothering. And now, for the past six years, I have worked full-time and been a single-mom, burning the candle at both ends. The free spirit of my early twenties has all but disappeared.

Next summer, I will turn 40. Before me, has come a long line of early deaths in my biological family. Contrarily, my adopted family line tends to breed folks who live forever. Science has yet to settle the nature versus nurture debate. I'd like to side with the nurture part here; however, biology is a loud and clear voice in these days of genetics. The decision to hike the Appalachian Trail is a home-coming of sorts, something I want to do before the hour grows too late. When I was a child, mysterious, winding footpaths beckoned invitingly, disappearing into forests on the side of the road as our car whizzed past. I was certainly not allowed to follow any mysterious, dark paths for something might "happen". And so, as a young adult, I was drawn to a life of risky behaviors and great adventures to counter this very loved, but sheltered, childhood. I'm merely compounding that theme now as a mature adult, I suppose—revisiting an old method with new perspective.

My two sons are Joseph, who will be turning 16 while I am hiking, and Grayson, who is solidly 13 during this fleeting moment in time. Amazingly gracious and unceasingly delightful, they are my sunshine, my sorrow, my joy, and all of my fears. When I first seriously began to consider making this hike happen right now, I asked both boys for their thoughts about my leaving for six months. Specifically, I wanted to know whether they would feel I was abandoning them. When I heard their reply, I saw years of unconventional parenting paying out in gold. They both agreed, "No, Mom! You would not be abandoning us; you would be teaching us to follow our dreams." The boys gave me the trail name, Willow, after the willows in our front yard and the willow mural painted on my bedroom wall. In Gaelic lore, the willow represents both the nimble maiden and the weathered crone. It is known for its affinity for water, its feminine grace and its ability to relieve pain. I can only hope to live up to their expectations.

The Appalachian Trail, for those of you who do not know, is a footpath that stretches 2175 miles from Georgia to Maine. It runs the length of ridgelines through the Appalachian mountain range and up through the Great Valley of the Appalachians. Its lowest point is 124 feet above sea level near the Hudson River in New York; then, it climbs the Green Mountains of Vermont to the White Mountains of New Hampshire, ending dramatically in Maine on Mount Katahdin at 5267 feet above sea level. The highest point along the trail is Clingman's Dome, North Carolina in the Great Smokies National Park at 6643 feet. Over 500 miles of the Trail are in Virginia. Through more populated areas the trail corridor is only a few hundred feet wide in some places. Benton McKaye first envisioned the project in 1921 as a trail that connected ridge-top communities of libraries, craft centers and hostels where tired urban souls could come for renewal in nature. In 1930, Myron Avery took over the development and mapped out the route, organizing volunteer crews, and supervising construction of hundreds of miles trail. This undertaking was formally completed on August 14, 1937.

What do all these facts actually say, though, about the Appalachian Trail? What is the AT, really? Today, the 2175 miles of trail are maintained by the National Park Service and by hundreds of volunteers coordinated by the Appalachian Trail Conservancy. It remains as an ongoing effort of a group of dedicated people who tirelessly monitor changes in government policies regarding our national wild places and who go to bat for each and every acre that is threatened by the encroachment of big business or urban sprawl. And, the Appalachian Trail has become a culture all its own.

Thru-hiking the AT means different things to different people. Dan Bruce, author of "The Thru-Hiker's Handbook", defines a thru-hiker as "a person who is currently attempting to become a 2000-miler in a single continuous journey by putting on a backpack, leaving from one terminus of the Trail and hiking essentially unassisted to the other terminus". There are variations on this theme which is a source of great debate within the hiking community. Some hikers hike sections of the AT each year, eventually completing the whole 2000 miles, one section at a time. These are known as 'section-hikers'. Some hikers carry packs part of the way, but have their packs shuttled by vehicle for them when they reach more difficult areas of the Trail, a practice known as 'slack-packing'. Some hikers focus on putting in long days and big miles, earning the title of 'power-hiker'. Still others are known as 'purists', making a point to hike every mile of the official, white-blazed Trail. A 'blue-blazer' is a hiker who substitutes a section of blue-blazed trail for a white-blazed section between two points on the Trail. Blue-blazed trails often take the easy way around obstacles rather than over them. These variations serve as trail metaphors for the various approaches we all have to tackling life.

As a child I had the fortune of living on a dead-end road in a quiet neighborhood next to a great, dark wood. Gresham Woods was really just a hundred acres of yet to be developed, second-growth, Virginia forest on the outskirts of Richmond. But, to us kids, it was the great forest in all our fairytales and held unimaginable secrets. I still remember my first venture down the trail into those woods alone, heedless of parental direction to the contrary. I remember the enormity of the stately oaks and the silence. The trail glowed an eerie white where the sandy soil of Virginia lowlands peeked from the parted carpet of leaves. And, I remember the way that path snaked away before me, beckoning me around each curve, only to lead away again around another, more intriguing, curve up ahead. Spirits whispered from all sides, and sounds I had never heard before came from the soaring canopy above. Possibility was breathing all around me, and my hypersensitive body soaked in this energy field knowing somehow that I had found THE something no one else knew about. When I told my friends I had gone into Gresham's, they were shocked, awed, frightened for my safety and did their best to instill fear in me again. They recounted stories of children being abducted from those woods and found dead, months later. Supposedly, there was a house deep in the forest where people did drugs, and these people had no care for snooping children. Though these stories gave me pause, they did not stop my occasional foray back to see the tall oaks and watch the scampering chipmunks. I could not understand how something I found to be so magical could be so insignificant to others.

In college, following the guidance of Self Realization guru, Yogananda, I renounced worldly possessions and lived out of my backpack. I made a vow of celibacy and gave up meat. I built a debris hut on the ridgeline below Howard's Knob in Boone, North Carolina, and I learned to walk through the woods in the dark simply by the way the path felt beneath my feet. Every evening, I left campus and carried a backpack up the mountainside to sleep in the woods. I lived this way for almost a year, eventually graduating to the relative comforts of living in a canvas tipi with Adam.

Over time, I diverged from Yogananda's path, moving on to explore Native American spirituality and Old World paganism. Adam and I had been an item since I was 19, a tumultuous and torrid affair from the beginning. We married when I was 23. After the children were born, I continued a close relationship with the outdoors, and Adam and I backpacked with the boys for the first few years. We met up with college friends and organized summer gatherings in Pisgah National Forest, sometimes camping for a week at a time. But then, Adam took a job working in a wilderness program for the state, and I found myself home alone with our children four days of every week. I could not carry all the gear necessary for three people to go backpacking, so the children and I stopped going. As my responsibilities increased, my world view narrowed. When Adam was not at work, he wanted to enjoy the comforts of home with his family, not schlep a wife and two kids back out into the woods. My backpacking days ended so quietly that no one really noticed, not even me.

After our divorce, I found the Kelty pack that had served for so many miles years before. It was completely covered in mold from being stored in the basement. I allowed indignant rage to take over as I examined the damaged pack, and in a fit of martyrdom decided that I would never be backpacking again, so I might as well throw the pack away. Over the course of the next few years, I convinced myself that I had never liked backpacking anyway, a way of licking the wound so it would heal.

Late summer of 2004, while vacationing at the beach for a couple of days, I went hang-gliding. When the tow plane cut loose, the glider dropped away, and the wind across the wings was the only sound. The landscape suddenly seemed brighter and clearer; colors were more vivid, and it seemed I could see forever. An epiphany occurred. Somehow, I remembered this feeling. This was what it meant to be alive! This was ME! This made me HAPPY! I felt truly alive for the first time in years. A few weeks later, while on a business flight, I thought about the pilot of the plane as I looked out the window over the cloudscape at cruising altitude. I decided to learn to fly an airplane so I could have more of this in my life.

The same way I booked the hang-gliding, I booked a flight instructor—just picked up the phone and told them what I wanted to do. I flew a Cessna 152 for about a year. I never finished the hours required to get a pilot's license, but I did reach the point where I could fly solo. Several sunny afternoons, I flew over Hickory Nut Gorge at Lake Lure, North Carolina. It was during one of these flights I came to understand that to grow

beyond the known requires risk, but that most importantly, at the heart of risk lies opportunity. If I could
fly this plane, then I could pursue any dream, no
matter how seemingly elusive. Just as Gresham's forest
of my childhood held the zero point field of possibility,
somehow it really was possible for me to leave home
for six months to chase this lifelong dream of hiking
the Appalachian Trail.

❀ ❀ ❀

N O V E M B E R   2 0 0 5

Slowly, some things are falling away that perhaps
should have fallen away long before now. I may have
underestimated the power of what hiking the AT will
do to my life. This process of planning requires the
elimination of things that once served but are no longer
needed. I find that I am mourning the loss of the person
that always does what is expected by others, the one
who always comes through. Many details are becoming
clearer as I grow into a new way of thinking. The old,
"super-girl", tomboy role of my childhood, invented
to compete with the boys in my neighborhood, became
the real thing in super-mom of today, a role that is
slowly destroying me. Now, I am learning to accept my
many failures and hold them dear without judging
myself for not continuing to be the perfectionist of
bygone days. If I can fully embrace the person that has
been trapped within everyone's expectations, impris-
oned within the script, then perhaps I will regain that
21-year-old spirit that once sought adventure. Ulti-
mately, I hope to lose the fear of who I really am, and
be simply that, and be happy.

My mind races these nights looking for tasks left

incomplete and finding none, looking for projects to start and finding only my life facing me. I feel maturity settling in, weighing my flightiness down. It is strange to tick off major obstacles from the lists and narrow the gap between a dream of the future and the reality of the Now. I feel a sense of vague desperation as the gap begins to close. Ever so slowly, I am left facing only me. No more lists, no more preparation, no more things to discard or pack away, only me—the one real item this trip requires—the reason, the goal and the "mystery" of the trip.

DECEMBER 14

This past weekend, Dad came for a visit. During our time together, some rather quantum occurrences brought to mind the question of whether time is actually concentric circles that share points along various planes rather than being chronologically linear. My father's reality has been quite fear-based for most of the time I've known him. He has this knack for coming up with every conceivable "what if" before you can possibly begin to fabricate a relatively believable answer, and so you are left standing before him stuttering and shuffling your feet and questioning your own resolve over your risky proposal in the first place. But recently, my close college friend, John had gently reprimanded me for not having told my father of my hiking plans already. He reminded me that Dad deserves more respect for his role as my father than I was giving him by being so secretive and fearful. His nudge made me realize that I will be "daddy's little girl" as long as I agree to play the role of "daddy's little girl". If I want my father's perception of me to grow as I have grown, I must continually reinvent my relationship with him and be open to the changes maturity has to offer in that aspect of my life as well. Thank you, Johnny Be. Hmmm....ok, so I was marveling at quantum events.

I invited my father to come visit, even though I had no intention of telling him anything face to face. I had a nice, neat plan to write him a letter. I would include my mail drop schedule, mileage chart, resources list, the places-I'm-staying list (complete with phone numbers), and have all his "what ifs" answered before I ever opened that can of worms. Dad's visiting; we're at the soccer game, and I introduced him to a family friend. The first words out of the friend's mouth are "so, are you going to be hiking any of the Appalachian Trail with Amy?" My father, bless his soul, didn't even blink. I was busy collecting my jaw from the floor and reigning in racing thoughts when Dad said "no, not likely, but I did meet a man once when I was fishing who was hiking the whole trail." So, the friend says, "Well, that's going to be Amy here pretty soon!" Luckily, the atmosphere of an indoor soccer center amidst a team of teenage boys is rather conducive toward distractions being turned into great escapes. We left soon thereafter. Dad didn't mention it at all, and I don't even think he really put it all together at that point (quantum event number one survived).

All that night we talked about various things, and nothing was mentioned. We had a good visit. The next morning, over coffee, Dad said, "so what did you want to talk to me about?" (quantum event two) "Did I want to talk to you about something?" "That's why you wanted me to come down isn't it?" "well, no but..." By this time, I was laughing—it was all so ridiculous, me playing this game. So, I told him...after a long prelude regarding comfort levels of risk and other procrastination techniques.

In all honesty, the things Dad wanted me to consider were quite valid points. His main concern was for my children and that their needs continue to be met in my absence. I have my own reservations surrounding this issue, and it's one I struggle with as a mother, this letting go and allowing their father, my ex-husband, to fill this place. He asked if I have a will, a rather morbid item on my to-do lists that keeps recycling itself and popping up undone for ages.

Mom sent a holiday card. It is a picture of a woman in a long black wool coat and a hat and gloves, in the woods in the snow. The wind is blowing snow fiercely, and her coattails are flapping wildly all about her. She has her arms raised at quite happenstance, odd angles as she fends off the gale.[†] It's positively delightful.

NEW YEAR'S EVE 2005

In this time of letting go of the past year, I find myself reminiscing about my dearest friend and companion, my dog, Blaze.

A huge part of reaching for one's dreams seems to involve a process of purging the things that hold us in one place—the aspects of ourselves that keep us from reaching our full potential and that cement us in the very past from which we seek to evolve. This process is often the stumbling block that many of us cannot seem to get over for there is much fear involved in letting go of our possessions, our past, our familiarities, our habits, our comforts, and our routines. Something as simple as getting rid of clothing that we never wear can be an issue—the voice inside your head saying, "but I might need that someday." Or, a bag of yarn that was going to become an afghan—do we censor our potential or embrace our limitations when we move beyond the long unrealized small goals in order to reach for the larger goal? Is there a difference? What about quitting a job that has fed and housed my family for seven years? It has not fed my spirit, but it has fed other aspects of my life, providing me with the money for a beautiful home, food, entertainment, massages, airplane rentals, gasoline, and the myriads of things that go into creating comfort and satisfaction. How exactly do I acknowledge all of my job's contributions to my life and simultaneously walk away from it, saying that it isn't for me anymore? This ambivalence about reaching for the larger goal has been where my thoughts reside in the past two weeks of little time off and late nights at the office. It is similar to my grieving process over my dog, Blaze.

Our animals are often the manifestations of the pulse of our lives. Blaze was almost 12 years old this October when he died. He was a mixed breed Dalmatian/Golden Retriever. There was the constant worry in my mind over what I would do with Blaze while I was hiking. He was suffering from old injuries and would not be able to make such a trek, though he had hiked hundreds of miles with us during his lifetime. I did not want to take him, but I did not want to leave him with anyone else either. Blaze had never left my side in those 12 years. He was my constant companion, following me from room to room in the house. He was my guardian against fear and loneliness. I had gotten Blaze when I was a new mother, living alone in our new house every week while my husband was gone three to four days a week with his job. His presence distracted me from noises outside the house at night and the worry that I was alone with two babies. He was always cheerful and never seemed to ask anything more of me besides my companionship. I was grateful to him for his patience and his tolerance of trying circum-stances. (Full-time mothering of babies two years apart was often trying.) He had been in serious pain off and on for several years, and his hip would pop out of joint once in awhile, or his legs would just give way on him. I kept him as spry as possible with weekly short hikes and glucosamine and vitamins. He was beautiful and shiny and black even as he aged. How could I just leave him for six months? He would not understand where I had gone and would worry until I returned, possibly dying while I was away. These concerns ate at my resolve.

As his health deteriorated, we hiked less often. He had good days and bad days. Sometimes he was visibly depressed, and other times he seemed quite content. I began to send him releasing thoughts and reassure him that I would be ok, that he could leave when it was his time. We took him with us to the top of Table Rock one gorgeous day in October. He walked slowly, hanging back and staying right by my side all the way up even though Adam had his leash and was walking in front of me. At the top, he gazed out over the horizon, taking in the 360, something he usually ignored, after all, he was a dog. I thought then that was strange for him to notice the view and to appear so pensive.

Blaze died that night of bloat. He accepted the pain as he had all things in our lives together, with one of his long groaning sighs, as he lay down. We had to take him to the emergency room, and euthanize him, or his death would have been long and excruciating as his organs shut down one by one. My family left me alone with him as he departed. He died with his head in my lap, as he had spent so many evenings in our time together throughout the years. I was glad that I had told him the things I wanted to tell him all along and not waited until now. I marveled at life and all that it contains. The ultimate letting go was upon me, readying me for my journey. Blaze was leaving me, telling me that it was time, that his work was done here, and that I had nothing left to fear, his life a manifestation of the journey I had made to overcome fear and to reach my potential. He had walked me through the door, and now he was returning to the One. I find myself poised on the precipice, just as he was, ambivalence over all I am letting go coursing through my mind; I believe through my commitment to the trail, I honor Blaze, as he leads the way into the unknown.

❀ ❀ ❀

2 0 0 6

Email from my friend John, affectionately known as Johnny Be:

> Sounds to me like you are getting your gear squared away and your base weight of 24 lbs sounds great. I had a call from Uncle Wally on New Years Eve and we talked about trying to link up to hike a portion of the trail with you somewhere on the NC, TN, or VA leg of the journey. We were envisioning how you would be breezing along with your squared away thirty five to forty lbs while we would both be carrying about eighty lbs and carrying a Walmart bag in each hand...also, I would be wearing a cast iron skillet for a hat and Walter would be balancing a watermelon on his head! We got a good laugh out of that...even though it is probably TRUE!

J A N U A R Y   9

At Joseph's high school dance performance, I sat in the audience waiting for the show to begin; some of his girlfriends came from across the auditorium to sit with Grayson and me. I was flattered. The show was "awesome", to coin a teen expression, and it is always a high for me to see my sons in their element, laughing and loving life.

The last dance was complete with break dancing, posturing and strutting, and girls gyrating in the background. In one number, Joseph did a head stand, spinning around on his head in sync with another of his buddies. One dance was a "gangsta" set, and another had an Eastern feel with yoga poses and flowing music. One was performed by a young woman who had been attending this high school earlier in the year, but she had been advanced to the School of the Arts in Winston Salem. She had come back at the bidding of the dance teacher to perform for this show.

Adolescent energy is contagious and fun. Everything is new and exciting to them, and they are so in the Now, without even trying—no Eckhart Tolle calendars needed. Perhaps it is a bit of this gift I would like back, by hiking off into the woods for six months. Tonight it was Adam, their father, who missed out on yet another wonderful first in their lives; while I am gone, he will have the opportunity to be there for things I will miss. The hard realization of just how much I will miss them sets in; I wont have anyone to argue with over who gets to use the computer, no one to use up all my cell minutes, or take my car keys as I reach for them, and no one to laugh at my grains of wisdom that coagulate into huge, cumbersome rocks late at night when I am tired.

Last Wednesday, I managed to squeeze in a training hike. It was getting dark, and I was quite frustrated that time had run out; I'd spent too many hours at work in front of the computer. The boys were at Adam's for the night. As I stirred a dehydrated meal on the stove, trying out the vegetarian "Scrambled Eggs & Bac-un", I decided to hike despite the darkness. I used to love hiking in the dark years ago when I lived out of my pack. I remembered walking up Howard's Knob each night in pitch darkness where you couldn't see your hand before your face, keeping my feet on the trail by feel. I packed up without the usual sense of hurry that has come to accompany almost everything I do (another habit I aim to shed) and headed out to a local trail with a nice climb.

As I donned my pack and headed up the trail, the quarter moon shone so brightly, low in the crystal clear winter sky, that I took off the headlamp and put it in my pocket. The mountain warmed me quickly, and I shed a layer. Once at the top, looking down on the valley where my house was nestled amongst the lights, I soaked up the darkness of the winter moon set, grateful for the ribbons of forest that lace our communities and run the ridgelines. I felt as if I were part of a great reverse contrast painting, inside the dark spaces; as Carlos Castaneda learned from Don Juan, the true art of "seeing" is to truly see those spaces in between.

I found the surface of my desk after a 12 hour day that began with introducing myself to a classroom full of people at the chipper hour of 7am. Once at the surface, I think there's supposed to be something about breathing....

J A N U A R Y   1 7

Saturday brought three inches of snow. I packed up and headed out in it first thing Saturday morning while the storm was still in its peak. It was wonderful to be in the snow with the promise of a warm house to go home to. It silenced the yammering noise of my thoughts.

I am hoping Mom can be convinced to send me home-baked zucchini bread along the trail. I've never forgotten the delicacy of her zucchini bread she used to mail in care packages when I was in college. I'm sure that along about Pennsylvania such a delicacy will be as precious as gold.

Dad called. He received the packet of AT information that I mailed to him. He's making a list. Hmmm, sound familiar? He's making a list of questions. Supposedly this list of questions is so long, that he is going to have to deliver it to me in person. He would not ask them to me on the phone. Great. But, true to form, he has already bought two books about the Appalachian Trail. He could tell me the trail passes the historical marker honoring Audie Murphy, the most-decorated WWII soldier, and he knew how many miles of trail were in Virginia. He had purchased special flashlights that shake up to activate the charge so they will light. He had found the best deals on calling cards and wants to send me some. He wants to donate some money to my cause... and do I have all my gear, yet? He just cant resist being interested in something that bears such similarity to the Lewis & Clark expeditions that he so reveres. I think he might be excited about this after all.

F E B R U A R Y

The heat is on now between the boys and me as the time grows nearer for my departure. My "almost-16" year old's attitude is deteriorating with the speed of hormonal light. One day he's on my lap, and the next day he's yelling that he's glad I'm leaving. In the awareness of our pending separation, I suppose I'm mothering a little too much. I tend to give both boys a lot of space in general, but it seems the two of us are on some strange, uncomfortable edge. Tonight, he injured his ankle playing soccer, the same ankle he was on crutches for about a month ago. My concern and disappointment when he continued to play on it was too much, and he got quite snappy with me, causing me in turn to become seriously MAD at him. Meanwhile, the 13-year-old silently watches with a maddening smirk on his face. Sound familiar, anyone? Even so, while I'm fuming mad, I'm thinking of what a great soccer player Joseph is, and how much I will miss seeing him play while I am gone. I am thinking about how my concern goes further than his—he thinks of the next period in this game while I am thinking of his ankles holding out for college leagues.

There is a growing pile of boxes in my living room. I still do not have a renter. Adam tells me that finding a renter is not going to be a problem, and for me not to worry. I worry anyway. If I do not rent my house out while I am gone, there will be a serious money shortage while I make house payments during six months of unemployment. However, not finding a renter will not stop this trip from happening.

There is still much to do before I leave, but my mind has already bailed on the effects of everyday life and is off somewhere chasing white blazes. I am having dreams about mountain lions—good dreams about mountain lions; the big cats are symbolic of intense focus and courage. I am battling great apprehension, and yet am more confident than I have ever been. My job is asking more than ever before, and somehow I am delivering. It helps to know that the job is now finite. The dissatisfaction and difficulties seem smaller now; the end of this particular life assignment is within sight, and the beginning of a great adventure calls. It's akin to the feeling of waking up on Saturday morning as a child knowing you have the whole weekend before you, or the pure joy of leaving school on the last day for the summer.

I purchased a full supply of dehydrated meals from maryjanesfarm.com: 188 breakfasts, 190-something dinners, 50 servings of mashed potatoes, 87 servings of salsa, and 110 breads for $715 plus shipping. Shipping was unbelievably high. And then, I have to pay again to ship it to myself along the way, so the less than $2/serving turns out to be more like $3/serving. I'm at peace with the food thing though, finally. I'm done. Whatever else I want to eat, I will purchase along the way. Mary Jane's meals comes in three pound bulk bags, which I will divide into serving size Ziploc bags. Fun stuff! Organic. Vegetarian. Ethnic meals. Some of their stuff, I don't like at all. The meals that I do like, I really like.

I have dehydrated bacon and hamburger to add to some meals. There are also dehydrated apples from Mom, gorp mixes, and homemade hot chocolate mix laced with protein powder. I found a great deal on candy bars, but it will be a miracle if the boys and Adam don't eat them before they make it into the mail drop boxes.

T H E   P A C K   S T O R Y

For over six months, I've waited for the 2006 Osprey brand packs to come out. When their new catalog arrived in the mail I was astonished by the specs. The packs were heavier this year. Betrayed. The next weekend Adam and I went to Frugal Backpacker and took all my gear. We packed and unpacked and repacked several of last year's Ospreys, and I also tried a Dana brand Bridger. The Dana had some features that I really liked. I bought the Dana.

Buying something impulsively after researching, waiting for, and planning on something else felt like selling out to the "woman changing her mind" prerogative. I spent the first two days in shock. By the third day, I was second guessing my decision. By the next weekend, I was back at the store asking them to take it back. The salesperson was very understanding about me wanting to try the 2006 Osprey before finalizing my decision. I kept the Dana with the agreement that he would give me store credit toward the Osprey if I liked it better once it came in.

The itch is getting to me, and I had to buy a pack, no matter what, get it on my back and play. Which I did... over and over again. Pack the pack this way, put it on, take it off. Pack the pack this other way, put it on, take it off. Change this around, move this, put it on, take it off. I like the Dana. I like it a lot. It has a really different kind of hip belt that has cutouts where my hip bones are. There's nothing there to create those lovely bruises that usually color my hips after the first day with a pack on. But, the moldable hip belt on the Ospreys was the whole reason I was waiting for the 2006 models to arrive.

On Tuesday, Feb 21st, I packed up the Dana and

took it back to Diamond Brand. Darren, who I had bothered for two months over the phone, packed the Osprey and fitted it for me. It was perfect! I was relieved that there was a marked difference between the way the Osprey and the Dana carried. I was afraid that they would be so similar that I would again be in a quandary, but there was no question. The Osprey felt 100% better. I found by having the Dana at home, and having time to play with packing and re-packing it, that it was very sensitive to weight distribution. If I got the distribution just so, then the pack felt great, but if I was off by just a little, then the weight pulled me backwards and didn't center on my hips. The Osprey has two metal stays, one going down each side of the back of the pack. This gives it more stability, more like an external frame pack, which is what I'm used to. I don't have to do that weird dance to get the damn thing on like I was having to do with all the other internal frame packs I tried. The pack moves the way you expect it to and doesn't flop around when you try to swing it onto your back. It weighs 4lbs. 9 oz. and is 4400 ci, which gives me a little more room than the Dana.

During a four day weekend, I was able to get the gazillions of Ziploc bags of dehydrated food off my living room floor and packed into mail drop boxes. Each box is packed with dinners, breakfasts, miscellaneous, some lunch items and snacks. By using these mail drops, I shouldn't have to spend much money for food other than a few fresh items for lunches and eating in restaurants. The boxes are not currently labeled or taped, except with a box number. Box numbers correspond to numbers on the master list, which is on a spreadsheet—a habit left over from my cube-dweller job (the spreadsheet is named Dilbert.xls). The spreadsheet tells what is in each box, with items that have to be put in later in boldface, where to mail it and what date to have it arrive. Adam and the boys will have this list as a guide. I'm sure everything will get tweaked as I go, but this will provide a baseline. The boxes sit stacked against the wall. One more thing out of the way.

This getting ready to leave process has not been all roses with me just smiling all the way. I've been depressed by the looming departure date in relation to the things that have to be done versus time continuing its disappearing act. It seems that no matter how much time I have available, it isn't getting done. I spent four hours last Sunday cleaning the boys' rooms and going through their things. We got rid of three garbage bags of trash, and tons of clothes and toys for Goodwill. Are their rooms empty? No! We have hardly begun. I have not been able to locate anyone who is interested in renting my house for seven months. That's been a huge stressor. I have it listed in a local newspaper, and on two websites. I'm hoping to have that answered in the coming two weeks. I have begun packing the house into various boxes, which always boggles my mind. Example: I've already packed the blank check registers (of course, who would think), and behold, I have run out of pages in the check register. Hell if I know which box they're in. Most of the boxes are already in the storage unit, too. Murphy's law says that they are in the box on the bottom of the stack in the back of the unit, right? So, I drive my son to the bank on Friday because he's having a "have to pay everyone back that I borrowed money from" emergency. What do I do? I sit in the car planning my "don't borrow money" speech and forget to go in and ask for a new check register.

Another trip, another day.

As time grows shorter, I am catering to my sons more, which has created varying degrees of disaster. I am hyper-aware of the length of time I will be away from them and how significant that amount of time is to a growing teenager. Joseph is experimenting with the bottom of the bell curve as it relates to his grades and how this in turn, when multiplied by two parents, exponentially effects his social life. The parent who is not leaving for six months has no problem being stern; the parent who is up at night addressing voices of guilt (that would be me) tends to undermine said stern parent's efforts by being a wuss with the follow through on consequences. This takes on the characteristics of a landslide in slow motion when played out; then, everyone is mad at everyone. It makes me want to pack myself into one of the mail drop boxes and be mailed to Maine which would be much simpler. The family dynamic of mom pursuing her 20-year-old dream is worse than the actual hiking will be. I think this letting go thing has something to do with trust.

MARCH 19

My last day of gainful employment, March 16th, has passed with hardly a flutter of fear in my heart. I should be frightened, but somehow, I am not. The support and encouragement from co-workers and from the corporate office was overwhelming. Each person miraculously seemed to be individually touched by my announcement to hike the AT. Despite the fact that my leaving was going to cause some workload rearrangement, everyone was excited about my adventure. The girls with whom I work most closely decorated my pod with footprints of hiking boots interspersed amongst bear prints. They hung pictures of bears and hiker signs. There was a stylized picture of a man and woman hiker consulting a map whose caption read: "Amy, lost on the AT, asking a cute guy for directions". And, they made a booklet called 'Amy's Critter Guide' with printed web pages of bear and mountain lion attacks on humans. At lunch they orchestrated a party complete with a cake that said "Happy Trails, Amy!" and gifts of gorp, and hiking paraphernalia. The management staff at the corporate office also sent a package. Each person had signed the front and back inside covers of a travel journal with encouraging thoughts for my journey and included a package of Gevalia coffee. Yum! Numerous cards and hugs and well wishes from literally hundreds of co-workers filled my last few days, and my head buzzed with the reverberations of energy until well into the wee hours of the morning. Conversations with my supervisor and my manager at the corporate office gave me the reassurance that my time with the company had indeed been valuable. It seems I am leaving with everyone's blessing, and that feels good and right, cementing the certainty that my actions are in synch with what should be at this time in my life.

This morning concluded my last scheduled 'event' of delivering the sermon for the Unitarian Universalist Church of the Swannanoa Valley, sharing my vision of this hike with my community. The congregational response was extremely supportive and welcoming. An undeniable change is taking place in my psyche as the responsibilities fall away one by one. All that remains is having the oil changed in my car, renewing my driver's license and helping my sons move into their dad's house.

Mom came to my house on Friday to help me clean

and ready the space for the renter. The man and his fiancé are from New Orleans. All during Hurricane Katrina's aftermath, I had wished to open my home to someone temporarily, a way to give something to the people of New Orleans, a gesture of compassion for our shared humanity. The opportunity has presented itself now, just in a different way. I am pleased to have the means to help at the same time that I am being helped. Mom has performed her usual miracles in my home. She has cleaned tirelessly for two days, bringing the cleanliness of my house up to the standards in which I grew up but have never been able to maintain. She came armed with easy to prepare foods like sausage/cheese balls, for quick breakfasts, and home-made macaroni & cheese. The wisdom of her 50 plus years of homemaking is apparent in everything Mom touches. Even now, she is upstairs cheering on my youngest son in his last ditch efforts to pack his roomful of collectibles, rocks, strangely shaped sticks, toy cars, bottles, and posters. She listens to each story, honoring the great importance of each keepsake with her rapt attention. The plan is to move the boys' things to their dad's house tomorrow.

Meanwhile, at their dad's house, our pre-divorce marital home, a similar equally frantic last ditch effort has been going on. Rooms are being painted, hardwood floors sanded & poly'd, furniture moved, and space created. We are down to the wire, and Adam is coming through; he even managed to show up for the church service this morning amidst all of his work yet to be done. The stacks of things in my house are divided into boxes for storage and boxes for Adam's. I hope he's aware of just how much personality two teenage boys can fit into a few boxes! I'm not sure he remembers that part; it's been six years since our divorce. Joseph has already salvaged two giant speakers from a friend's house and hauled them to his dad's. Better his house than mine!

MARCH 24

My house is empty except for all our packs and some food in the fridge at this point. I am numb. The whirlwind of lists and things to do has abated and my mind is mostly blank. I am a canvas, stretched taut and waiting, standing silent in the slanted light of the studio while the artist has morning coffee and reads a book. It's a very odd feeling, one I can't say I've ever experienced before. Everyone asks if I am excited; no. There is far more apprehension than excitement. Am I ready? Well, I damn well better be; that's all I can say. How is my family? How are the boys? Hmmm—we are all in some sort of daze, shell-shocked by the empty house, the move, the prospect of such change descending upon us fast, attempting to remain normal amidst such encroachment of the unknown into our midst. Adam and I are stressed and tense with each other. There's been a lot to accomplish to get the boys moved to his house. He's worked incredibly hard to focus and get it done. I helped for a couple of days, getting them set up in their rooms, and then retreated to my empty house, my yoga and a book. He's happier without me in his house giving orders and moving things around. He works at a different pace than I do. They will figure it out on their own.

The weeping willows outside the condo are sprouting. Each spring they are the first to leaf, and each fall they are the last to drop. The sap started to run a couple of weeks ago, and the wisps turned first a pale yellow against the backdrop of stark black branches of trees around them, then a vivid yellow that morphed to a vibrant spring green. Feeling this same quickening in my own pulse as six months of freedom beckon, I realize that my journey this year will coincide almost exactly with the leaf cycle of the weeping willow—even more fitting than I could have imagined. I am reminded of walking a labyrinth—there are no tricks or dead ends. The walker is assured of reaching the center. The walking becomes the destination.

The Osprey sits packed waiting quietly by the front door.

Slow Georgia Burn

The drive to Springer Mountain, Georgia was an emotional nightmare I'd much rather forget. After trying all morning to finish things up at the house and leave the house turnkey for the renter, it seemed as if I would never be through with myriads of last minute details. It came time to pick the boys up from school, and I was still vacuuming. An hour after we should have been gone, I was cleaning bathrooms. By this time, I was a basket case; I could not bring myself to leave. Eventually, I sat immobilized in a chair in the living room and cried, a release I'd been holding back all day. Adam and the boys could not understand what was happening; they thought I should be excited and happy to be ready to go. My mind latched onto fears I had entertained all day while I cleaned: Adam won't remember to send the maildrops, he's going to back out, I can't do it. Everyone sat in the car and waited, while I sulked in the chair. Adam had to come in and reassure me more than once before I made it out to the car and even then, I refused to drive, handing the keys to Adam. All the way to Georgia, all I could think of was how scared I was. I did not relax and no one spoke, the silence in the car feeding my runaway thoughts. We stopped for gasoline, and I went to the back of the car to dig something out of the trunk. In my distracted frustration, I hit my head on the open trunk of the car so hard that a gash opened in my forehead. I spent the next 50 miles obsessing over the hand of God smiting me on the head for my childish acting out, much in the way my father used to reach over and thump me on the head if I was misbehaving. Slowly, the bump on my noggin' began to seem funny. Adam reached over and put his hand on my knee; crisis faded.

When we arrived at the Hiker Hostel in Dahlonega, Georgia, the cabin was warm and comfortable, and the people were so nice that a thin layer of fear and anxiety dissolved. Adam and I had a good talk that night, whispering to each other in the curtained bunk bed while the boys slept in the other bunks. Another layer fell away.

Atop Springer Mountain[†], we were greeted by Many Sleeps, the grizzled gate-keeper of the legendary begin-ning point of the AT. Many Sleeps, an accomplished thru-hiker and traveler in his own right, counts hikers and gives out complimentary matchbooks from the Leave No Trace organization. He diligently explains to each hiker that if they will keep the matchbook and turn it in when they arrive at Walasi Center at Neels Gap they will receive a free Leave No Trace bandana to use for the rest of their journey north. In a daze, I accepted a matchbook and the number 422. Another layer peeled away and was carried off on the fierce, March wind.

Together, Adam and the boys and I hiked north from the summit of Springer. Grayson wore his dad's sweatshirt and let the sleeves dangle; he was quiet. Joseph chattered on and on, a verbal distraction from the impending separation. We came to the parking area where the rest of my family would catch the shuttle back to the hostel and go home. I would keep going, alone. The look on Joseph's face as he told me goodbye haunts me still; if I could do so without shame, I would go home to my babies right now—if there were a home to go to.

The sun still seems high—I'm guessing 4 or 4:30? I've never carried a watch in my life and have always been proud of that fact. I've weathered numerous discussions on the topic with my father while he disseminated all the reasons a person should carry a watch, me stubbornly clinging to my postulations about the irrelevant nature of time. Why now, out here in the middle of the woods do I suddenly have a need to know what time it is? A desperate grasping for the familiar? Somewhere between last night at the hostel and this morning loading into the shuttle, I lost my headphones, so I have a Trail Audio mp3 player but no way to listen to it. I'm bored, but slowly making peace with discontent. I am glad I made camp early giving myself time to come to terms with being away from home and family.

So far this has been an exercise in re-discovering all the things at which I suck. I missed the first shelter that our shuttle driver had mentioned because I didn't think I had gone far enough to be there yet. When I saw the sign for the shelter, I read it, but stubbornly decided that couldn't be it and kept going. Only later, when I stopped for a break and took out the guidebook, did I realize that indeed I had passed the turnoff for Stover Creek Shelter. Personal discovery # 1: assimilating information from trail signs isn't my forte.

I only did four miles, stopping very early in the day. My bones ache where the pack weight rested on my hips and shoulders. Rather than creating a worse problem by doing too much, I opted for too little and stopped at what I think is Chester Creek campsite and made my first camp.

On Springer, the only other hiker we met was Ol'Lee. He had planned on staying at the Stover Creek Shelter tonight—like me, not putting in very miles the first day. He's hiked before, section by section. It would have been nice to have someone to talk to, but obviously I botched that.

Then I set up my tent—no real issues there. Since I had stopped so early in the day, I decided to build a fire to stay warm. Personal discovery #2: building a fire is not like riding a bike. Three times a charm. The water filter business was a-whole-nother experience, holding the intake tube still with one foot, holding the output tube to the top of Platypus with one hand, balancing in a kneeling position on the edge of the creek holding the pump between my knees and pumping with the other hand. I felt like I had completed quite a performance by the time I had a liter of filtered water in the Platypus, but there was no one to applaud. The Nalgene bottle and Camelbak both have an opening large enough for the output attachment on the filter to fit— so naturally, I chose the most difficult of the three, the Platypus, to use. All the while I was doing this I was thinking "What if it were pouring down rain?" [†]

Next, I proceeded to hang a bear bag rope, ready to attach the bag of food once I was finished preparing my dinner. That was uneventful—but, when I actually did hang the bag from the tree I had chosen, it was obvious that any self-respecting bear would be able to get to it quite easily for it hung too close to the trunk of the tree. I moved it later in the day—after all, what else did I have to do?

I cooked couscous/lentil curry on the fire, getting

filthy in the process. The food was good and hot, and it improved my disposition greatly. I kept thinking I would quit with the fire business and just let it go out since the wood was so wet, slow burning and smoky. But, the day dragged on, and I didn't want to freeze to death—geez what time had I stopped hiking anyway? So I kept playing in the fire, getting dirtier and dirtier. When the wind blew, the fire burned great—otherwise it smoked and sputtered along. 35 degrees. The temperature had been 30 at 9:30 this morning when we parked at Springer. Several hikers had come by but none had stopped to camp; they all passed on, the last guy alone and carrying too much weight. I nibbled dry apples.

Ok, this water thing can't be that hard. I decided to try it again. Remember...what else did I have to do? It's not like a phone was going to ring at any minute with my next pressing engagement. This time I took the Camelbak. I went uphill to a small branch rather than to Chester Creek. I hung the Camelbak on a tree branch and propped the output valve into the opening in the top. Presto! One hand free. I stood up this time, placed the intake valve on top of a flat rock in a small pool and counted 90 pumps to fill the three liter. No big deal. I went back and played in the fire some more.

M A R C H   2 6

I've witnessed a few other hikers visibly wrestling their own demons as they make their way along the trail. As I sat quietly on a log in a clearing eating my lunch, I watched this guy come by counting his steps out loud. When he was directly across from where I sat, he glimpsed my movements out of the corner of his eye. He jumped straight up in the air and came down in a half-crouch facing me. I watched him silently as I ate my tuna. "Ha-ha! You startled me" he exclaimed before moving on. I wondered what he thought I might be. At least my fears don't include unknown creatures lurking in the forest.

It is dark—night of the second day. I have made dinner, filtered water and hung the bear bag. I filled the Nalgene with boiling water then placed it inside a sock to keep me warm. I am settled in the tent; it's 48 degrees according to the tiny thermometer on my pack. After only hiking four miles yesterday, I hiked 8.7 miles today, according to the book.

I'm not doing so well with this mileage thing. It took me all day to do the 8.7, and I am so dead tired I can barely think. I could not have gone any farther. The only reason I came as far as I did was because I had run out of water. It surprised me, and I wondered if something was blocking the flow. It turned out the Camelbak tube was kinked, and there actually was a dab of water left. Luckily, I had also filled the Nalgene so I was able to ration the last little bit for the final two miles. A blunt wake up call to be more aware that my priorities are going to have to shift—and soon.

MARCH 27

The things that are going through my head defy all description. This is the hardest thing I have ever done—bar none. Fears run rampant. As I walk, my mind vacillates wildly between horrific ideas of what might happen to me while I am alone out here and still more distinct images of imminent failure and my eventual demise. Many of these scenarios begin with some sort of plunge from an unnamed cliff onto rocks below or involve gangrenous limbs blackened from frostbite. For the life of me, at this time, I cannot come up with a single reason to be hiking this trail at this time in my life. I have kids at home that need me. What could I have been thinking? At times I have to drag my mind back to the meditation of one foot in front of the other just to stop panic from consuming all rational thought. Other times—like when I'm sitting on a log resting—I am confident I'll make it to Katahdin. Mostly, I keep thinking that six months is a godawful long time, and that I miss my boys.

Right now, the weather is beautiful; I cannot even imagine how hard it will be when it is raining. This morning the thermometer read 28 degrees. Once again in the wee hours of the morning, after the warmth of the hot water in my Nalgene bottle dissipated, I was cold and could not get comfortable. I'm not getting along very well with the sleeping bag—a Marmot Trestles 15 degree bag. Both nights I've been cold, despite the additional fleece liner that supposedly makes it warmer. Alternately, I toss and turn trying to find a position that is both comfortable and warm, only becoming more hopelessly entangled in the liner inside the bag, eventually figuring out that the lump under my right shoulder is the zipper of the bag that has migrated around underneath me in the melee. As I lie awake, I debate the pros and cons of purchasing a different bag when I get to Neels Gap and make a list of items I can send home to lighten my pack, as well. There really isn't much else I can do without. Obviously, I am going to need all the clothing I have; if it gets any colder, I'm in trouble.

I've now been alone for three days—talking only to one hiker named Brian at lunch and briefly to some weekenders from Pennsylvania yesterday. Everyone passed me early on, and no one else has come along. My mind plays with the math of 8-9 miles a day, deciphering again and again the reality of not being able to finish in six months at this pace. I do feel my muscles getting stronger, but the uphills are incredibly difficult, and I go very slowly. My collar and hip bones are bruised from the pack. I am wearing my fleece tied around my waist as padding of sorts, and I have wrapped my polypropylene shirt and tights around my shoulder straps. It helps some.

The sunshine is warm and the sky is blue. I've eaten lunch, rested and done some yoga. It's time to try this again.

E V E N I N G —

For some reason I've been able to get it together a little better today, possibly the warmer weather. It's just now dark and the temp inside my tent is still 49 degrees. I am fed, warm and clean. I've hung the bear bag, and arranged things in my tent differently so I could bring in the empty pack. I am doing what I can to get an efficient routine down before rain comes on Thursday. Once it starts to rain and be cold, the party's over, so to speak.

My attitude is slowly improving. Yesterday was pitiful. I was on the verge of giving up and catching the shuttle at Cooper's Gap to go back to the Hiker Hostel in Dahlonega. I arrived at Cooper's Gap late in the afternoon but had no idea what time it was. Stewart, from the Hiker Hostel said that he brings the shuttle to Cooper's Gap every day at 5pm for anyone who just needs an out or a night in a bed. No one was at the gap when I walked through. I started up the hill on the other side of the road debating whether to turn around and wait. Just then, a dark gray SUV drove by slowly. I don't know if it was them or not. The sound of the car on the gravel faded. A wave of nausea and fear sweep over me at that moment. There I stood at the bottom of a huge mountain, very little water left, the sun going down, and two miles to go before I could get water and make camp. The feeling of nausea became stronger the more I thought of my situation, and I could feel a full fledged panic attack coming on, so I sat down where I was to eat the Clif Bar that was in my pocket. (New mental note: when all else fails, eat!) The food was exactly what was needed, and it wasn't so sweet as to require a lot of water to wash it down. I took one swallow of water, saving half the Nalgene for the remaining miles. All I could do was get up and try.

With calories feeding my brain, I recognized that it might not even be 5pm; it could be more like 3:30pm. I wasn't as bad off as I originally thought. I got up and walked, making it to Justus Creek that night, gaining the mile lost the first day when I was only able to do four. Now, I was back on "schedule."

From that moment of stress I learned that EMDR works wonders for my anxiety. EMDR is a technique used by psychologists to reverse psychological damage caused by severe emotional trauma. This crazy idea of mine to hike the trail just might qualify as severe trauma. The patient watches a light move back and forth across a screen while being talked through troubling images of their past. When my imagination is running away with me, I focus my eyes on the ends of the trekking poles; first to the left, then to the right, then back to the left. I had found a long time ago, that the calming effect of EMDR could be reproduced by watching one's own footfalls while walking a labyrinth, and now I find it applies to watching trekking poles, as well. With this discovery, when my mind races away chasing some fantastical and terrible thing, I employ the principle of EMDR as a walking meditation and keep going. After all, do I really have a choice? Even if I were to decide to bail, it's not like I can just hail a cab.

More signs of spring have become apparent which have also served to cheer me up. Last night was another cold, cold night, and I was awake much of the night attempting to stay warm. This morning, when I went to take down the bear bag, there at my feet, by the creekside were five yellow violets nodding their little heads in the morning chill. Later in the day, as I walked, I saw several patches of bloodroot pushing their beautiful pure white blooms up through the forest soil. A couple of them had the tightly furled first green leaf poking through right beside them. Bloodroot is one of the few plants that sends up a flower before the foliage is even visible. In plant lore, bloodroot symbolizes healing and growth; I carried this thought with me. Later, when I stopped for a drink of water, a giant trillium was budding between two logs.

I saw birds I have not seen in years, downy woodpeckers and nuthatches, whose antics I used to love to watch as a child. I came very close to a rufous-sided towhee, and tonight, a pileated woodpecker flew over, giving a raucous laugh, as I set up my tent.

I chose a hilltop tenting spot. The first campsite I came to was in a low gap on a ridgeline that would have served as a wind tunnel all night, so I skipped it. Luckily this one was only a quarter mile farther. Brian was just ahead of me, but he went on down to camp in the cove by the creek. I just couldn't go another step. I'm glad I stopped when I did—this is a good level tent site. The wind is dead calm right now and hopefully will stay that way all night.

Part of the ritual of going to bed includes fretting over the mileage and terrain anticipated for the next day. Tomorrow, it appears I am slated for Blood Mountain. Great. Granny Franny, whom I met at the hostel, said she'd gotten a blister the size of a quarter going up Blood Mountain. She came off the trail after that to order new boots and a new pack and was staying at the hostel waiting for them to arrive. Blood Mountain is 4461 feet and steep. So far, I have no signs of blisters; I've been taking off my boots and socks whenever I stop and letting them air dry in the sun. I've also been mindful of the way I am placing the weight on each foot, and if one part of either foot is hurting, I try to walk more evenly on the sole of my foot. The same seemed to work when one of my knees started hurting today. I changed the way I was putting my weight on that leg, and it stopped hurting. So far so good.

Instead of the hot water Nalgene bottle, tonight, I am going to try one of these chemical hand warmers I've been carrying. The package says the heat will last up to 10 hours. We'll see. Hopefully, I'll make it to Neels Gap tomorrow and can get a shower. Beginning to see the value in small joys.

MARCH 28

Just as I was turning off the headlamp and rolling over to go to sleep last night a ruckus erupted downhill from the tent. It sounded like a dog fight in fast forward with high pitched barks and snarls. About five minutes later, the problem child had been banned from the group for causing trouble, and the clear lonely howl of a coyote pierced the night. It's the first time I've ever heard one in the wild; it punctuated my own emotion, soothing me in an eerie way. After hearing the coyotes last night, I have been so psyched about "my hike." Today, I finally met and talked with other hikers, all of which were in the same area, but they had all stayed in shelters, and not one of them had heard the coyotes. Later this morning, I saw what I am sure was a coyote den under the upturned roots of a fallen tree. The hole in the ground was back up under the roots. In front of the hole, under the umbrella of the roots was a dirt pit—a bowl of sorts—filled with paw prints where pups might play or worry a bone. I felt a silent kinship with these creatures, privileged to share the forest that is their home.

The sky was overcast until afternoon. It rained a little, so I put my pack cover on at a trail intersection. The climb up Blood Mountain was foggy—essentially in the clouds. At the bottom of the mountain, huge stone steps marked the trail by a large, gnarled oak; a dramatic spring poured from a slab of rock, and a wooden sign read "Blood Mountain", all of which was enshrouded in mist—the perfect vignette for a Led Zeppelin album cover.

After so many people had said that Blood Mountain was a kick-ass hike, I was surprised at how easily I moved up it. When I stopped to put on the pack cover, I ate a Pemmican bar and drank spring water, only carrying a half liter up with me. I put it in low gear and never stopped going, all the way to the top. The stone shelter at the summit recalled Avery's vision of what the AT might be like, with great hostels and libraries along the ridges. The Blood Mountain Shelter is a square stone building with two rooms. The first room has a stone fireplace which has been blocked off, prob- ably for years. The second room has two pane-less windows and a raised wooden sleeping platform. The two windows in the back room, which were needed to admit light, were positioned in such a way that the wind coming over the rock ledge funneled right through the room, making quite a frigid place for sleeping. Dramatic but cold—sort of like a castle, I suppose. So much for Blood Mountain. [†]

Bama was the first person I'd seen since meeting Brian at lunch the day before. She stopped for a break on a log and talked while I wrestled the pain in my shoulder. This was the first I realized that there were lots of other people behind me still, and that my alone-ness was defining my experience in ways very different from others'. After a short while, I had to get up and move on; there was a cold drizzle, and I needed to keep moving to stay warm. Bama and Banjoman caught up with me at the spring at the base of Blood Mountain. They were both slack-packing from Woody Gap to Walasi Center and only had daypacks with them. I knew about slack-packing, which is the practice of not carrying all your gear with you by having someone drive your gear ahead and meet you, but I had not considered it this early in the trip. I was intrigued that this other way of hiking called so distinctly to some folks. They had actually stayed in a hostel that night and been driven back to the trail. No wonder Bama was so fresh and clean. I caught up to them again on top of the mountain, and we hiked to Balance Rock together, then they went ahead. They will be staying at the hostel again tonight and will be shuttled back from the trail when they finish their hiking for the day. It was easy to see how the expensive luxuries of hostels and slack-packing would make this trip quite comfort-able and more fun. But, even with that option dangling like a carrot on a stick, I felt immune to the temptations of civilization.

For $3.50 at Walasi Center, I got a hot shower and a wet towel. The shower was heaven! I was too grateful to complain about the wet towel. One of the guys in the store repacked my pack and adjusted the Velcro back; it fits me totally differently now, which will hopefully help with my shoulder problems. I have had to stop every couple of hours to stretch my arm and rotate my shoulder to ease the pain. After a long, long downhill to Walasi Center, my right foot has begun to have problems. There is a weird, twingey nerve thing happening in the outside part of the foot; at times it sends a tingly feeling up my leg. Again, all on the right side and probably related. Still no blisters. My feet are just dog-tired. When I take the pack off, I feel like I am floating.

After mailing a few things home, my pack weighs 37 pounds with five days of food, according to the scale here at Neels Gap. I must have left Springer with 45-50 pounds, including water. No wonder I could only do four miles the first day. My legs grow stronger each day—or is it that the pack simply gets lighter? I traded in the matchbook I'd carried from Springer and received the Leave No Trace bandana, which I mailed home to the boys.

One temptation that I could not ignore was the possibility of communication with my family. I called Adam briefly from the hostel but it was difficult, at best, to have a conversation. The phone was a wall unit situated in the middle of the main room surrounded by other hikers all watching TV. A curtain of isolation separated me from the gaiety; instead of joining in and establishing friendships, I was overwhelmed with disappointment in not being able to share my experiences with Adam and the boys. I miss my family so terribly.

Of the hikers in the hostel, Ol'Lee and Brian were the only people I had met before. Brian is going home because he injured himself this morning; he had intended to be out for two weeks but was cutting it short. I met a young guy named Justin who is from New Hampshire. His tent is the same as mine, and we are camped beside each other. Justin seems much more my speed—not wanting to pay to sleep in a hostel and not putting in big miles. At 10 miles a day, he's still doing more than me though. Tomorrow, I will try for 10, but don't know if I can make it; today was only eight and my feet hurt a lot. The good news is: there was still four or five hours of daylight left when I arrived at Walasi Center, meaning I must have averaged pretty good mileage per hour, even coming over Blood Mountain. Tomorrow looks like there are a lot of ups and downs the hikers call PUDs (pointless ups and downs). We'll see how it goes.

It has grown dark, but I'm not sleepy. I slept well last night after two cold restless nights. The chemical hand warmers were helpful but not as comforting as the hot water Nalgene. Temps tonight are predicted to remain in the 40s again. Noise from the road below is distracting after four nights alone in the woods, but I'm finding comfort in being surrounded by other tents and people tonight.

MARCH 29

One of the tools of the trade is a mileage book. Some use the Appalachian Trail Conservancy's publication called the *AT Data Book*, and others use the latest version of the *Thru-Hiker's Guide to the Appalachian Trail*, a book written and updated each year by Dan Bruce. I suppose if the AT were the military, Dan Bruce, whose trail name is Wingfoot, would boast a chest full of medals and be a fearless officer. His authority on all matters trail is a source of constant debate among thru-hikers, some in support of his wealth of knowledge and others scoffing at his boastfulness and counting his errors. When you are miles from anywhere and relying solely on the information that Wingfoot has decided to include in the book, omissions of seemingly minute details can cause hours of frustrated hiking. In this instance, according to Wingfoot, there would be four miles without water from Whitley Gap Shelter to Low Gap Shelter.... Somehow, even knowing this ahead of time didn't prepare us for running out of water on an inordinately hot, dry Georgia spring afternoon. To add insult to injury, the book also warned that the water at Whitley Gap Shelter was 1.5 miles off the trail. We dropped our packs for a break at the trail intersection, and it was determined that Bama would stay with the packs while Banjoman and I went to retrieve water for all three of us.

Banjoman and I struck out on the ridgeline trail with the fleet-footed pace of backpackers recently liberated from the weight of their packs. After a short while, the trail emerged onto an open rock plateau with amazing views off to the south. Several large crows circled lazily in the air at eye level out over the valley. It was the perfect vantage point for lingering on a hot spring afternoon, but alas! We were on an important mission. Find the water source.

Hmmm. Rock plateau. The water source seemed to grow farther away with every step. Even our conversation could not disguise the needling thoughts in our minds of "too far! too far!" Finally, the trail dropped over the side of the ridge and began its descent. More promising maybe, but sobering. We were going to have to climb back up this. The descent was steep with few switchbacks. Eventually, through the leafless trees we could see the horizontal plane of the shelter walls. Almost there!

Of course, the condition of this shelter was immaculate compared to the more heavily used shelters situated in more reasonable proximity to the trail. Ironically, this isolated shelter boasted covered cooking counters along its outside walls, a useful feature allowing for a much less crowded dinner experience that would have been a welcome accommodation before now (especially in the rain, I imagined). Banjoman and I headed to the spring another three tenths of a mile away, pumped our water bottles full, and then came back to the shelter to check the register. As expected, very few signatures graced its pristine pages, a mute testimony to the folly of shelters so far from trail proper. This may have been the result of a trail re-route.

We began our trudge back up the mountain, both of us wistfully musing aloud about Bama's long luxurious break sitting by the trail, waiting. On the way up, we passed another poor soul who had been sent by the others in his party to retrieve the precious H2O. We reassured him that he was "almost there", a trail euphemism used in all manner of sinful ways.

By the time we reached Bama resting with our packs, she had made friends with the folks from the next group of hikers to come along and was chatting away with a southbounder who was completing the trail for his millionth time. Most importantly, he came bearing news of what lay ahead at the bottom of the mountain on which we sat...trail magic! Our first. Trail magic, as it is known, can be any manner of desired comforts made available to weary hikers through no doing of their own, whether it be free food, shelter, clothing, rides to town or what-have-you. In this case it was fresh water and sodas! Banjoman and I exchanged jaded looks. You mean we just added three miles to our day's hike for nothing? "Oh well, what can ya' do?" words of wisdom from a hiker much younger and more cheerful at the moment than we. My pack seemed to weigh a ton, but the anticipation of trail magic spurred us down the mountain.

We arrived at Hogpen Gap on GA 348 road crossing and, sure enough, there sat a couple that had driven up from Atlanta with a trunkful of sodas, water, cookies and fruit just as the southbounder had said. They even had brought lawn chairs for easing trail-weary bones while partaking of the coveted goodies. We visited and snacked for 30 minutes or so before facing the next uphill out of the gap with 4.2 more miles to reach Low Gap Shelter for the night.

The bones of my feet screamed when I rose to leave. Our trail magic host watched as I struggled under the weight of my pack before gaining my footing. "Isn't there a body weight to pack weight ratio a backpack shouldn't exceed?" he asked my companions. "Don't look at me," Banjoman said. I could only respond with a faint smile. I wanted nothing more than to just ditch the entire pack right there, stick my thumb out and hitch home. Instead, I steadied myself against my hiking poles, and climbed the mountain slowly and painfully, preoccupied with the harsh realities of the lessons of the trail. I vowed as I climbed that never again would I allow fear to make my decisions for me while on this trip; I would trust that the trail would provide—four miles between water sources or not.

Hanging a bear bag, per se, can be a debatable

necessity if one is expecting to thwart an actual bear when there simply are no bears; however, its importance for keeping other critters at bay is paramount. In areas where there really are bears, they cause much damage and require far more than a string and bag to hold at bay. Mice, skunks and raccoons create more worrisome situations than most people ever have with bears. The hanging of said "bear" bag can be quite the trick for an exhausted and hungry hiker in the fast-fading light of an early spring evening. This activity actually caused more anxiety than did the idea that any bear would ever visit my camp. True to Murphy's Law, alone with no audience I was queen of throwing a rope over a tree branch. Bring an audience into the picture and no matter how disinterested or possibly oblivious they actually were of my plight, I was no longer queen of anything but could provide free, clown-like antics for indeterminable lengths of time. The embarrassing "damsel in distress" theme of these occasions generally dampened my enthusiasm for these shows tremendously. The vulnerability that may be cute in a pert, 20-something female decidedly does not fit my style at this juncture in life. On this particular fated attempt, the rock that was tied to one end of the rope as a weight not only carried the rope up and over the branch, but continued its arc around the branch several times in fact, securing itself quite firmly at a height of about 12 feet above my head. The folly of attempting to change the situation successfully wedged the rock into the crook of the tree trunk still at a beautifully scenic height of 12 feet or so in the air. And so, to my chagrin, I was thus "introduced" to Zippo, Asher and Just Bill.

A P R I L   1

Bama and Banjoman hiked ahead with a group of other thru-hikers the next morning. Somehow, I managed 11 miles, tenting on Tray Mountain with Just Bill, Asher and Zippo, my bear bag saviors. I've hiked with them since, and we are doing roughly 10 to 11 miles a day, a pace that I seem to be gaining comfort with. I expect to reach Nantahala Outdoor Center by next Saturday or Sunday.

At Deep Gap Shelter, we listened to the rain on the roof. Key word there is 'roof'. After being out for an entire week, this was the first time I elected to stay in a shelter as opposed to tenting, and it was sweet. There weren't even any mice. Bill and Asher are both from Asheville, North Carolina, my home town, and it's been encouraging to connect with people who are familiar with home. The rain stopped at dawn; it was a hot muggy hike down into the gap where we hitched a ride in the back of a pickup truck into Hiawasee. [†]

The Blueberry Patch hostel, a few road miles from the trail, is a converted garage behind Gary and Lennie Poteat's home. I arrived at 11:30 this morning (clocks have been elevated a notch in my stubborn "no time" mind), excited about my first trail hostel experience. The sun shone on the side of the wooden bath house and glinted on the wet grass in the blueberry fields. I took my time taking a hot shower, musing on matters of being a woman hiking the trail while I pampered myself with scented shampoos, lotions, razors and combs that Lennie had provided for hikers. The guys had elected to stay at a motel in town. [†]

I'm taking even more stuff out of my pack and sending it home via Bill's girlfriend who is going back to Asheville tomorrow. The weight of the pack is pushing my lumbar out of place, and my right leg keeps going numb. I've got to get the pack weight as low as possible. I've been in incredible pain, first with my shoulder, then my back, then sunburn, and now my feet and my numb leg and big toe. I'm surviving on Tylenol but need to get something stronger. The hiking is hard, harder than anything I've ever tried to do; but slowly, my mind is working its way around how to handle this, and the problems drop away, one by one. Having the pack refitted at Neels Gap took care of the shoulder issue. The sunburn has healed under the past two days of overcast skies.

After a shower, I made phone calls: first Mom, then my friend Walter, who is planning to meet me soon along the trail, then Adam and the boys. Mom is planning to send packages of home-baked goodies along the way, so we initiated her first mailing. Walter commiserated with the pain I was experiencing, as he is a veteran backpacker of the n'th degree who carries way more weight than I could ever begin to tote. I also called my chiropractor and discussed the fear that I may be doing permanent damage to my spine by continuing to hike with my right leg completely numb. He reassured me and offered some tips; somehow, just connecting with the stability of the life I had left behind calmed me and boosted my morale.

Miraculously, this afternoon while hanging out in the hotel room with Zippo, Asher and Bill, it came to light that Zippo is a chiropractor. He graciously adjusted my back, using a stuffed sleeping bag roll placed under my back against the floor. The adjustment rippled all the way up my spine, and I believe I may have glimpsed God. Hopefully, the yoga twice a day and the adjustment will help with the nerve thing in my leg.

APRIL   2

The long hours walking alone lend themselves to thoughtful and detailed examinations of what creates home, what comfort means, and what luxuries we take for granted as a nation caught up in the throes of the technological age. I have never been so glad to be 'home' in my whole life as when I crossed the border into North Carolina. Georgia seemed light years behind simply because I had made that first milestone of reaching the beloved mountains of home. Suddenly the uphills didn't seem quite so steep and the downhills didn't seem quite so pointless; home seemed to be as simple as knowing the names of the towns and the landmarks. The state border was nothing more than a small wooden sign nailed to a tree on the right side of the trail with NC/GA carved into its weathered surface. An iron pipe was embedded in the side of the tree where perhaps an old register would have once been tucked; it was empty now. Two tenths of a mile farther, at Bly Gap, was an impressively gnarled tree marked with the white blaze—the sight of this tree grounded me even more.[†]

A great horned owl hooted as dusk began to fall. The shelter came into sight.

At Muskrat Creek Shelter I met Linc and Jeanne, an amazing couple that I instantly felt to be my kindred spirits. About my age, they are health-conscious, earth-loving people who are committed to doing things their way in order to hold true to their principles in all they do. Jeanne is a strong woman with a very determined character. She has dark brown hair that flows past her waist which Linc braids into two braids each morning.

Linc is soft-spoken with a slender athletic build and long hair; he has previously hiked the AT, years before he met Jeanne and is hiking again to be a part of her life-long dream. Their quiet integrity soothed my anxiety, and the fact that they are a pair somehow embodies the essence of home for me. I am drawn to them as a source of good energy and stability in this new and changing environment. Their routine is solid and unchanging. They carry whole wheat flour and sourdough starter and bake their own loaf of bread every couple of days in a backpackers oven or over a fire. They carry fresh vegetables and meticulously plan and balance their meals for the most nutritional power-punch food can deliver. Their knowledge of plants and wholesome foods offers much in common to discuss. They have lived an alternative lifestyle that most just daydream might be possible someday. Linc and Jeanne are a world unto themselves. I am privileged to meet them and hope to see more of them along the way.[†]

A storm rages outside the tent. Thunder echoes off the mountainsides and lightning erratically illumi-nates the nylon walls, casting wildly waving shadows of naked branches. Between storm clouds passing, a large bird, possibly a heron lost in the wind, flies by making a frantic duck/bird croaking noise. I am quite content in this raging reshuffling of energy. It suits the circumstances quite properly. Spring fury.

A P R I L   5

Tenting a mile north of Winding Stair, I am alone for the first time since those first four nights. It feels good; it is quiet but a little unnerving. There was a sign posted at USFS Rd 71, back before Standing Indian Shelter, that said there has been a bear in the area that displays no fear of humans and whose range runs all the way to Wayah Bald. According to the sign, the bear has made off with several people's backpacks. Camped here, I am still within that range. My bear bag is hung on the other side of a small creek from my tent, and I've not cooked any food here.

I was able to do today's 13.1 miles with relatively no problems; it's my biggest mileage day yet. Jesse, a new hiker friend I met at Blueberry Hostel, left our campsite early this morning to do the 12 miles into Franklin with plans to stay at the Budget motel tonight. Asher, Zippo, and Bill who caught up last night also camped with us at Betty Creek, and they also entertained visions of motel comforts. Coyotes serenaded us after dark while we sat around a small campfire. At the road in Winding Stair Gap, Crutch, the shuttle driver offered everyone rides. The guys didn't want to share a room with another person, so instead of going with them, I opted for the hamburger, fries and pie they had brought from town, and they left. I ate the burger and fries there in the parking area at the road crossing and saved the apple pie for breakfast. Linc and Jeannie are camped on the south side of Winding Stair Gap. They're going into town to grocery shop first thing in the morning and then coming back out.

Zippo, Asher and Bill had stayed in Hiawasee an extra day and night, which is why I didn't see them on the trail the next few days. So far, they're spending as much time in town as they are on the trail, it seems. I felt discarded by them today—not a member of the boy's club, but I knew I would be alone on this trip, so I am simply doing what I set out to do, hike the AT. As a peace offering, Jesse offered to share his motel room so I could use the phone and take a shower and go to the post office, but I decided against the expense, not wanting to get caught up in the town habit. My agenda is different from most people's out here because most of my food is already purchased. My town needs have been zero and my only desires have been to communicate with friends and family via phone & email—and a hot shower. With two more 10 mile days—which will seem easy after today—I will be at Nantahala Outdoor Center Saturday morning. There I can shower, make phone calls and pick up my next drop box. Logistics take up most of one's "spare" time, it seems.

As I was setting up my tent, a turkey flew in, intending to land here, but changed his mind in a flurry of feathers and landed farther up the hill. When we were camped at Muskrat Shelter, Linc taught me to recognize the call of the barred owl, and its eerie monkey-like hooting stays the silence now above my tent. Planning to be up and out early, I've taken two Tylenol and am so tired I can hardly stay awake.

A P R I L   6

The sun illuminates just the very far end of the tent. Plans to leave early were forgone, as I've slept late with no one up stirring around. I dreamt of deception and betrayal and of cleaning run down apartment units to get them ready for rental.

I lay here thinking of the chipmunks that have watched me pass over the last couple of day's hiking, one down by the spring in Beech Gap and another in Wallace Gap. They are busily spring cleaning their burrows and searching for winter's remaining nut stashes in the warm spring sunshine. Seeing chipmunks transports me back to childhood when Mom and I would walk together to the end of a dead end road in our neighborhood where a chipmunk lived in a rotting tree stump. We went to see him specifically and would bring him cookie crumbs and nuts, watching for him to come out of the stump to daintily check out our offerings. He turned each nut over and over in his tiny paws, sniffing, nibbling, and finally stuffing the whole piece into his fat cheeks before choosing another. For me as a pre-school child, this simple excursion was a highlight of lazy afternoons at home with Mom.

The sun has warmed one side of my tent. Upon beginning to stir, I find that I am incredibly bone-tired. I am glad today has only 10 miles in store—I can take my time this morning, take care of me—wash my face & hands, eat a good breakfast, write, and listen to music. I tried to get a radio station last night, but this tent site is too deep in a hollow for any reception. When I climb out, perhaps I can hear a weather forecast. I am really looking forward to getting a shower at the NOC and possibly meeting up with my friend, Charles, sometime soon. There will be baked goodies there from Mom, too—I wish I had some of them right now. OH! The apple pie is in my bear bag. Getting up now!

E V E N I N G —

The fire tower on Wayah Bald offered a humbling, 360-degree view. Albert Mountain, Standing Indian Mountain and other unnamed, purple mountain silhouettes brought visual perspective to how far I have come and just how far two thousand miles really is.

I dilly dallied after my late morning in bed, taking pictures, stopping at the fire tower on Wayah Bald, and spending an hour or more for lunch, but still made it

9.4 miles—a great day and my first day completely alone again.[†] Bill and Asher passed this morning. A mother/daughter team from New Jersey said they heard that Zippo was going to stay another day in Franklin because of problems with his knees. When I last saw him, he was in pretty bad shape coming down into Winding Stair Gap, using two sticks as hiking poles with a bandana wrapped around the meniscus of one knee. Jesse's probably back on the trail today, but I haven't seen him. Maybe he'll catch up by tomorrow. I am camped with the mother/daughter duo, Pokey & Dancer. They have never done anything like this before, don't believe in bears, and are currently talking on their cell phone. I could hear them long before I could see them both times I happened upon them today. I set up the tent and crawled inside just as rain began to fall.

Have I said yet that I'm looking forward to getting to Nantahala so I can get a shower? I'm supposed to call Charles too and perhaps get a chance to meet him. I know Charles from trailjournals.com but have never met him in person. The anticipation of meeting someone who has become a good friend via email has fueled my excitement about reaching the NOC...a little over 11 miles tomorrow, and then five on Saturday, to get there. It was so good tonight to saunter into camp with lots of daylight left and to set up the tent and cook a meal without rushing. There was even time to make Mary Jane's focaccia bread, which is a flour mix that only requires water. I am carrying measured Ziploc bags of mix that make three round patties of bread, cooked in a bit of oil in my small frying pan. They rise about like pancakes and make eating dehydrated fare more like real food. I will have two meals left over unless I eat extra tomorrow night, which won't be hard to do.

A P R I L 7

According to the radio, a huge storm system is moving in with quarter-sized hail and tornadoes that have already claimed many lives in Tennessee. Hikers have holed up in shelters for the night. I am with Old Grandad and his elder sidekick, Eel. Old Grandad is thru-hiking, and Eel is going with him as far as Damascus, Virginia.

Bald Shelter—11.1 miles and my first blister. It appeared on a serious downhill into Tellico Gap on top of the second toe on my left foot. Since it's in a place that doesn't usually rub, I've left it alone for now. Tomorrow's downhill into NOC is rumored to be worse. For some reason, today was difficult for my feet. It seems they are still not adjusting well. The pain in the soles of my feet often is so excruciating that I can hardly walk. The rest of my body is ready to do more miles, but my feet won't hear of it. I ate an extra meal when I arrived at the shelter, satisfied by eating until full and not being concerned with running out of food. There is one more dinner left that I won't need.

Suddenly awake, lying on my back, I could just make out the outline of the shelter roof against the sky. The sound of the wind grew louder, and I remembered the storm warnings. Thunder rolled in the distance to the west on the backside of the shelter. It was now or never if I was going to go pee, so I crept out of the sleeping bag as quietly as I could. No one else was yet awake.

Outside the shelter, I faced the wind. The sound of the storm coming up the mountainside from the valley to the west was a dull roar as high winds fingered the mountainsides and combed the tops of the budding trees; just to hear it coming sent a shiver down my spine. A hiker was sleeping not far away, just behind the shelter, in a hammock with a tarp spread over it. The rest of us had tried to convince him there was room in the shelter, but he assured us he would be just fine outside. On the hillside to the east, between the shelter and the trail, was a smattering of tents of all colors, shapes and sizes. Some were thru-hikers, some were weekenders and some belonged to a scout troop out for spring break. There was a light on inside Dancer and Pokey's tent as they readied their gear for the rain. The tops of the trees began to sway, and a clap of thunder sounded farther down the draw, echoing off the mountainsides; the roar of the storm moving toward the top of the mountain sounded as if a freight train were bearing down on us. I was a young child again, standing at the picture window in our living room watching birds tossed about on the winds of a summer thunderstorm, thrilled by the unleashed power and sense of danger.

Others were awakening as I crept quietly back into the shelter. The rustle of sleeping bags and the soft glow of headlamps provided a cozy backdrop to the drama unfolding outside. A smattering of rain hit the tin roof as a crack of lightning silhouetted the wind-bent trees and someone whispered "here we go". A torrent of rain was released in an instant and all other sound became indistinguishable from the deafening roar on the tin. Another shiver of excitement raced up my back, and I couldn't help but wiggle with childish glee and snuggle down into the sleeping bag. The noise became even louder as the rain changed to hail briefly, then back to large drops of rain. The wind whipped the treetops and buffeted the campers' tents. Some in the shelter sat up in their bags watching the storm, others paced under the cooking awning. Eventually, as the heaviest thunder moved over the crest of the mountain and the downpour pounded out a steady rhythm on the tin, I fell asleep again, thankful to be warm and dry and safe on this stormy night.

A P R I L   9

Morning dawned foggy and wet. The young man who had opted for the hammock appeared to still be alive. Tenters emerged one and two at a time, disheveled and damp, comparing tales of battling mini floods inside their nylon sanctuaries. The forest was fresh and clean. Old Grandad and Eel[†] donned their full regalia of bright blue rain gear and headed up the hill back to the trail. I opted for no rain pants, just long pants and a rain jacket to fend off the early morning chill, trusting that the heavy fog meant the rain was over. Pokey and Dancer were already up, packed and gone by the time I passed their tent site.

The trail traveled along the ridgeline through trees covered so thickly in moss that the tree trunks and branches appeared to have sage-colored hair. Paw prints were outlined distinctly in the wet sand, possibly coyote, possibly a dog. A huge oak had been split by a bolt of lightning during the storm, its trunk laid open, shattered and pungent, its branches blocking the trail.

On the ground by my footfall lay a sprig of mistletoe blown from the treetop by the impact. I picked up the 'golden bough' and tucked it into the front of my jacket, carrying the ancient herb with me to present its magic to Charles. What more powerful juju than mistletoe delivered to Earth by the hammer of Thor? The trail then plummeted toward the Nantahala River via a rock cliff known as The Jumpup. Views of the river gorge and surrounding mountains were crisp in the damp air; patches of fog drifted below, filling nooks and crevices with tufts of wispy white outlined against dark, wet mountains tinged with pale morning sunlight. Huge, cumulus clouds piled up against one another on the horizon, parting here and there where shafts of sunshine pierced through.[†]

I arrived at the Nantahala Outdoor Center around 11am. I called Charles from the pay phone, and he offered a stay at his mother's house for the evening. It was perfect timing. Rain began to pour down again not long after I had gathered my maildrop from the Outdoor Center and made the call. Mom sent tiny loaves of zucchini bread, banana nut bread, and apple walnut bread. Thanks, Mom! I sat nibbling banana nut bread under an awning and chatting with another thru-hiker while he hitched a ride, and I waited for Charles.

Mrs. Hodges is the quintessential, grandmotherly woman, kind and warm, sharing her home with a complete stranger. I luxuriated in the hot shower, then Charles treated me to a meal at Ryan's Steakhouse in Sylva. We visited over the all-you-can-eat buffet and solidified this new phase of our friendship. Sleeping in Mrs. Hodges guest bedroom was the first time since March 24th I'd slept in a real bed. Despite being indoors, I awoke at first light to the sound of birds chirping, refreshed and ready to get back on trail. I took another shower just because it was there. The smell of breakfast cooking wafted tantalizingly through Mrs. Hodges' house, calling to mind all the comforts of home.

The kindness and hospitality of this family exemplifies all that is right and good in this world. This kind of human connection serves as a ground for the insanity of this journey. Charles and his mother dropped me off in front of the NOC, and we posed for goodbye pictures. Knowing that there are many people, strangers even, who are touched by my efforts to hike to Maine, feeds my resolve with the energy of their good wishes.[†]

N I G H T —

Hiking up from the NOC, I was pumped for the climb and enjoyed every minute of it. Anything that isn't downhill makes my feet very happy. I climbed steadily, catching up with Old Grandad and Eel after about half a mile in. We walked together to a sunshine-drenched ledge and ate lunch gazing down on the Nantahala River across to the ridge we had come from the day before. After lunch I got a burst of energy and did the last section up to Cheoah really quickly, even leaving Old Grandad and Eel behind; I was psyched about putting in a long day. When I arrived at Cheoah Bald, my friend Walter was there waiting.[†]

I first met Walter when I was a college student at Appalachian State University, a young and innocent freshman, easily influenced and wide open to the world. He immediately corrupted me with his wit and twisted humor, his vegetarianism, Eastern religious practices and BMW motorcycle. Walt had been celibate for 13 years; a vow of celibacy suddenly seemed like a great way to save myself from continuing down the carousing college path I had already begun. I signed on, and that became only the first of many ways in which Walter's quirky wisdom and unconventional lifestyle influenced the directions I took and the decisions I made. I became a vegetarian, studied Yogananda's teachings and began my opposition of the status quo in earnest. Next came living outside; he taught me to backpack by lending me his old army Alice pack (the most uncomfortable pack ever made) and a feather sleeping bag (note: there is a vast disparity between feathers and down—do not confuse the two— let's just say that sleeping bag singly discredited the saying "light as a feather") and ferrying me out to the middle of the great Pisgah National Forest. There, I came face to face with my first real mountain, with Walter trudging doggedly up ahead, his schizophrenic sidekick, Don, puffing and sweating behind me, and Walt's new Army buddy, steady Johnny Be beside me, comforting my tears with assurances that this was one grueling mountain, and it should be respected for the punch it delivered. The four of us spent many a happy, summer eve crouched by the sweat lodge fire there, diving into the swimming hole, or sitting silently in the shadow of the 50-foot waterfall behind our campsite. Walter's legend endures, as he still lives in the woods after all these years, carries a mammoth pack everywhere he goes and frequents the loneliest folds of the Appalachians he can find on a regular basis.

Walter had staked out the best tenting spot on the bald, and the views are so fine that I agree we should just take it easy, visit and stay here. To the south, the furrows and undulations of the mountain ranges are breathtaking. From the other side of the ridge, we watch an orange sunset with No Falls (thru hiker) and Tom (section hiker). A three-quarter moon is rising, and it is a perfectly clear night. Life is good.[†]

A P R I L   1 2

Day 18-162.9 miles—I am sitting on the bottom step at Fontana Dam Visitor Center waiting for the sound of Adam's pickup truck.

I arrived last night at Fontana Shelter around sundown. As I was coming down the mountainside to the marina, I was so hungry my stomach was digesting itself. At the marina a big, homemade sign read "R U Hungry?" According to the sign, 'Hikers for Christ' was offering a free, hot meal at the shelter from 5pm until dusk. WOW! FOOD! It was another 1.1 miles to the shelter, a cruel 1.1 of silly uphills and immediate down-hills through an ugly section of dead pine trees along the edge of Fontana Lake, but the anticipation of food carried me forward.

When I camped with Walter on Cheoah Bald, the people I had been hiking with passed. I put in 12.6 miles yesterday and caught up with some of them at the shelter by Fontana Lake which is known as the Fontana Hilton. Old Grandad and Eel were there, as were Thomas, Firefly, Julia and Mark. Everyone that stayed at the Hilton last night was headed into Great Smokies National Park this morning. I will still be a day behind them though, because today will be my first ZERO DAY!

The concept of the zero day matches the modern work world's "mental health day" or "personal day". It's the day that you take just for you—to recoup what you've put out, to gather your wits, to rest, to regroup.

Many of the hikers have already allowed themselves several of these days of rest, but I have been staunchly sticking to my schedule despite my bone-weary level of exhaustion in the beginning and the pain I have been experiencing in my right foot and knees.

Adam and I have reserved a cabin at Fontana Village, compliments of a friend from home. As I've walked, I've come to realize how much of my motivation to fulfill this dream is tied up in seeking Adam's approval and respect. So far, on the phone, he's been distant and seemingly unconcerned with my progress or well being for the past three weeks. Neither he nor the boys have bothered checking my website to see how or where I am—ironic since I created it for them. As I walk, I think of these things a lot, and focus on letting go of any expectations I obviously have of how he should be. I try to walk myself into acceptance—acceptance of what he is regardless of my own expectations. After all, he is taking care of the boys for me/us, he is sending maildrops, and he is coming here to meet me today. There are many reasons why we are no longer married. I want today to be fun, so I try to release any disappointment I may have subconsciously set myself up for...beginning with the fact that it is already 10am, and there is no sign of him.

There was still plenty of daylight when I arrived at the shelter last night even with two long breaks with Walter during the day's hiking. I left him camped at Cable Gap Shelter and did the 6.6 from there to Fontana after lunch. My feet and legs were very sore all night, and my leg muscles were cramping. But still, there is a difference; it's a tolerable soreness now, and I'm not taking any Tylenol. I should be ready now to tackle the Smokies. I passed Justin and his girlfriend, Eliza yesterday. Evidently, Justin had taken a few days off to meet up with Eliza, and now she is hiking with him some.[†] It was good to see him again, and I really like Eliza. The rumor ahead of me, I hear, is that I got off the trail; funny, considering I hiked 17 days before taking a zero day at all, and I've only stayed in town twice, Hiawassee and at Charles' house. Do we ever escape misguided chatter?

The second night Walter and I camped together a little past Brown Fork Gap Shelter, tenting at a wide spot in the trail where we were witness to an amazing barred owl serenade. At first there were only two owls. One was very loud and was just above the spring, which was down the hill; the other one was answering the first and was perched right above our tents. Their calls were like nothing I had ever heard before, sometimes dragging out for 15 seconds and ending with a raspy screech that sounded like an angry monkey. Then, a third owl could be heard rivaling the first to be the loudest and most adamant. Perhaps, an owl courting ritual with two males competing for the quieter female's attentions?

E V E N I N G —

Adam arrived at 11:15am coming through with flying colors. He brought different clothes for me to wear while I was in town, lots of food, wine, maps, permission slips for me to sign for camps for the boys for the summer, and his warm kisses and his beautiful smile. Adam met Linc and Jeanie when they showed up at Fontana Village to do laundry. We stood together for a short while outside the laundry room talking and watching a blue-tailed skink in the doorway; they will be staying at the shelter tonight. I will have folks I know to hike into the Smokies with in the morning after all.

Jesse is right behind them also, they said. Justin and Eliza are staying at Fontana Inn, too. Since Adam had his truck, we gave Linc and Jeannie a ride from the post office back to the shelter. We went to the outfitters, ate lunch at the Bistro in the Lodge at Fontana Village, did laundry, checked into our neat little cabin, and went to Robbinsville library for internet access and then out to dinner.

The current plan is for Adam and the boys to meet me on trail next Wednesday to accompany me into Hot Springs during their spring break.

A P R I L   1 3

Adam walked from the dam to the trailhead at the entrance into the Smokies with me. It was hard to say goodbye yet again. Three weeks ago, when I left Springer Mountain parking lot, I was caught up in the eagerness to begin my journey and had not felt inclined to look back as my family pulled away; but this time, on every switchback up Shuckstack Mountain, I watched for Adam to cross back over the dam. I never did see him.

On the way up Shuckstack, I saw the first deer I've seen on the trail. Squirrels scampered about, and a pileated woodpecker darted through the treetops. I read later in the Mollies Ridge Shelter trail register that some hikers saw two wild boar early that morning. All I saw of the boar were tufts of hair lying on the trail. Shuckstack was not the four-mile nightmare I had expected. After Georgia, the long climbs don't seem so bad. I really thought I was doing well. I stopped to rest at Doe Knob, ate a snack and took off my boots. Spring beauties in full bloom carpeted the forest floor. The forest was predominantly birch, lending a fairy tale quality of light to the woods, and the carpet of white and pink flowers made the whole place seem surreal. Afternoon light slanted through the trees and shimmered on the silvery bark. I found myself thinking of how birch are the last to lose their leaves in the winter, envisioning this forest with dry brittle leaves rattling in the November wind with a silver moon peaking through clouds scurrying across the sky. I passed a huge tree with a hollow center and a peaked opening in its base, the perfect gnome home. I half expected Owl from *Winnie the Pooh* to appear. If only he had appeared with advice for how to accept what the trail handed me next.[†]

Just after the miles of spring beauties gave way to oak forest again, my left knee completely gave out. Someone asked me later about the mountain between Doe Knob and Mollies Ridge. I honestly don't remember any of it being difficult.

Shamans and Mohawks

"The real miracle is not to walk either on water or in thin air, but to walk on the earth."
— THICH NHAT HANH

There was no specific reason why my knee suddenly collapsed, aside from the simple, cumulative effects of 175 miles with a pack that was too heavy. I took a step and an excruciating, ripping pain shot through my entire knee. As it gave way, I caught myself with my poles. I thought, 'wow, that's not good'. I tried again to put weight on it—same pain accompanied with a wave of nausea. I tried again—same pain and a symphony now of nausea, dizziness and panic. I sat on a log and took off the pack. I tried again to put weight on it; no go. I lay down and cracked my back and tried again; no go. I sat on the log and took two Tylenol. I took out the book and figured I had about two more miles to reach the shelter. I sat on the log some more. Disbelief and a mild sense of panic began to take over my thoughts.

Jaguar came down the trail. I sent him on, saying to give me three hours to get to the shelter and if I didn't show up to come back for me. He left.

Along came Hippie Longstocking, Granite, and Pro from Dover. Hippie wouldn't hear of leaving me there. She gave her pack to Granite who left carrying both hers and his own. She took my pack, and we walked at my pace for the last mile and a half (it turned out). I limped along, supporting most of my weight on my poles.

As we walked, Hippie talked me through a shake-down of the items in my pack. It came down to clothing being the culprit category. "Tell me what clothes you are carrying in here," Hippie said. I listed them off: two pair of socks, one pair of underwear, one sports bra, long johns, two long sleeve shirts, a tank top, rain pants, rain jacket, polarfleece, hat, and gloves. It didn't sound like much to me. "Why do you have two shirts and a tank top?" she said. "One shirt is the one I hike in when it's chilly, and the other one is my dry one for camp. The tank top is what I wear when I'm washing all my other clothes." "That's good," she said. "You're on the right track, but you can go lighter. When you wash clothes, wear your rain gear; lose the extra long sleeve shirt, the extra tank top and the polarfleece. You may not even need the long underwear after the Smokies, and you can lose it, too. If you are cold at night, use everything you have to stay warm; sleep in your clothes and wrap your rain jacket around the outside of your sleeping bag. It will hold in any warmth that is escaping from the outside of the bag; it traps moisture, but it will keep you warmer if you need it."

My mind did not want to accept what Hippie was saying. My array of clothing seemed to already be much smaller than most people's; some were carrying entire ensembles for town, had several dry shirts and more than one polarfleece. I didn't want to embrace yet another level of deprivation on this trip, feeling compromised enough. But in the latter years of my life, I've learned to listen to those who have gone before and to apply what they have to offer so that I don't have to relive their mistakes out of my own stubborn pride. Her words gave me food for thought, a new and more extreme method of ultralite backpacking. I was familiar with the concept of items having more than one use, but this seemed to be bordering on not having what you needed when you needed it. There were other less extreme arguments she presented as well, however. We discussed the water filter, my heavy sleeping bag (2lbs13oz), the weight of the Osprey pack itself versus the ULA that she carried (only two pounds) and the amount of food to carry. I wasn't sure which pieces of her advice I would use, if any, but I certainly was intrigued when she said that her pack only weighed 22lbs! And perhaps, most of all, I admired Hippie's leadership and her confidence. Her unconditional assistance in my time of need served as an inspiration, showing me that challenging circumstances could be overcome with the right knowledge and the right attitude.

Hippie Longstocking, Pro from Dover, and Granite all pressed on after leaving me with their blessings at Mollies Ridge Shelter. Linc and Jeanie were there waiting. They retrieved water from the spring and set up my tent while I gratefully sat and cooked and discussed my situation with everyone. I was sick with the thought that this could be the end for me.

Sitting at the shelter all day on Friday was very difficult, watching as everyone packed up and headed out. Eliza, Justin, Linc, Jeanie, Danny Miles and many others left with best wishes and promises to send the

Ridgerunner when they saw him. Ridgerunners are employed by the park service to patrol the trails in the Smokies. All day I sat; I set up my stove and started cooking food, handing it out as people stopped for lunch, eating a lot of it myself, too. I knew this was the only way I could reduce the weight of my pack before attempting to hike out. I got rid of four meals that after-noon. By the end of the day, word came back via some southbounders that the Ridgerunner would arrive in the morning to carry my pack out. The park rangers would send a horse up to get me if they had to. It was hard to accept that I was leaving the trail. I think that if everything had not already been put into motion to get me out, that by Saturday morning, I would have attempted to continue on my own if at all possible.[†]

Down the trail came a person I recognized but couldn't place. I said, "don't I know you?" He said, "yes, you're Amy, and we met at Trail Fest last year and again at Trail Days." It was Lamar. He was a seasoned back-packer who had hiked every mile of the trails in the Smokies more than once. He understood thru-hiking and its challenges, the level of deprivation of comforts and the needs that accompany being a traveler on foot. He offered to drive me out of the park once I got to the trailhead. I guess if you have to be injured it helps to have friends come to your rescue.

Friday night I was able to reach Adam from Catskill Eagle's (another thru-hiker) Blackberry. I could hear the shock and disbelief on Adam's end of the line as I explained what was happening on my end. Despite my stoic exterior with everyone else who had been so helpful, once I heard Adam's voice, I began to cry. We left it that I would call him back as soon as I got out of the woods to let him know where to pick me up.

The next day, I was packed and preparing to leave when the Ridgerunner showed up. My knee was feeling much better. I'd been eating Aleve that someone gave me and was wearing a brace a friend of Lamar's had let me borrow. Graybeard, the Ridgerunner, took my pack, and we set off for Russell Field Shelter—piece of cake without a pack. The 5.8 miles down from Russell Field to Cades Cove was more difficult since it was downhill. My knee screamed all the way, but I had to get out somehow. This was not the same level of intolerable pain of two days before, so it was manageable. Lamar hiked out a different way with his hiking partners, got his car, and met me at the Ranger Station at Cades Cove. He graciously took me to his home, let me shower and eat a meal. I stayed at Lamar's that night, and we met Adam the next day in Newport, Tennessee.

The ride home was fraught with anxiety and permeated with a sense of failure. Adam did his best to assure me that my time off the trail would be temporary and to convince me that I just needed a week of rest. Once during our marriage when we had ended up in therapy sessions together, the psychologist had labeled me as suffering from "attachment to outcome", a concept whose dichotomy of relevance, both productive and non-productive, I simply could not grasp. In theoretical application in my life, I clung to productive attachment, unable to even glimpse its dark side which had haunted my sub-conscious since childhood. The term "attachment to outcome" has continued to pop into my mind at the most inopportune moments henceforth, this being one of those times, when its whisper became a raging current upon which I was about to be carried away.

Damn it! Of course I was attached to this outcome.

That was the WHOLE POINT! Thru-hike the AT: that means all of it. Settling for less was not an option. Consolation grounded in physical safety and reason was not an option. Crawling back to my pod and trying again another year was definitely not an option. The outcome had to be summiting Katahdin after walking there from Georgia, and nothing else would suffice.

Time became an enemy masquerading as a close friend. I knew that my knee needed rest, and that I must stay off of it for probably a week, but the variables of the equation pointed insistently to the deadline of October 15th for reaching Baxter State Park in Maine. Due to the nature of Maine winters, the trailhead to the mountain summit at the northern terminus of the trail closes on October 15th and woe to any dreaming hikers that do not arrive before then, for they will not be completing their thru-hike that year. Already knowing I am a slower hiker than most, I cannot afford to cut into available hiking time very deeply without considerably affecting the average number of miles needed per day to make it there in time.

Even though I had not actually fallen and injured my knee, I still wanted to have it x-rayed to be sure nothing was out of place and to hopefully eliminate the idea that I may be causing permanent damage by continuing to hike. Adam, no stranger to sports injury, had experienced good results with acupuncture and recommended his friend. I set up these appointments as soon as I arrived at Adam's house, not wanting anything to take very long and keep me from getting back on the trail within a week.

My days were occupied with cleaning Adam's house, helping the boys continue to get their rooms in order, a task hardly begun under Adam's watch, cooking meals for our family, and visiting with friends. There was no internet access, so I spent time at my friend, Cathy's, updating my journal online and catching up on email. Cathy pointed out during one of my lengthy lamentations that this knee injury was not a stand alone separate experience, but an integral part of my AT journey, and perhaps I should just relax and let the knee heal while I enjoyed being with my family. She helped me to understand that I was stubbornly holding on to my expectations of how this experience would be while the actual experience was offering a new challenge; it was up to me whether or not I chose to do what it would take to accept this challenge and succeed. This perspective gave me the freedom to enjoy this time off the trail; I had missed my family and friends so much during the first three weeks, and here I was home with them for a week! I stopped the needless fretting and began my plan of attack.

I took my pack back to Diamond Brand and relentlessly re-evaluated what I was carrying, keeping Hippie Longstocking's advice in mind. Together the sales associate and I cut every piece of extra webbing, straps, and fluff off my pack. I took off the top of the pack (known as the brain—now I'll be traveling without a brain!), all the buckles and straps I wouldn't be using, the inside divider, the inside water carrier pouch and buckles. The Osprey had weighed 4lbs 8oz, and now it weighs 3lbs 10oz empty. I also revisited the gear I had chosen. I gave up the ThermaRest (an older style that weighed over a pound), the water filter, two heavy stuff sacks and the Tevas. I replaced these items with Aquamira (chemical water treatment), ultralight stuff sacks, and Crocs (superlite camp shoes) and kept only my thinsulite foam pad to sleep on. Comfort may demand that be changed later, but that's the plan for now. I changed my pot for a smaller pan, changed the Nalgene for a plastic Gatorade bottle, and the Camelbak for two Platypus (clear plastic water bags). As far as winter clothes went, leaving the polarfleece at home became conceivable since I would most likely not be going back to the Smokies but would probably be getting back on the trail in Hot Springs. I took out the hat and gloves, replaced the heavyweight long under-wear with silk weight and kept only one long sleeve shirt. Hippie would be so proud! Another weight-saving measure that I opted for was the practice of shipping a bounce box from town to town ahead on the trail. I put (almost) all my incidentals in this bounce box, which I will send to myself at each mail drop along the way, thus not having to carry such items as shampoo, nail clippers, or extra tent stakes. I've gone from a base weight (no fuel, food, or water) of 24 pounds (at Charles' house on the bathroom scales) to 18lbs 4oz on a digital scale today at Diamond Brand. Loaded, with five days worth of food and fuel, but no water, my pack is at 26lbs 8oz. meaning that with 1 1/2 liters of water my pack weight will still be under 30 pounds.

The acupuncturist was my first appointment. Having always preferred alternative medicine to conventional, this was no leap of faith, but it was some-thing I had never tried before. Lying still for 15 minutes with needles in my knees and feet, first on the left, then on the right, was akin to listening to someone scrape their fingernails down a chalkboard—not excru-ciating pain just something you wish would hurry up and end. Afterward, the pain in my knees lessened considerably, and I felt a ray of hope begin its magic. An interesting tidbit of Chinese traditional medicine draws a parallel between the knees (considered to be a kidney meridian) and the emotion of fear and its connection with will power. This gave me much food for thought concerning my push for this goal and the emotions I'd been wrestling these first three weeks of hiking.

As the release of this blocked energy was facilitated, the way was cleared for a more constructive energy flow. Many interesting things began to happen in rapid succession. I received a phone call from Calen Rayne, a shaman who attends our Unitarian Universalist church. He had learned that I was home with an injury when Joseph stood up before the congregation and lit a candle asking for everyone to send their healing prayers my way. Calen offered to perform a sound-healing session on my knee to see what we might accomplish. No way was I going to pass up another opportunity for healing. I eagerly scheduled the appointment that very evening.

The session began on a massage table around which was positioned many statues, symbols, bells and instruments, some of which I recognized and some I didn't, from many different faiths around the world. As an anthropologist and a Unitarian Universalist for 15 years, personally, I maintain a firm faith in that which defies explanation and accept the concept of Mystery in its many different cloaks. My countenance was one free of expectation or judgment, only quiet acceptance, much akin to a hiker trudging up a mountain. As I lay still with my eyes closed on the table, the silence in the room was punctuated with various rhythms, bells and rattles. I had no concept of time and don't know how long I lay there, but a sublime sense of peace and well-being made time irrelevant. The final blissful tone of a Himalayan singing bowl resonated throughout my bones. I opened my eyes, curious to what Calen may have discovered. Sound, or vibrational healing, I learned is used to facilitate a particular meditation technique employed by the shaman called kala-vancana. Various vibrations serve to "re harmonize" the energy flow within the person experiencing the imbalance. Meanwhile, the shaman receives medical intuitive readings about their subject.

"The problem is not coming from your knee, Willow," he said. "I am finding that the problem is in your right foot, here." He pointed to the third metatarsal bone on my foot, the very place that had been giving me so much excruciating nervy pain and tingling sensations the first week on the trail. The memory of my entire right leg being numb for days and the pinched nerve sensation in my right toes surfaced. Calen had not read my journals, nor had I told him about these other problems, as it seems I had successfully blocked the details from my memory. While my mind then raced through all the issues I'd experienced with my right leg and foot in the first weeks on the trail, he crossed the room and placed his hand on a diagram of human body systems that covered the far wall, pinpointing the metatarsal of the third toe. This was where the problem with my left knee was originating, a strain on my knee generated by compen-sating for and favoring the right foot, he said. We agreed that tomorrow during my appointment with the conventional doctor I should discuss the problems with my foot just as importantly as the problems with my knee. We compared our plans for the Sunday I was to begin on the trail again; Calen would be able to send a protective bubble to surround me as I walked, an energy field which would deflect negative influences and possibly further injury, providing me with a safe place to step wherever the trail led. I left his presence reluctantly, rather stunned and thoughtful.

Armed with this new information, I went back to the acupuncturist to have her focus her treatment on the nerve sensations that plagued my right foot. I explained what the shaman had discovered and asked if there were a way for her needles to, in effect, tell the nerves to "shut up!" She meticulously placed new needles which generated great heat in the spot she had chosen on my foot. Again, I lay still for an indeterminable eon. This time I was very aware of the nerve sensations in my right foot afterward, and how they had changed from the painful tingling I had learned to ignore to a dull tingle similar to a limb falling asleep. My knee seemed unchanged this time, although, simple rest was working its own form of wonder there, I was sure. I now looked forward to speaking with the sports doctor to see what his expertise could add to the farrago.

I approached this mainstream doctor with the knee issue but also recounted the initial troubles with my right foot. After x-rays, his verdict was that there is no lasting damage to the knee, and the right foot, which indeed started the problem in the first place, is suffering from interodigital neuritis, a fancy word for a pinched nerve caused by the bones being compressed, causing a crushing effect. In my attempts to avoid that sensation, overcompensating with the left leg, strained the knee. Interestingly enough, this doctor said to me, "Whatever you do, don't stop hiking the Trail!" I guess that's the difference between a modern sports doctor and your mother's general practitioner. I was grateful for his ability to understand the drive that I have to do this and his support of my quest despite the obvious dangers; we all live one human experience after all. He gave me a metatarsal pad to place on the insole of my boot under the ball of my right foot. It functions to spread the metatarsal bones over the slightly raised section and lessen the pinching sensation in the nerves. He also prescribed a ridiculously expensive orthopedic knee brace for me to wear which feels so great I wish I had one for the other knee, too. Now I can set about acquiring weird tan lines on my left leg that include a circle on top of my knee cap. Charming, don't you think?

The plan is to go to Hot Springs, North Carolina in two more days, camp with my family and friends and enjoy the Appalachian Trail festival held there each spring called Trail Fest. The Trail is routed right down the main street of Hot Springs, and the hiking community supplies a large portion of this small mountain town's local economy. I'll visit with any hiking friends that have reached Hot Springs, and those that have passed the town already will catch shuttles back so they can participate. In order to have officially hiked the entire Appalachian Trail, I will have to go back after my summit of Katahdin in fall and pick up the missed miles. By starting at Davenport Gap, I will be skipping the 58 remaining miles of the Smokies. My thinking here is that I can't go back and start 10-mile days right away with the injury. Restrictions on how many days you have to get through the Smokies as a thru-hiker would require a daunting number of miles per day, and I don't want to be under pressure to hike if I don't feel up to it. I'll pick up just beyond the Smokies, where I can regulate daily mileage myself, and I'll come back and do the 58 miles of the Smokies this fall with Adam and the boys. Yes, it's a compromise. It has required a few days of deliberation to reach a mind space that accepts this change of plans, but I am at peace with the decision and will be relieved to be back on the trail.

For some reason (maliciously yet to be revealed), things were supposed to happen this way, and coming to terms with that has been the mountain I've been climbing this week. I've struggled to keep faith in myself, but I have met many incredible people who were willing to help me find that faith again. Everyone offered positive energy and lots of encouragement. I have to believe that a part of my lesson has been to learn to accept the Flow no matter where the current carries me. Losing the last of the "luxuries" has made me resentful of other hikers who can carry more weight. I'm fighting this attitude though for it does not serve me; sometimes I'm winning, sometimes I'm losing. It doesn't seem fair that the 175lb guys can have luxuries because they can carry them, but technically, I guess it is. As a 98-pound female, I simply can't afford that any longer. When I catch myself thinking I am at a disadvantage, I remember this: we all have to carry our own shit, whether we are climbing Katahdin or traveling the River Styx. How much shit do you carry? Where are your priorities?

❀ ❀ ❀

THE PACK STORY CONT'D

At Bluff Mountain Outfitters in Hot Springs, I made another commitment to the ultralite concept by purchasing a new pack, choosing the woman's Granite Gear Vapor Ti because it weighs only two pounds. It was kind of sad giving up my long researched and anticipated Osprey; but realistically, I have to be willing to do what it takes to make this work, and saving another pound and a half off my base weight is important right now. Fully loaded I am now at 27 pounds! There are two outside zippered pockets at the top, one on each side. In those I'm carrying things I will need during the day—AquaMira, headlamp, pocketknife, Ziploc bag wallet, and pack cover. The pack also has a more padded hipbelt and a weight limit of 35 pounds, therefore it does not have the capacity to carry more than I can handle.[†]

A P R I L   2 3
H O T   S P R I N G S ,   N C

With the help of family and friends, another big decision was reached at Trail Fest after much discussion. I will get back on the trail from here instead of Davenport Gap at the northern edge of the Smokies. By leaving from Hot Springs after Trail Fest, I will remain on "schedule" for my maildrops and for summiting Katahdin before October 15th. I won't have to rush to make up miles, and I will remain in proximity with hikers I've already befriended. After completing the rest of the trail, I'll return to hike the 93 miles from Russell Field Shelter, where I left the trail in the Smokies, to Hot Springs. The quintessential trail town of Hot Springs will be a fitting finish for my journey, and hopefully I will then be able to celebrate my victory with family and friends here in a town close to home. I am satisfied with this compromise, which releases me of any guilt or feelings of shortcoming that might have undermined my resolve. I do not think I am sacrificing the integrity of my thru-hike, a subject of continuous debate among hikers. Others may believe differently, but the motto is: "Hike your own hike."

Back on the trail, I am battling mixed emotions. Having such a wonderful time at home with my family emphasized that I really didn't want to be away for the next five months. Although I am happy to be able to continue hiking and pleased with how well today's five miles went, every step was accompanied by thoughts of my family.

I left town around 1pm, I think, maybe a little later. I hiked slowly and carefully. When I finally stopped for a break and added up the mileage, I was surprised by how far I'd come. I was a bit familiar with this section of the trail because I hiked it last summer, which probably made time seem to pass more quickly. I was lost in thought when suddenly my focus blurred in a shimmering arc that extended on both sides around me. I hesitated, wondering if I was about to faint. A thought popped in from nowhere, and I found myself thinking of the protective bubble Calen had promised. A sensation of air rushing by to fill an empty space, much like the sound you hear when you enter the chamber of a revolving door, overtook me. My bubble of protection had arrived! I walked on wondering why I never pursued my love of anthropology to become some female Indiana Jones or another Jane Goodall, for most certainly the world's secrets have not all been revealed.

I made camp just off a dirt Forest Service road to the west of a gravel road on Mill Ridge. The dirt road led to a small secluded field. On a level area on one edge of the field, I pitched the tent in a little dip where it could not be seen from the road. As I rest here, the wind blows large, cumulus clouds across the sky. For most of the afternoon there has been more blue sky than clouds, but that seems to be changing. There are still hours of daylight left, but I set up camp anyway, knowing I need to take it easy at first. Adam will meet me at Sam's Gap where the AT crosses I-26 this coming Friday morning. I have four full days and a morning to go 38.4 miles. That should give me eight- to nine-mile days. Afterwards, with two more 10-mile days, I will reach Erwin, Tennessee. For most hikers, it's only four days from Hot Springs to Erwin, but I'll be taking a week. At this pace, I won't make it to Katahdin before winter.[†]

However, the slower pace has changed my attitude. I found tonight's beautiful campsite by taking my time. I have daylight to spare and am enjoying lounging in my tent in this field watching the clouds. I cooked and ate leisurely and will probably snack again before dark or have some hot chocolate. Tomorrow morning I anticipate some yoga before packing up. No one else is here to pace myself by. I'll get up when I get up, and not when a whole shelter full of people start shuffling around to start their day. I'll get my rhythm back before joining the crowd again. I can't camp alone all the time—I will get too lonely, I think—but tonight is good.

A P R I L   2 4

My Grandaddy always said, "To bed with the chickens, up with the chickens." Sometime early this morning, before I was fully awake, a fox barked. I rose early and hiked a couple of miles in the cool morning air before stopping at a spring and snacking on zucchini bread Mom had mailed to Hot Springs. Fiddleheads unfurled in the damp humus at the spring. The sweet bread contains black walnuts my late grandmother cracked. I kept the walnuts in the freezer and gave them to Mom before I left so she could use them in the cakes she baked. Three generations of homemaking—black walnuts cracked by Grandma's patient hands, baked into goodies by Mom, and then eaten by daughter while hiking the AT—powerful sustenance.[†]

Four roses Adam gave me are fastened to the top of my pack where he tied them yesterday afternoon. He bought them while I was staying with him and the boys last week. He had gone to the grocery store to get some things for lunches for the maildrop boxes; when he got home, he set them in a vase on the counter while I was busy cooking dinner. I worked all around them without seeing them for a long time. Finally, when I did see them, I was really surprised to find them sitting there—like "Where did these come from?" He laughed and told me a man in the store had said to him, "Whatever you did wrong, it's alright now!" The flowers came with us to Hot Springs and graced our picnic table all weekend, and now they remind me, every time I see their shadow cast from the top of my pack onto the ground ahead of me, that Adam and the boys love and miss me.

A turtle toiled along the gravel road on Mill Ridge. I snapped a picture and told her she was beautiful. Something about finding turtles is rooted in the sweet nothingness of childhood summers in the Blue Ridge Mountains of Virginia. Upon discovering one, there is always a distinct sense that all is right with the world. Many native traditions associate turtles with the origin of the continent. As an animal totem they represent balance and harmony and are symbols of self-reliance and strength. I carry these reminders away from Mill Ridge.[†]

April's glory is in full swing, sprouting flowers and butterflies everywhere. Wild geraniums, trillium, rue anemones, several varieties of violets (white, yellow, and purple), wild strawberries, snakeberries (they look like wild strawberries but have yellow flowers instead of white and they fruit above the leaves instead of below), fire pinks, wild mustard, black cohosh and lots more I didn't know. Fluttering around them are lesser fritillaries, dog sulphurs, cabbage sulphurs, dianas, spicebush swallowtails, tiger swallowtails, painted ladies, and the tiny purply-blue butterflies I never learned the name of. A skipper landed on my toe when I had my boots and socks off during a break in the sun. Black and white spotted, its legs were loaded with bright yellow pollen. Skippers are kind of like daytime moths and are named for their erratic flight. They are cate- gorized between moths and butterflies, displaying characteristics of both such as plume-like antennae like moths but with an upright wing carriage similar to butterflies.[†]

T he west slope of the knoll in the oak forest where I am tenting is covered in lily of the valley. I've set the door to face the rising sun. Pro from Dover passed by sans Hippie and Granite; he stopped to ask about my knee. He passed along the info that there is a "hiker feed" set up at the next gap. All the big milers that didn't leave Hot Springs until this morning are stopping there to eat. I am reminded that soon everyone will pass me again.

My knee did alright, and I really like the brace, but the downhills did hurt quite a bit. After I settled in my tent, I used some Aspercreme someone had given me at the campground in Hot Springs. It seems to work pretty good to relieve the soreness. The knee isn't swelling too much, but ice on it would feel good. Haha! Ice! What a concept. As I sat fingering the tender area around my kneecap, my perception became wavery; I smelled the familiar metallic smell of fear and an inky blackness crept in from both sides of my vision. I was losing consciousness. When I was a child, I would faint quite often, and developed quite an elaborate routine for fighting the undertow. Tonight, miles from nowhere, with no one around, for some reason I didn't fear the void, only regarded the realization with a calm sense of curiosity. As quickly as the sensations arrived they dissipated. I wondered again about that bubble of protection. And, I wondered about personal strength and exactly what that means.

The radio says there will be thunderstorms tonight and tomorrow. The temperature is supposed to be much lower tomorrow. I hiked with the radio on, enjoying what few luxuries I do have as often as I wish out of pure self-pity. I do wish for a book to read, though. Stopping early in the day leaves a lot of daylight to kill before bed. I intended to do seven miles, but I think I ended up with a little over eight. I was beat by the time I found a tent site. In case it storms, I've taken extra care staking down the tent. A woodpecker's percussion provides a background rhythm for the droning of a fly caught between the tent screen and rain fly. In the distance is the white noise of a swiftly flowing creek. The sun sets slowly.

A P R I L   2 5

The hiker feed Pro from Dover had mentioned turned out to be an ongoing thing, and I was going to get to participate after all. Sweet! A sign at the bottom of Allen Gap indicated there would be food at a house 300 yards down the road. Even though I had just eaten re-hydrated scrambled eggs with Tabasco for breakfast, the prospect of waffles was too tempting. At the road, I met Clay and Branch. They are a younger couple hiking together. Their pace is slow and steady, and they both seemed to take a lot of care to look out for the other one. Once again, being in the presence of a couple made me feel at home. Clay and Branch accompanied me to the beautiful log cabin for a sit-down breakfast, complete with coffee and waffles and even blackberry jelly, my favorite. Other hikers were already there, and more arrived as we ate. There was an offer of lunch immediately after we finished breakfast. Everyone else chose to stay and eat more food, but I packed up and headed up the mountain in the rain. Knowing it would take me much longer to hike than everyone else, I wanted to get started.

On the way up, I discovered I could affect how my knee felt by using different leg muscles. By leaving my heel on the ground on the uphills and using my quads to pull I could isolate that set of muscles and not continue to use only my calf muscles to push off. This balance seemed to appease my knee greatly. In Hot Springs a friend had suggested that an imbalance in quad and calf muscle strength might be at the root of my knee problems. Operating under that premise, I decided to make a concerted effort to strengthen my quads to counter balance the pull of the strength of my growing hiker calf muscles. The technique seems to have worked, as I was able to do over 10 miles without feeling much of a strain. I didn't originally intend to go that far today, but when I hit my eight- to nine-mile goal, I was on a high rocky ridgeline with no place to stop.

On the ridgeline of Black Rock Cliffs the trail was constructed of boulders placed in such a way that each step was perfectly spaced. The rocks were so precisely positioned that no boulders moved underfoot. Most had been blasted and placed one on top of each other.

Some were ground into small bits and shoveled between naturally positioned boulders to form a flat walking area. This meticulous trail design went on for miles along this ridgeline. The 360 degree view included Tennessee on one side and North Carolina on the other. In some places the passage between rocks was just large enough for a person. In other places, what appeared from a distance to be a pile of jumbled rocks, actually was a very clear path that lay chiseled out before you once you reached the top. It was the most amazing feat of trail construction I've ever seen.

The ridgeline was incredibly exposed so there was an alternate trail for use during bad weather. Of course, even though there was thunder rumbling that evening, all the thru-hikers chose to take the exposed ridge trail. Several were caught up there during the storm. I had just finished eating and was settling into my tent for the night when the storm started. I had come all the way off the mountainside and set up camp in a saddle gap on the east side. The wind ripped through the trees on the west side. The dip of the saddle protected my tent site, and the wind roared above me—I was relieved. The ground where I had staked down was so humus and soft, I wasn't so sure the stakes would hold in a hard blow. Once the wind abated and went roaring off over the next mountain, a thunderbolt cracked right beside me to the west, and the sky opened. Lightning must have struck on the ridge. I lay there listening to World Cafe on NPR, turning the volume up all the way to hear it over the din. Rain pelted the tent hard. I watched a mosquito hawk crawl around on the outside of the mesh between the mesh and the tent fly, riding out the storm perfectly safe. When the wind blew particularly hard, he would crouch down low, clinging to the mesh with long spindly legs. I wondered if he even knew it was raining at all since he wasn't getting wet. Bob Dylan sang "Things Have Changed", and the rain continued to pour.

A P R I L   2 6

As I lay silently debating whether or not to get up, the rain that had stopped during the night began again. I stayed in the tent dozing off and on until again the rain stopped after another half hour or so. I ate a pemmican bar for breakfast, nibbling it as I packed up, postponing cooking until I could reach the shelter two miles away. I packed up my wet tent, and as I set off up the trail, rain again began to fall. At the shelter I met three other thru-hikers while we tried to wait out the rain. They had stayed there during the storm and were the last of the hikers to leave the shelter for the day. I cooked some oatmeal, filled up my water bottle, and procrastinated, listening to the two male hikers belittle and tease the female hiker "all in fun". She laughed and punched one of them, a confusing reaction which pissed me off. Being a leftover from times before the backlash against feminism, I'm not comfortable addressing young women's issues about which I tend to have ridiculously strong, possibly unjustified, opinions. These young people were only a few years older than my own kids. I didn't want to be involved and was grateful I was hiking alone. I decided to just do it and headed back out into the rain and the peace.

For another mile it rained, but when it stopped, I was in the most beautiful forests interspersed with small meadows. The trail traversed through a meadow on top of a mountain, and then plunged into a birch forest carpeted with sleeping trout lilies and spring beauties, then slipped around huge boulders back out into another misty meadow. As clouds blew off the mountaintops, the air grew crisp and clear, and colors popped in the glistening dampness. At only 7.9 miles it seemed like an incredibly short day.

I am holed up at Flint Mountain Shelter for the night. We are full because of the rain, which began again just before dark. It was good to get some rest, though. My knee seems to be holding up, but rest is wise, I'm sure. Another short day tomorrow—just to the next shelter, so I can be at Sam's Gap on Friday morning to meet Adam.

A P R I L   2 7

I was happy to run into Linc and Jeannie not far after passing Devil Fork Gap. I had not seen them since my knee injury left me sitting at Mollies Ridge Shelter in the Smokies. We chatted about emerging wildflowers we saw along the way, enjoying plant identification and catching up on trail stories. Linc held Jeanne's hand at a stream crossing. He even waited to see if I wanted a hand also. They both hike in Keen sandals rather than hiking boots and wear wool socks when the air is cold. Neither one carries hiking poles. We hiked together the rest of the day, actually hitting a rather quick pace at times, me tagging along behind, arriving early in the afternoon at Hogback Ridge Shelter. Linc and Jeanne set about their routine of making camp and baking sourdough.

Since I didn't want to push my knee, I planned to tent for the night and meet Adam 2.4 miles away at Sam's Gap the next morning for resupply. Once again though, the wonders of modern technology reached out and sucked me in, playing me like a violin. Sage, a hiker resting at Hogback Ridge Shelter, offered the use of his cell phone. I contacted Adam and let him know I had arrived early; he said he could be at Sam's Gap in a couple of hours, take me to town for the night and bring me back in the morning. I did not resist.[†]

The 2.4 miles to Sam's Gap moved fairly quickly, most of it being a gently graded downhill; no doubt my motivation of going to town for the night sped me up some, too. Adam was at the parking area at Sam's Gap where other hikers were gathered getting rides into town or coming back from beer runs. We stopped at a local diner and ate—first things first—and then went home to the boys.

Once at Adam's house, a strange restlessness set in. I was glad to be with family, but something is shifting within me. With my injury on the mend and the unexpectedness of this visit, a mysterious impulsion is gaining a hold on my consciousness, dividing my loyalties between family and trail. I did not feel present this time. Last visit, I quite contentedly cooked and cleaned for the boys and Adam, but somehow this time I felt obligated rather than giving freely from my heart. I called Gaia, a friend who had hiked the trail the previous summer; we were trying to arrange going back to the trail together. Gaia knew several of this year's hikers that had come into town from Sam's Gap, and they were staying at her house. I felt the pull of the trail community battling the pull of my family. On the phone, Gaia observed that my family was placing a lot of demands on me during a time when I should be focusing on reaching my goal. I waved off her observation; she was young and had not been blessed yet with children of her own. But, a part of me did recognize it was time to move on; I needed to break this habit of coming home before it jeopardized my resolve to continue the hike. My family needed me, and I needed them, but in this endeavor we would have to embrace needing each other in different ways than physical presence.

Caller ID displayed the high school calling. A bad feeling crept over me as I answered. The athletic director was calling to let me know that Joseph had been caught stealing food from the cafeteria and was being suspended for two days, Monday and Tuesday. The athletic director and I are no strangers to conversations regarding the actions of my oldest son; we've debated the concept of discipline more than once, and he is aware that my methods are vastly different from the public school system's. However, I have always been unfailing in my support of the school's efforts to involve parents, and I recognize the schools have little resources for dealing with the hundreds of problem children that come to them from broken homes, poverty, and abusive situations. Being a single parent whose kids fell into the category of "broken home", I've never hesitated to cooperate when these kinds of phone calls came. I assured him the issue would be addressed at home.

Crap. What now? Grayson would be in school all day Monday and Tuesday; Adam would be at work. The idea that sending a child home to spend the day unsupervised as punishment has never made sense to me, especially when said child is a teenager, quite capable of getting into even more trouble while on suspension. Being out of school is exactly what they want. And what the hell is Joseph doing stealing food anyway? I was with them this morning. Didn't he pack his lunch when Grayson did? A vague awareness that things were spiraling out of control overtook me. Gaia's words echoed in my mind. I could so easily see how my family could just continue to have need after need, and I would never make it back to the trail.

When Adam came home, we discussed options. He did not have anyone lined up as backup that might fill in and stay with Joseph those days. This lack of forethought for emergencies made me furious, but it was too late to question whether he could parent the children effectively while I was away. "Ok," I said, "there is no other choice. He's coming with me. You'll just have to figure out how to come get him on Tuesday so he can be back in school by Wednesday." "I think that's a great idea! He'll benefit from spending the time with you, and he won't be sitting home playing video games," Adam replied. 'Yeah, I'll just bet you think it's a great idea,' I thought to myself. Again, I heard Gaia's words. Damn, now I was stuck hiking with my delinquent son, whose delinquency was probably related to my absence in the first place, while I chased this stupid dream, and his father struggled to keep up with two kids he had never parented alone.

Clearly, I needed an attitude adjustment or this next four days with my son would never work. When Adam and I unveiled the concept of his very own juvie wilderness camp to Joseph, he visibly balked. That was vindicating. "I was going to play Nintendo!" he fussed. "Yes, well, now you're not. Find your backpack; you're coming with me." The evening wore on while Joseph hunted down various pieces of camping equipment, found warm hiking clothes, and packed food. Adam and I discussed further. It was obvious Joseph needed to spend the time with me; I had been his only source of discipline for the last six years. I was the one he responded to, and I was the one who was available to be with him these next few days. Adam admitted he felt things were going awry at his house, and that he was having a difficult time establishing rapport with Joseph. His grades had been slipping, and he was never where he was supposed to be. I could see that bringing Joseph along on the AT was just one more step, another way this thru-hike was uniquely my own. You do what you have to do to reach Katahdin. I actually began to look forward to Joseph's company.

A P R I L   2 9

Ah, the stamina of youth! Joseph's first day out we did 11 miles. For the first few hours there was continual complaining; I'm not sure if that was for his benefit or mine. He perked up after we came across hikers 56 and Katori doling out trail magic on Big Bald at lunch time. Hot dogs cooked on a grill on top of the world, Little Debbies and sodas.[†]

A scarlet tanager winged by us on the trail, the first I've ever seen in the wild; the bird was so bright it caught Joseph's imagination, and he stalked it through the forest so he could watch it as long as possible. As an animal totem, the scarlet tanager heralds a serious lesson that needs to be learned, just the bird for him to be stalking. Thank goodness he wasn't sitting home playing video games.

Alone on the trail all day, we tented at a campsite in Whistling Gap.

A P R I L   3 0

My delay in getting out of bed this morning only brought rain. We ate cheese grits in a cold drizzle and broke camp shivering in the cold. Today was my chance to make a difference for Joseph. I asked him about stealing food, already guessing it had been going on for weeks. He admitted quite readily this was not the first or the only time he had done it, and he launched into quite a disenchanted soliloquy regarding capitalism, prices and unnecessary rules. Beneath all this, I heard a cry of deprivation. It turns out, after piecing together the story, Joseph was spending his extra time in the mornings spiking his mohawk instead of packing his lunch, and Adam had refused to pack his lunch for him. He was ending up at school every day with no food and no money. We discussed the immorality of taking things that don't belong to you, me citing times he had things stolen from him. We discussed time management, constructive usage of time, why Adam shouldn't have to pack his lunch so he can spike his hair, and alternative plans for mornings. I declared the spiking days to be over. He walked ahead and didn't speak to me for a few hours. After awhile, he simply stated he understood and could we please not talk about it anymore. I could only hope I had gotten through and honor his request, otherwise everything I had said would be lost. We were freed to enjoy the rest of our time together.

We put in seven miles by 2pm to the next shelter where we cooked a huge lunch and ate and chatted with thru-hikers Bare Bear and Dick Tracy. Then, we were off again to do the remaining 5.7 miles to Erwin. Joseph's constant chatter stopped completely today under the mileage. Mine did too, for that matter—13 miles. We hitched a ride into town that dropped us off at Miss Janet's at 6:30pm where we ate a huge spaghetti dinner and watched movies.

Hitching into town with my teenage son was a trail experience that causes a mom to think twice while the mind dredges up all the fears we are supposed to let govern our lives. Miss Janet operates a shuttle from the trailhead to her home on Elm Street every evening during the peak hiker season. When Joseph arrived long before I did at the bottom of the mountain, he sat on the guardrail by the side of the road and watched as Miss Janet's shuttle left. He caught an earful from me when I finally made it to the road and found out he had let our shuttle leave without us. We passed Uncle Johnny's hostel but had our hearts set on staying in town, and I had a maildrop that had been mailed to Miss Janet's.

How do you teach your teenager about hitchhiking without feeling guilt? We walked a mile while I wrestled those logistics. The car that stopped was a beat up station wagon filled with junk. But Hiker Trash, the driver, started spouting out names of thru-hikers both past and present, telling stories of his hikes, and praising Miss Janet for her involvement in the hiker community before we ever got our packs loaded in the car, so I knew we were going to get there in one piece, despite his questionable presentation. I saw the hesitation cloud Joseph's face, and I nodded. Joseph has grown up in the mountain counties of the southern Appalachians; he knows first hand the goodness of heart of some of the roughest looking characters. By the time we arrived at Miss Janet's, he was having a good laugh at the sight we made.[†]

Tomorrow we will hang out till noon or so and then hike out to the next shelter so Joseph will have a chance to stay in a shelter, a tent, and a hostel all in his four days of juvie wilderness camp. We will meet Adam at Indian Grave Gap on Tuesday around noon.

On the way to Curly Maple Gap Shelter, Joseph hiked with Sweet Tea, a young man whom I had met a few weeks earlier. They hit it off really well, and I found it interesting that their conversation took off after going through a listing of the cartoons they both liked. Later when I met up with Bare Bear and Dick Tracy, my own contemporaries, we reminisced over black and white TV, 'I Love Lucy', 'The Lone Ranger' and 'The Wild Wild West' shows. An unnamed cultural ritual to establish generational priorities?

Staying at the shelter was a rather odd experience for a mother of a teenager in captivity, considering most of the people that stayed there that night were smoking a bong and drinking liquor. A teaching opportunity? I struggled more with my own inability to confront their inconsiderateness than I did with how to talk to Joseph about what we were witnessing. I know I have done the right thing by bringing my son out to hike with me rather than leaving him home alone during the school days, but hanging out with him in the midst of a partying crowd of 20-somethings had not really been a part of the boot camp plan. Fortunately enough, Joseph found their stoned antics only mildly entertaining, and he saw quite distinctly things he did not want to emulate. We were able to discuss the event from the perspective of outsiders, a luxury many mothers of wayward teens don't get. I continue to be ever grateful.

Besides Sweet Tea, the inconsideration of Joseph's impressionable age occurred to only one other hiker. Last night was the first time I'd run across this group of young male hikers and their accompanying substances. If others were using, they had the decency to not be so flagrantly disrespectful. One hiker struck up a conversation with me about it the next morning on the trail. He was the one person in the crowd my age or older. The thought had actually occurred to him, but it had not deterred him, nor had it inspired him to rein in their antics as their elder peer. I voiced my displeasure regarding the whole evening, and he apologized on his own behalf and stressed to me that the rest of them were too young to even realize what had transpired. Dubious forgiveness of my own paralysis fringed my thoughts after the opportunity to talk to him, but I was still keenly aware of my failure to stand up for myself and my son. Obviously, I'm struggling more than I realized with this responsible aging thing.

Joseph and I arrived at the road in Indian Grave Gap from Curley Maple Gap Shelter about 11:30am according to Joseph's cell phone. I was actually sad to see my hiking buddy go home; it had been fun to have someone to talk to, and this might be the last time I see Joseph for months. I will not see Adam again until he comes to meet me on my birthday in June.

M A Y   2

The ethereal beauty of Unaka Mountain eventually obscured any worries about maturity. Switchbacks snaked up the rocky elevation gain. Gradually the grade lessened and the ground was covered with bright green grass.[†]The trees were mostly birch. Higher on the mountain, the trees were stunted and short; the grasses were long and blowing in the breeze with intermittent patches of cedar then more birch and grass. Ahead the edge of a dark forest was visible.[†] Soon I was enveloped by a forest of giant red cedar covered in a pale pistachio-green lichen.[†]Carpeting the rocks was emerald green moss and lacy ferns. The effect created a cathedral hush to footsteps on the spongy ground. I slowed to a crawl, absorbing the boreal magic through every pore. On the other side of the mountain, the rocky trail returned and the steep descent took over my attention. This last 1.5 miles took absolutely forever. I thought I would never get to the shelter. There are seven hikers at Cherry Gap Shelter sharing a fire. Rain has passed by for now.

They Say 40 is the New 30

MAY 4

The concept of switchbacks was abandoned completely for this section of trail. The poor attempt at a switchback up out of Hughes Gap simply meant the trail went straight up, changed directions, then went straight up some more. That, combined with the idea implanted in my head by the 1.8 miles listed in the book, qualified the endless climb as a time warp. I was sure the sun had not moved in the sky for hours but was hung somehow over Hughes Gap forever. My mind kept singsong chanting "Help! I'm in Hughes Gap and I can't get out!" The mountain, which was named Beartown Mountain, became 'Mother of All Bears Mountain', as I trudged up it, cursing under my breath. Toward the top, the change in altitude (5300 feet) brought the bright, green grasses and the birch trees back. The beauty finally got the better of my foul mood as I climbed higher into this mossy, grassy wonderland of huge boulders and grand vistas. I stopped often and took pictures and walked slower from my own reverie than from the terrain.[†]

M A Y   5

Morning dawned foggy and rainy at Overmountain Shelter. This renowned shelter is a big, red barn.[†] Although it was fairly warm, I was uncomfortable all night (no ThermaRest on hard wood). I awoke in the darkness, suddenly alert. I turned over and looked out from the barn loft door at multiple lights bouncing along the hillside. Without glasses, I thought it might be fireflies, which didn't seem likely this early in the season. With glasses, I witnessed the progression of a large group of hikers coming down the mountainside trail toward the shelter. Their headlamps alternately bounced and twinkled and beamed as each person picked their way through the forest. I counted seven; no wait, here came two more farther toward the top. I could now hear their distant voices, muffled by the damp air. It was the most eerie sight, watching them approach, as if I were an initiate into a secret society, witnessing some clandestine ritual known only to night hikers. Five of them dropped their bags in the bottom of the barn and brought their sleeping bags up to the loft. Then, they went back outside where the rest had already spawned a small tent city and were lighting their stoves. The group split into small circles, each circle forming around a glowing stove while they cooked and ate. Shadows from their headlamps outlined their features against the darkness, and only their hands were lit. After all that, I slept, but only briefly; then, I read a little from the glow of my own headlamp inside my sleeping bag—even more uncomfortable. I was glad I had kept the paperback *The DaVinci Code* after Joseph finished it. Close to dawn, I fell mercifully asleep for a third time. I was up and on the trail by 7:45am.

I imagine the English moors to be much like the trail over these balds. Steve, who is visiting from the UK, attests this area is much like his homeland. I love the overcast sky, the varied tones of gray and the Moorish land features—mist hung in the still air. Hiking up the balds kept me quite warm in the gentle drizzle without the bother of rain gear. Peaks of distant mountains could occasionally be glimpsed through shifting clouds.[†] Huge boulders appeared out of the fog on the tops of hills in groupings hauntingly reminiscent of Old World menhirs.[†] I daydreamed of moving to Ireland as I dodged huge cow patties, putting the miles away with the easy hiking. By 12:30 I had gone all but half a mile from my destination. I postponed lunch in favor of a shower and pushed on in to the Mountain Harbour B&B. The rain began to come down hard not long after I was settled inside.

The Mountain Harbour Bed and Breakfast maintains a Hiker Barn, a quaint, clean and very comfortable hostel created from converted barn loft. I shared the accommodations with Steve, Sage, Grits and Wade. We all rode into Elk Park in the owner's king cab pickup truck and had dinner together at the local diner, each of us marveling at just how much the other was eating. Thank goodness for a mattress to sleep on tonight. And the rain came down!

I called my college friend, John, who lives nearby and arranged to meet him tomorrow morning. He will hike with me from here to US321—about three days. I am excited to have a chance to hike with him and happy it worked out so easily. I expect to be in Damascas, Virginia by Wednesday, May 10th. I spent the evening chatting with Steve and learning about the UK. Life is good.[†]

John, the Lion-hearted, Johnny Be Good, US Army certified Panama Jungle Expert. Johnny defies all explanation. He is the mythical prince on a white stallion, the ever-elusive free spirit, the "give you his shirt off his back" Samaritan, and the man you want to be next to when the world comes to a screeching halt, because there isn't a thing he cannot do. John and I have been close friends from the first time we were introduced by Walter on that fateful climb up Heartbreak Hill (as we came to know it) in Pisgah National Forest. Our friendship is one that transcends time and has a storyline of its own embedded deeply in an ongoing series of intense conversations and surreal memories of sunlit streams, national Rainbow gatherings and tipis. He has always inspired me with his free-spirited ways and his vast knowledge of all things wild.[†]

John came around a corner hiking south on the trail singing a cheery hello; we chatted as we walked back to his car. He had saved a half a Subway sandwich for me. Heaven! I devoured it in one bite. He retrieved his pack, and we headed up the trail together. He had packed pretty light in anticipation of the miles I would torture him with. By the end of that day, I had done 15 miles, and he did five. We camped at Hardcore Cascades, which is where hikers, organized by Bob Peoples of the Kincora Hostel, built a stone bridge over the creek, and the site where they will build a new shelter during Trail Days this year. True to his style, Johnny pointed out the centerpiece of the bridge was a giant boulder shaped like a heart.

There was a bright moon. I left my empty pot sitting outside of my tent, like I usually do. The mice always come and climb around in it at night. This night, I heard something messing around with the pot and figured it was another mouse. I did hear a strange caliber of ring on the metal I hadn't heard before, but still didn't think anything of it. I shone the flashlight on the bear bag hanging, and it wasn't swinging, so I figured all was good. The next morning when I crawled out of the tent, the pot was gone. Simply gone! It didn't take but a second to add it all up. Moon shining on metal, strange sound with the pot, raccoons' known penchant for shiny objects, and campsite by the creek where a raccoon would likely hang out. A raccoon had stolen my pot! I walked down to the edge of the water to check, thinking that's the first place he would have gone with his treasure; no pot. I came back and looked at the ground, thinking, 'ok, I'm imagining this, and it's really sitting right in front of me'. No pot. Then, on the ground, I noticed scuffs in the wet leaves where he had dragged my pot into the rhododendron bushes. There it was, in the bushes, not far from the water's edge. I left it there so I could share the saga with John when he awoke, a humorous start to our day.

As we packed up camp it started to rain; we hurried to get moving so we could stay warm. I was glad for company on a cold rainy day of hiking. The time went by quickly as we walked and chatted, and eventually the sky cleared. We had lunch on a rock overhang with a great view in the sunshine. John shared his sardines and rice cakes, and I shared my whole wheat alphabet noodle miso soup and frittatas and Texas Pete. We considered stopping at Kincora hostel, but nixed that idea as the day had turned out to be great for hiking.

We did stop and dilly dally at Laurel Forks Falls. A young family had come down to enjoy the falls, a man, woman and a small girl about three or four years old. We passed them once, but then because we stayed on the AT and they took a side trail, we ended up behind them and didn't see them again. We did find the little girl's soiled panties thrown on the side of the trail though. I spent the next mile fuming over the ignorance and general lack of respect that would cause someone to leave human feces tossed along the edge of a river for someone else to clean up.

Many signs of beaver activity were visible along the banks of the river. We found a creepy abandoned campsite that looked like something out of a horror movie where the person was chased away or attacked in the middle of eating their dinner. The mess had obviously been there for a week or more. Wanting to put some distance between us and the bad juju of Laurel Fork, we hiked halfway up Pond Mountain and camped just off the Trail on an old wooded logging road ending a 13 mile day.

Pond Mountain was an easy grade down from the top the next morning. We ate lunch at the shelter at Watauga Lake and continued to the dam. Along the dam is a rock wall that harbors many plants in its cracks and crevices. Situated perpendicular to the prevailing wind, it catches wind-blown seeds. Bleeding heart and wild columbine dripped from its vertical surface. We picked and nibbled on locust blossoms as we said goodbye, then John hiked off up the road to find a ride back to his car, and I continued up Iron Mountain.[†]

To the next shelter was going to be a 14 mile day. I arrived with plenty of light left. No one was there, and a slight breeze was blowing directly into the shelter. At the back of the shelter was an open rock cliff that looked over the lake, and the space seemed poorly planned, lonely and cold. I cooked dinner, ate, read, and signed the register. Still no one showed. Not wanting to stay there alone, I moved on to a lower altitude to tent camp for the night. I figured I would hike until the sun dipped below the mountain across the way, and then stop at the next campsite I found.

By the time the sun disappeared below the mountain, my feet hurt more than usual. I smelled a campfire and figured I had caught up with Wade, who always makes a fire when he camps. Instead, I was surprised at the top of the hill to find a couple of local hunters with a huge tent, a dog, and a giant fire with three entire trees crisscrossed on top of the firepit. I was not pleased with the situation, knowing it was pretty obvious I was hiking alone. It freaked me out so much to be this close to dark and to have my safety possibly compromised, I hiked another two miles to put distance between myself and them—just in case. The additional miles gave me an 18 mile day and two blisters. I set up camp and hung the bear bag in the fading light, calming myself by reading before going to sleep. I actually slept relatively well and was up and out of camp by 8:30, listening to BBC news on the radio while I cooked and ate breakfast.

I crept along the next day, feeling as if I were barely moving, and stopped for a leisurely lunch, stretching out in the sun to read. I ate a lot of food, knowing I had more than I would need to make it to Damascus and enjoyed a cup of hot tea which really gave me a boost for the latter part of the day.

Mid afternoon, I happened upon Linc and Jeanne camped at a nice spot in the woods just north of some open farmland. I took a break on a log and chatted. Jeanne wore a colorful furry fleece pullover around camp; I noticed because my fleece was something I missed since converting to the ultra-lite method of hiking. Jeanne carried more than one warm fleece along with all the heavy raw foods, flour, sourdough starter and metal cooking utensils they used. The more this couple revealed of themselves, the more respect I developed for the quiet uncompromising way they lived out their simple values. Nutrient-rich foods are heavy and rare on the trail. Despite the tempting, savory aroma of sourdough bread baking, they were not compelled to share when camped with other hikers; their diet was a lifestyle born of conviction and they did not seek approval or attention. On this day, blessedly, our friendship transcended their protectiveness and Jeanne offered a precious morsel of sourdough. Its heavy chewiness satisfied as much through the spirit of her kindness as it did by its richness in flavor.

After 15 miles for the day, I made my own camp in a beautiful little glen near Double Springs Gap. A wood thrush sang beside the trail as I set down my pack. He stayed and serenaded me for a long time, making me feel at home and welcome there.

A few hours after dark, a loud, strange noise sounded a little way down in the draw. The sound resembled the whine of an electric drill ending with a staccato "T" sound. Five or six calls later there were sounds of running and crashing around in the woods. I concluded it must be a deer or an elk and maybe two were mating or fighting. I imagined being trampled to bits in my tent if the ruckus moved up the hill. A light green, my tent would be difficult for a color blind animal to discern in the moonlight. I lay there composing bizarre headlines for the news article in my head. The animals crashed around for about 10 minutes, then all was quiet for about 20 minutes or so, and then more running and crashing even closer. They ran back across the way they came; then, one more loud call sounded, after which all was quiet the rest of the night. I guess that was the triumphant "hell yeah!" of the antlered ones.

I hiked into Damascus at 330pm on Wednesday, May 10th relieved to have made it in time to get my box from the post office which closes at 4:30pm. I checked out Dave's Place and the Hiker's Inn, two hostels. I didn't want to stay at either because Mom was coming into town to meet me. No sense in subjecting her to the hiker bunking experience. I got a room instead at the Victorian Inn, a sumptuously decorated B&B in Damascus off the main road, a Mother's Day gift for both of us, I guess. We liked it so much last night, we will be staying one more night. It's cold and raining and very windy outside today anyway, so that wasn't a hard decision to make.[†]

M A Y   1 2

Rain pelted the leaded panes in the old windows on the second floor, and the wind whistled around the gutters. Inside, I soaked in a bath tub full of the hottest water I could stand. Sleeping on soft beds at the Victorian Inn was fine indeed, but taking a hot bath was the absolute most divine. This was my first hot bath since leaving home in March. I stretched and massaged my legs and feet, then slept in a comfortable bed—so comfortable it felt as if the mattress had wrapped itself around my body, and I was simply unable to move. I thought of pioneer women and the hardships they endured, many of them relatively unwillingly, I'm sure, following their husbands, fathers or brothers across miles of wagon trail, their bones jarred all day. How a galvanized tub full of hot water might have felt to them is easy to imagine, but the most likely reality was that even such a simple thing would have been a luxury far beyond their reach at that time. I submerged my head and listened to water close over my ears, acutely aware of my modern, American privilege.

Mom gave me an early birthday gift of a Ther-maRest Pro-Lite sleeping pad that only weighs 13 ounces, so hopefully I will be able to actually sleep at night instead of tossing and turning in discomfort. I am no longer carrying the thinsulite pad; now, with five days of food, one liter of water, and lots of snacks my pack weighed only 30 pounds at Mt. Rogers Outfit-ters this morning.

It's going to be a cold night.

MAY 13

I awakened to blue sky and sunshine when I expected more dreary clouds and drizzle. The trail wound its way up White Top Mountain to Mount Rogers. Huge fleecy clouds scurried across the sky in the spring wind. I did 12.2 miles and called it good. Thomas Knob Shelter stands high on a bald next to a tree line of fir; it is a log cabin almost completely enclosed and with a full loft. I immediately chose the loft for the warmth and shelter from the incessant wind. Clay and Branch also chose the loft and busied themselves with setting up a drip tarp before the expected rain arrived; spots of daylight glittered above us winking through rusted out pinholes in the tin roof.

My mind has been full these last two days of hiking. Yesterday, I refinanced the house, acquired investors, started a bookstore in Damascus, and watched as it slowly sunk financially, all within 8 1/2 miles. Today, I created an inspirational slide show of pictures I took as I hiked and composed prose for the narration. Of course, by the time I get to the shelter each day, meet everyone, chat, eat, set up, and get ready to write it all seems so far away and long gone—just whimsical games my mind plays to keep me entertained as I walk. Yesterday's thoughts were problem-solvers that kept me inside my head and moving most of the day. Today was more leisurely and creative.

Three male scarlet tanagers were in hot pursuit of a female who suddenly took off through the trees at lightning speed, darting and twisting in and out, then making a sharp turn to the right and back to where she started from. Of the three males, only one managed to stick with her despite her sudden changes of direction. He then sat in the same tree with her, and they twittered back and forth. Like bungling idiots, the other two males who had flown straight instead of anticipating her movements were now fighting amongst themselves—both a lost cause. This little show produced a half hour's musings on natural selection during which I concluded that customs such as arranged marriages, female infanticide and clitoridectomies must all be ways the human male keeps his hand in the game of natural selection—otherwise the human female might be free to completely shun all sexual attentions of the bungling idiots of the world. Or not—as the case may, more sadly, be.

Wild red columbine and acres upon acres of white fringed phacelia abound. Dotting the sea of phacelia are yellow trout lilies, nodding trillium, white trillium, red trillium and violets. Wild strawberries bloomed on White Top Mountain. I wish I could be here when they get ripe. Nothing tastes better than a wild strawberry. I've only found them in any quantity once before when I lived in Watauga County, way back up in the hills of western North Carolina. One late spring day while exploring the mountainside behind my house, I found a pasture just full of blooming strawberries, some of which were just beginning to set fruit. I climbed up there twice more checking on their progress and was eventually rewarded with pints of wild strawberry jam for my efforts.

As I approached Whitetop, a young deer startled up from a spring. He bounded up the hill, so I stood still. He stopped and could no longer see me. He then let out the same strange whistle I had heard the other night—just much softer and less urgent—before he bounded away. Ask and ye shall receive.

Clouds are building on the horizon and the wind is picking up. I hope, if it storms, it does it tonight, so tomorrow will be clear when I cross Grayson Highlands. At the VA 600 road crossing, there was a man giving out trail magic. It was really too cold to sit for long, but I got a Pepsi, an apple, and a sausage-egg-and-cheese biscuit, saving the apple for the wild ponies that live on Grayson Highlands.

At Thomas Knob Shelter, three men were also doing trail magic. They grilled hotdogs and had a cooler of ice cream, cookies and sodas. Today, I've eaten six pieces of bacon (left over from the Victorian Inn), two blueberry muffins (from Mom), hot apple cider (powdered mix), a package of crackers, an entire box of Kraft macaroni and cheese, a package of tuna, five mini Snickers bars, half a Nutri Grain bar (left over from yesterday), two sodas, two hot dogs, two handfuls of peanut m&ms, hot tea, and about eight cookies. I would eat more now, but I've already hung the food bag away from the mice. Life is, indeed, very good.[†]

MAY 14
MOTHER'S DAY

Sunshine illuminated fog lying low in the valley; from Thomas Knob Shelter it seemed like a promising day. I started out toward the Highlands. From behind came long low rumbles of thunder. In the west towered a wall of gray-black clouds rolling and tumbling over themselves. I reached a rock summit (the highest around—the worst place to be) just as the sky opened and lightning began to flash. I knew a rock tunnel was up here somewhere from the guidebook. I found the tunnel and squeezed inside. Clay and Branch came in with me. Above us thunder and lightning boomed and cracked; it began to hail. Together in "Fatman's Squeeze" we waited out the storm, thankful for shelter. When I came off the rocks, the dark cloud was to the east, and another was rolling in from the west. Several groups of wild ponies grazed calmly. The apple I had saved for them was in my pack, but the dark sky kept me moving. I passed several more groups and saw a baby pony. Then, came a steady, cold rain that lasted for about 45 minutes of miserable hiking.

At the next shelter where a few hikers gathered, I learned another hiker had gone up to the ponies and given them his apple. I knew we would see more ponies, so I kept my apple out of my pack this time. When I left the shelter, I spotted a herd on a hill to my left. I left the trail and approached slowly, cutting the apple into pieces with my pocketknife as I walked. When I got to them, no one moved. Closest to me were two babies. I walked slowly to them and held the pieces of apple out in my palm. They came and mouthed and lipped and dropped it, stepping on it to get closer to me and nuzzle my arms. A pregnant mare came over. She knew this was good stuff, and she gobbled down the rest of the pieces as I offered them to her. The foals still couldn't quite figure out the mysterious apple. I petted them, and they cocked their heads to one side while I talked. They stood only a few feet high and were so cute. I thought of my two boys as the foals pushed each other out of the way so they could get closer. When the apple was gone, I said my goodbyes to the mare and foals and went back to the trail, my journey a little sweeter for my own special Mother's Day treat.[†]

The rain continued off and on all day, and the temperature dropped drastically. I only did 11 miles because the weather was so disheartening. The descent from Grayson Highlands to Old Orchard shelter was riddled with boulder hopping and terribly slippery footing. I had not intended to stop this early, but was relieved to have the opportunity. I tent camped in a clearing a few hundred yards from the shelter, planning to be up and out early.

MAY 16
JOSEPH'S BIRTHDAY

I've managed to set a personal record without really intending to by hiking 25.2 miles yesterday to reach a pay phone so I could call Joseph to wish him a Happy Birthday before he left for school this morning. It sounds like things are going much better for him since his stint on the AT with mom. The hair-spiking phase has passed, under my prompting, and he has managed to get his lunch packed each day and has raised his grades. He was even inducted into the Beta Club at school on Monday night. I planted a seed in his mind, mentioning that he might want to consider hiking with me this summer if he doesn't succeed in getting a job. With it going on mid-May, jobs available for high schoolers have just about been snapped up, I'm sure. I have recurring nightmares of my teenage son roaming the streets of our small town terrorizing the retirees all summer. He'd be much better off in the woods with me. Happy Sixteenth Birthday, Joseph!

The phone was at the ranger station next to Partnership Shelter, most famously used for calling in pizza delivery orders to the shelter. I arrived last night just as darkness was falling. Pizza had already been ordered, and I had not been counted in, despite the fact that the last two hikers had passed me on the trail only an hour earlier. I cooked the usual dehydrated fare and breathed in the aroma of their pizza, setting up my tent to distance myself from their inconsideration. In my exhaustion, even the warm shower available at Partnership lacked its usual appeal. I turned in not feeling much a part of this younger crowd of hikers and missing my boys.

The next morning I took advantage of a phone number posted on a card in the shelter advertising an offer of shuttle service to town. I called Gonzo; he drove me to the post office for my maildrop, and to his house, where Becky, his wife, gave me awesome, homemade, strawberry pie. Another quantum trail miracle—day dream of strawberries and strawberries will appear. A hot shower and internet access later, I packed my food bag and was dropped at the grocery next to a Walmart. When I finished shopping, I called Becky, and she drove me back to the trail. I was hiking again by 11:30am.

My feet acquired new blisters from yesterday's 25.2 miles, so today was slow going, but my knees seem to be doing ok. Always something, I guess. The rain held off again, and it was actually warmer this afternoon. I stopped at a shelter after seven miles, thinking I would go no farther, but the sun came out so I was inspired to keep moving; my leg muscles cramp quite a bit when I'm not hiking now. I came down the mountain to the I-81 crossing, and everyone that had passed me earlier in the day was there getting rooms at the Relax Inn. I stopped and got a hamburger at a restaurant called The Barn, making one more attempt to connect with other hikers, but then kept going. A tractor trailer truck driver slowed beside me as I walked along the road to the underpass. "You need a ride?" he hollered through his open window. Honestly? "No thanks!"

At dusk, I set up the tent in a cow pasture on the far side of I-81. I suspect the cows will be paying a visit tonight. Of course, I managed quite by accident, to pick the pasture the cows were in. I passed a cow grate—obviously, I'm on the wrong side of it. Cow grates are oddly fascinating contraptions. The metal or wooden grate lies level with the road with an open trough underneath; cows will not venture across the grate, thus enabling a truck or tractor to drive through an opening in the fence without the driver having to fuss over opening and closing a gate. There was an old wooden cow grate at the end of the driveway of my grandparents' farm, but I haven't seen one since childhood. This one is made of concrete. As a child, I asked endless questions about the idiosyncratic bovine device, so intriguing in its simplistic technology. Every step through these farmlands of Virginia reminds me of summers spent in these very mountains on my grandparents' farm. Roaming pastures and woodlands for endless summer days is one of the favorite loves of my childhood that brought me here to this very moment, camped in a pasture on the side of the Appalachian Trail, I suppose.[†]

This weekend is Trail Days Festival in Damascus, a hiker-oriented festival that celebrates all things Trail. The majority of this year's thru-hikers have left the trail to attend. Though I had many offers and opportunities for getting back to Damascus for the festivities, I opted to continue hiking during this time, hoping for fewer people on the trail and a chance to gain some ground on my schedule.

M A Y   2 0

Ahead, a doe walked straight toward me. She had not yet seen me, so I stopped and stood very still. She continued walking and nibbling on leafy branches on either side of the trail. She sensed my presence and stopped, but still could not see me. She and I stood there about three minutes while she nibbled and looked around. Then, she turned and walked back the way she had come. I followed quietly. She vanished then, the way deer seem to do.

Shortly afterward, I saw a beautiful Southern Ring Neck snake on the trail. He was a dark gray/brown with a bright orange band around his neck (do snakes have necks?) right behind his head. I picked him up with my hiking pole. His underbelly was the same bright orange. He, of course, was indignant that I had messed with him and slithered away quickly. These snakes are harmless and rarely out during the day, preferring to hunt at night.

This may be the first day since the beginning of this crazy endeavor where nothing hurts. My knees do not hurt; my blisters from last week have healed, and the trail has been soft enough that even the soles of my feet do not hurt. In celebration, I continued walking and put in a 20 mile day, camping with another hiker beside a wide shallow stream not far past Dismal Creek Falls.

M A Y   2 3

Two nights ago, a section hiker from New Jersey named Woodstock and I stayed at Wood's Hole, a log cabin built in the 1880s. The old barn, also built of logs, has been converted into a bunkhouse for hikers. Tillie Wood runs the hostel and offers breakfast in her cabin. She and her late husband, Roy Wood, Assistant Secretary of the Interior during Jimmy Carter's administration, lived in the cabin and studied and helped to preserve a small herd of elk during the 1940s when elk were being reintroduced to the area in an attempt to re-establish their native territories. The cabin was so intriguing I knew Mom would want to see it and to visit with Tillie.

Mom met me in Pearisburg at 2pm; by the time I arrived, she had already toured the town, met the mayor, been offered a job, reserved us a room and shuttled a hiker (Sleeper) to his motel. We shuttled Woodstock to Dairy Queen and took off to our motel so I could shower. I had been out for 12 days this time. I'd gotten a quick shower at John and Becky's in Marion but still...that was seven days ago. I had tried the solar shower at Wood's Hole, but it was icy cold. Enough! I drove Mom to Wood's Hole over the twisty curvy back roads from Pearisburg so she could see Tillie's cabin. It has always been Mom's dream to live in a log cabin nestled deep in the mountains, so I knew she would love visiting. We ate a late dinner at PizzaHut. It was the first beer and pizza I had since being home with my hurt knee back in mid April, a far cry from others' experience of the trail as they party their way along from town to town on drinking binges. I was still doing laundry at 10pm, a lighted, modern privilege compared to the accustomed hiker bedtime.

When I left Pearisburg around 9:30am, Mom walked across the bridge at New River with me. Cars whizzed noisily by, but Mom was excited that she was walking a half mile of the famed Appalachian Trail as a part of my journey. It had been a fun visit, and I was sorry to leave her to drive home alone to her empty house, while I walked on alone. Life seems so strange sometimes.

My first day back on trail from a town stay is usually a great day of hiking. The 6.7 miles to the first shelter passed quite easily; I stopped and ate leftover pizza for lunch, and then noncommittally headed for the next shelter, another 12.3 miles farther, knowing I could always camp if I didn't get that far. With an hour and a half of daylight left, the stone shelter appeared among the trees after a total of 19 miles. It is one of only a handful of shelters that have an interior fireplace. One hiker had a fire already crackling away invitingly, and another hiker showed up later. I cooked dinner over the fire, saving fuel and warming up with a cup of hot tea while sitting on the hearth. The warm glow in the stone and wood shelter creates a rustic, homey atmosphere. The forest is dark and the last glimmer of light is fading from patches of sky between the trees.

Chipmunks rule the forests around these parts. Each one has a different reaction when encountering the threat of the stinky hiker walking by. Some dash for safety without a sound; some run a few feet then stop, looking back to consider the danger; others run away chirping loudly, screaming all manner of obscenities at the disturbance and are still fussing even after you have passed. Still others dive for safety quietly, but once they feel they are out of reach then scream obscenities at you. They are so cute it is extremely difficult to take them seriously, and I find myself laughing when I see one.

It was no laughing matter, however, when I happened upon a mother grouse and her chicks. I was only about five feet from her before she startled. I had not even seen her until then because of her camouflage. She flew into an injured bird routine in a heroic effort to distract attention from her chicks. As she flopped off in one direction, her babies scattered in all other directions. She looked back and realized one of her babies had run toward me instead of away from me (he must have slept through the hiker drill), and she panicked. She dropped the injured bird theatrics and ran toward me hissing. Babies were running everywhere chirping loudly by now, and you could tell mama was reaching max on ideas for what to do. She fluffed up her feathers and plaintively looked at me and made the most awful distress sounds. I talked to her and started walking slowly through the drama which was all taking place in the middle and on both sides of the trail. She ran completely away then, leaving her babies, so I pressed on, getting away as quickly as I could so she could gather up her family again. I felt terrible about the whole thing, but I'm sure everyone was fine soon after.

M A Y   2 5

I wanted to get as close to 15 miles as possible without starting the climb up Brush Mountain. I'm 'stealth' camping a little off the trail past Craig Creek just before the ascent becomes steep. Stealth camping is thru-hiker vernacular for making camp in an unauthorized spot, whether that be an illegal campsite or just a spot where no one has camped before. It's dusk; there's a lot of movement in the woods across a dry creek bed. I just have the netting part of the tent up. I think it's going to be a fairly warm night with no rain. (Much to my relief, the noises turned out to be two large deer.) If it does rain, I guess I will be jumping up and rushing around to put the tent fly on in the dark. I am considering getting up really early and trying to put in a long day tomorrow since today was slow. I enjoyed taking my time, lingering over red columbine and bleeding heart blooming on Sinking Creek Mountain. There's a pink flowering shrub that looks like a pink version of a flame azalea, but I don't know if that's what it is or not. I've seen a lot of it today. I finally remembered the name of a butterfly I've seen twice now—a red admiral. It was incredibly hot on the mountain's rock ledges, miles of full exposure to the glaring sun, like hiking on a griddle.

This dry creek bed was very obviously once a good-sized mountain creek, maybe four feet across with waterfalls and pools. It is bone dry. Where did the water go? I've come across many small dry creeks and dry springs as well. It's a rather alarming snapshot of what is happening to our planet. The trail has been following ridgelines and water sources have been few and far between. I'm usually carrying two liters with me when I have a source—something I never did in GA, TN, and NC where water was easy to find. I recall my father telling me that when he was a child, his father declared quite often that humans would run out of water in the next few decades—this coming from a man who grew up farming and hunting these mountains in the early 1900s. Grandma always kept a cut glass decanter full of water in the refrigerator for Grandaddy; he had grown up drinking from a spring on the farm and ice cold water was a given. In his later years, living in the city sans spring water, that cut glass bottle seemed to represent the sparkling serenity of his beloved mountain spring. When he came in tired and sweaty from working in the garden, it was the first thing he reached for, and the refrigerator was never without it.

The trail crossed the pastureland of several farms. Cows and a donkey stood languidly defying the definition of boredom. Shaky stiles made crossing barbed-wire fences individual mini-adventures. One stile stood by Keffer Oak, purported to be the largest blazed tree on the Appalachian Trail. It is guestimated to be over 300 years old; the guide book says it is over 18 feet around. On the hill above, I turned to take in the grace and beauty of its branches that reached for the ground on either side. I marveled at its majesty, mourning the sobering fact that all our country's trees were once this grandiose but are no more.[†]

In a pasture, a chipmunk darted out from one side, ran about a foot or so, and then stopped just under a blade of grass on the other side, his tail still in the trail. He appeared to be sick or injured, moving slowly, slinking low to the ground, and shouldn't really have been in a pasture at all. He wasn't even hidden, just under a dip in the tufts of grass; he lay there stretched out flat, perfectly still. I stopped less than a foot from him and peered down—he didn't move. I guess even chipmunks get sick and feeble ("out to pasture" came to mind). I left him alone and moved on pondering my 'sick joke'.

As I sat eating my lunch, the food bag began to move. At first, I thought it was my imagination, but then, it moved against my leg several more times, more insistently. I picked it up, and the earth moved up and down as a mole tunneled by.

Slowly the light is fading. Darkness arrives quicker in the forest—the sky above the canopy is still dimly lit.

The last of the birds are settling down, their chirps becoming less frequent. Most of the sounds are of twigs falling, leaves rustling softly, or bugs buzzing by. The rhythm of the night is taking over. Some birds twitter in a flurry as they sort out the last of their day. From far away a dog barks. A moth flutters at my light. The leaves crackle. A bug buzzes outside my screen. Night falls.

M A Y   2 6
M O R N I N G —

The rain came on slowly after a few rumblings of thunder woke me in the night. I was easily able to get the tent fly up before getting wet. It's been a warm night and the soft rain has been soothing. It's a little before 6am, and I am up and packing for my long day. Reaching The Homeplace Restaurant, 21.7 miles away in Catawba, Virginia before they stop serving dinner is my goal for the day.

L A T E   A T   N I G H T —

The Homeplace is just about all there is in Catawba besides a small grocery/gas station and the post office. It is an all-you-can-eat, family-style restaurant, housed in a huge, rambling farmhouse, famous on the trail for its scrumptious array of home-style food. I started hiking at 5:50am while listening to NPR on the radio. The trail went straight up for miles to a ridge where I saw the Audie Murphy Memorial, descended to a road, then climbed straight back up. Hours of rocky ridgeline scrambles culminated at Dragon's Tooth and a difficult, steep cliff scramble. Metal rebar was drilled into the rock face to step on because there was no other way down. I hiked all day with only two liters of water. With temps in the 80s, I stayed drenched in sweat. As I picked my way down the cliff past Dragon's Tooth, a young male hiker, the only person I had seen all day, came bounding down behind me. He was gone in an instant on down the trail with only the cursory "how are you?" and a flippant comment about the "killer descent". At that point, I broke. The long hike had taken everything I had; the cliff was scary and extremely challenging to navigate and, as the hour grew later, my chances of making the restaurant in time looked grim. What is all this hype about the camaraderie of the trail community anyway? What trail community is there for a middle-aged female? I spent the next couple of hours cursing Wingfoot's Thru Hiker Handbook, feeling sorry for myself, and crying for Adam to come save me from my foolishness. Despite my melodrama, I had little choice but to keep walking. Eventually, I emerged from the woods into a bright, sunshiny pasture. As I checked off landmarks for the next two miles, my disposition improved with the easier walking. A summer thunder-shower raised my optimism for reaching the restaurant. Some weekend hikers told me I was within a mile of Route 311, the road I needed. The rain came down harder, but I welcomed the cool-down. At the highway, a pickup truck stopped to pick me up after only a half a mile of road walking.

The restaurant is a very nice establishment, but for some reason, they allow dirty, smelly hikers to eat there. I sat alone at a table filled with bowls of green beans, mashed potatoes, gravy, corn, fried chicken, roast beef, pinto beans and biscuits. I ate everything on the table with the exception of one piece of chicken and a biscuit, which I wrapped in a napkin to take with me. Then, I had peach pie.

M A Y   2 8

Dad and Audree[†] live in Roanoke, Virginia not far from the trail crossing in Troutdale. We had discussed my arrival only as a date approximation, but Dad was eagerly tracking my progress through my online journal entries. From high up on the ridges that circle the valley city, I rose early to hike in the cooler temperatures. The day heated up quickly, and the snakes were out in force. A four-and-half-foot long, black snake stretched across the trail but allowed me to walk carefully by. A small garter-looking snake with a checkered pattern sunned on the rocks; I didn't recognize his markings.

One mysterious encounter left me dumbfounded, awestruck, excited, and disappointed all at once. Very seldom do I hike with earphones in and the radio on—usually only if I am struggling, bored or just plain over it for the day. This morning, I was over it before I even started because I just wanted to be in town, have a shower, visit, and eat good food. I had the radio on, walking the ridgeline, dodging rocks and watching for snakes. It was hot already. When I passed under a tree, the leafy part of a branch came down swiftly and smacked the pack hard, just missing my head. I heard a thud behind/beside me as something hit the ground, something big, and then a smaller thud, like its back feet hitting the ground. As I turned, only a whisper of motion was visible as the form bounded down a sheer drop, off the side of the mountain, and disappeared through the undergrowth with hardly a rustle. I paused, really baffled, then continued walking replaying the sequence and sound in my mind. The thud of the landing sounded like a pack hitting the ground at the end of the day; I was guestimating that the animal was 35-40 pounds. What could be that heavy and in a tree? Ok, I thought, a raccoon climbs trees. But...raccoons don't jump 10 feet off a limb, and then vanish; they sort of shuffle off. Possum, no; possums move quickly for no creature. Bears climb but don't jump and disappear. They might run away, but you would hear their body mass in the leaves and bushes. This was a calculated jump and a major leap off the side of a very steep drop for a quick getaway. The words 'mountain lion' teased me as I walked. No way. ok....bobcat? Yes, perhaps it was a bobcat. I even wrote in the trail register that I encountered a bobcat. But you know...the average bobcat is only 15-20 pounds, and the more I think about it, I think it was bigger than a bobcat.

When I described the event to Dad, he immediately remarked that there have been a few mountain lion sightings in the area due to a new reintroduction program locally. He seemed to think it was likely one of the big cats. The mystery of the elusive mountain lion remains intact even though I was possibly within five feet of one.

M A Y   3 0

Strangely enough, after sitting around all day for a much needed zero day at Dad's, my feet and ankles swelled and were still swollen this morning. I did not lace my boots very tightly because my feet were so squeezed into them. After about an hour of hiking, everything began to loosen up; I was able to tighten my laces, and the swelling disappeared. But, by the end of the day, my legs were swollen and splotchy. This has happened once before, just after Blackstack Cliffs in Tennessee; I assume it's something to do with the quantity of ibuprofen I'm taking.

With temperatures in the 90s, lizards sunned themselves, barely moving when I passed. The trail was less rocky and followed contour lines in and out of coves with very little water to be found. According to the book, there won't be any water tomorrow for 10 miles.

There were no snakes, despite the warmth, but I did see two scarlet tanagers and another mother grouse and her young. This time the babies were a little older and had the hiker drill down; they pretty much stood still while mama ran off into the rhododendron and made strange decoy sounds like a lost puppy whining. And, there were two toads—one, that was peeking from inside the hollow base of a tree, was a bright rust-orange color.[†]

On a water break at Wilson Creek Shelter, I chatted with Bright Eyes and Chardonnay. I had met these female hikers previously at Flint Mountain Shelter in Tennessee. As I was shouldering my pack, Just Judy, whom I met at Knot Maul Shelter a couple of days before my stay at Wood's Hole, showed up alone; she is section hiking part of Virginia. Her hiking partner had injured her foot and gone home. I was encouraged by seeing these women again. It has been a long time since I've had any female company. We each hiked on at our individual paces.

At the day's end at Bobblet's Gap Shelter, the energy is very different than usual as the shelter is full of all women hikers. There is cheerful chatting, helpful exchanges of pearls of hiker wisdom, and much laughter, none of which you get in a shelter full of men after a long, hot day's hike. You're lucky if you don't get loud snoring. Bright Eyes is a very striking, tall, thin woman in her mid-thirties—I guessed—radical, stoic and fiercely independent. Her repertoire includes all things organic, horticultural and artistic. We had lots to talk about, sharing recipes for healthy trail food and talking edible plants and gardening. I instantly respected her knowledge and poise. She was very definitely hiking her own hike and had been hiking by herself, rebuking attentions of the many male hikers following her like bloodhounds. Chardonnay, a younger woman, had been hiking with a girlfriend since the beginning but they eventually parted ways when their hiking preferences diverged. She too was now on her own; we discussed the difficulty of her decision to change plans and the challenges of honoring her budding independence as a woman hiker alone. These conversations were some of the most engaging exchanges I've encountered since beginning this hike, all in one evening spent with other women. Completely lacking was the doom and gloom of a shelter full of grouchy, tired men poring over trail maps and data books trying to conjure up the topography the of next day's hike. This perfectly delightful evening offered hope that my hike might not be all boredom and loneliness after all. It's no wonder men gravitate to where the women are.

A whippoorwill calls in the growing darkness.

J U N E   1

The day held a certain playfulness as I would only be hiking 10 miles and would have time to spare. Climbing Floyd Mountain in the morning coolness, I arrived at Cornelius Shelter by 10am, according to another hiker's watch. A deer grazed behind the shelter, its presence lending a peaceful air. A few days earlier I'd been musing on the beauty of the mourning cloak—

a fairly rare butterfly I have only seen once before whose larvae actually prefer the willow. Brains and Brawn, an older thru-hiking couple arrived, and we chatted; Brawn hung his shirt in the sun to dry. A mourning cloak appeared, flitting around his shirt.[†] It landed on my pack straps, unfurled its proboscis and began sampling the salty sweat; I reached out, and it moved the operation to my hand.[†] I sat with this butterfly on my hand for about 20 minutes before it fluttered away. Our universe is an amazing and mysteriously intricate place.

With 5.3 miles left to go, I lingered over lunch, chatting first with Brains and Brawn and then with Donkey and Hot Springs. They had seen Dad fishing at Jenning's Creek that morning. Evidently, he was there handing out apples and oranges, hoping to catch me on my way through. I was disappointed I had missed him, having passed Jenning's Creek the afternoon before. The rest of the day everyone told me they had met my dad. I was proud of his trail magic efforts.

I stashed my pack behind a tree at Parker's Gap and walked the one mile down a side trail to Apple Orchard Falls. Without a pack my sense of balance was off for the first two tenths mile or so. Once my equilibrium adjusted, it felt as if I were flying down the hill. In the trail lay a black snake, half in and half out of his hole in the ground. The back half of his body was stretched out on the side of the trail and the rest of him was underground, no doubt listening to the vibrations of my approaching footsteps. I stood over him and watched him slowly slither the rest of his body down into the ground. As I walked away, I recalled a similar event many years ago about this same time of year. Every summer at the end of May I spent two weeks in the mountains of Virginia on my grandparents' farm. One such summer day when I was about eight, I was on the rope swing that hung from a gargantuan, black oak in front of the farmhouse. I was daydreaming and letting the momentum of the swing bring me to center as it slowed. When I went to jump down off the barely moving swing, there was a black snake underneath in the worn spot of dirt. He was half out of his hole which was right in the center of the dirt area, and stretched out right where I would need to step to get off the swing. I was stuck there hollering for Grandpa to come. This memory offered a satisfying poignancy to today's snake encounter, parallel to so long ago. Ouroboros— the snake had eaten its tail. As a child, the snake was half out of its hole—a " coming out" to the world of my own undeveloped chi. As a grown woman turning 40, the snake is returning to its den. Closure, as if a chapter of time has ended, a time in my life perhaps when snake energy, or chi, was feared or not fully realized. With maturity comes a relationship with chi that no longer resonates fear but is based instead on knowledge and respect. The snake returns home from the hunt. Full circle.

Apple Orchard Falls is a 200-foot cascading stream. The US Forest Service built steps down to the base of the cascade, and a beautifully curved deck crosses the water and provides access to another deck with a bench for viewing the waterfall. The full afternoon sun drenched the space in golden warmth, and there wasn't a soul anywhere for miles. I took off my boots and socks and lay in the sun. As my body warmed, I stretched and did some yoga poses. I listened to music on my mp3 player, and danced in the sunshine at the base of this amazing waterfall in this secluded ravine in a forest high on a mountaintop. It is these times that give purpose to my insanity. What a day! What a life I am living! Mind-body union—the yoga of life itself.[†]

At Thunder Hill Shelter it is all females again tonight...cheerful chatter until way past dark.

J U N E   4

At the James River foot bridge, Brains and Brawn were having no luck at hitching. Brawn held up a bandana printed with "HIKER TO TOWN" in large block letters. The flip side of the bandana said "HIKER TO TRAIL". We chatted while we he waved his bandana at passing cars, and I waited for Adam. This couple's care and concern for one another on the trail is obvious as soon as you spend just a few moments with them. Neither can say anything without mentioning the other. Their individual sacrifices for the sake of their love for one another speaks volumes about the value of true commitment in marriage. Brawn, a hulking, cheerful, chatty man had always dreamed of hiking the Trail. Though Brains was a strong hiker, long distances were not her forte; she had agreed to accompany her husband on this journey so neither would have to bear the loneliness of six months of separation from one another. In return for her graciousness, Brawn felt his wife's every painful step, and kept his own long strides in check to match her slower pace. Both were soft spoken and kind, exuding patience and generosity into the very air around them. In their presence, I always felt like everything was going to be alright.

We loaded all the packs in the back of Adam's pickup truck and drove to Glasgow so Brains and Brawn could get a motel room and grocery shop. Adam and I headed off to the small mountain town of Buchanan (pronounced locally as buck-ann-un). We ate "second" breakfast at a local restaurant and stopped at the library so I could check email and post to trail journals. When we passed a parked passenger train car, I pointed and chattered on and on, absent-mindedly calling it a caboose; Adam laughed at me and pulled into the parking area in front with a gleam in his eye. As it turns out, the train car is the Buchanan Railcar Inn and staying there is my fortieth birthday surprise.

Beautifully redone, the car had once been an N&W railway dining coach but was now paneled in dark wood, plushly furnished and carpeted in dark red. A small bar area was by the door with microwave, fridge and coffee maker; the living area included a TV, movies and chairs and couches, and a bathroom and bedroom were on the far end.[†] Adam gave me a dozen roses, wine, fruit and cheese. It was a very special birthday gift—how does he keep outdoing himself?

The weekend was a smorgasbord of luxuries; the simplest of pleasures, like having someone's company, was magnified by the previous long weeks on the trail alone. Together we visited Peaks of Otter Visitor Center on the Blue Ridge Parkway; it was surreal to play tourist knowing I had arrived there on foot. We found the trailhead for Apple Orchard Falls and hiked down to enjoy the sunlit cascade. As much as we are both in the woods, we are rarely in the woods together. Being in the woods transformed from the "everyday grind" back to adventure.

On the porch railing of the Pink Cadillac restaurant in Greenville, Virginia, a giant, wooden Humpty Dumpty precariously perches. In his hand he holds a list of breakfast items. Humpty Dumpty has crossed off all items that contain eggs and has circled the last item on the list—HAM. Dinner was a salad that could have come from heaven as far as I was concerned, home-made clam chowder and fried mushrooms. Adam ate this huge thing called an Elvis Burger.

Forty has arrived, and although it arrived in unexpected style, the ambivalence I have about welcoming its reign is no less prevalent. I am distinctly aware of a process that has begun, an undefined silent process that slowly disconnects one from this mundane existence. Not morbid really, but sharply real, like the penetrating gaze of a hungry child.

JUNE 6
EARLY MORNING —

As the moon set, it cast shadows of the pine canopy above onto my tent fly, like the shadow puppet shows my sister used to create when we were children. I arrived at the Brown Mountain Shelter last night at dark. The last four miles was a push from Little Irish Creek after stopping there to cook and eat dinner. The terrain was very easy walking along the edge of Pedlar Lake; a light drizzle veil sparkled in the pale golden slant of the setting sun. The trail was flat and thick with pine needles, as it undulated around the short draws that dumped their small streams into the lake. The trickle of water was around every turn, a welcome change to the bone dry ridge walking of late. About a mile before reaching the shelter, I heard a small rustle over to my right that caused me to glance over. Light was fading into twilight and critters were starting to move about. The sound turned out to be a bear sharpening his claws on the side of a tree. He wasn't large, maybe 110 pounds, but he stood on his hind legs with his front paws extended up the tree. He had already seen me by the time I saw him, and his ears perked forward as he peered over his shoulder. My mind tried to make him into a leaning tree with an odd silhouette like so many other shapes at twilight. But, as I continued without slowing down, this shape elongated as he strained around the tree to keep his gaze on me. I felt the adrenaline hit my system as the positive identification of 'bear!' hit my brain; he was no more than 25 yards away. I kept going and the bear stayed put. I had planned to tent at a campsite by the creek up ahead, but with the adrenaline rush, I was plenty energized and motivated to go the extra 1/2 mile to the shelter. When I arrived after dark, the shelter was full, so I tented on a hillside, doing the last of the day's chores by headlamp.

E V E N I N G —

Yesterday's 20 miles took their toll on my feet which were screaming before I'd even done eight miles today. Mentally, I was beat down every time someone passed because I wrestled with my physical limitations. I really wanted to make it to the B&B in Montebello with the other hikers, but I just couldn't. It was all I could do to go the 15.8 to the shelter instead. The last two miles I was barely moving. The reality of emotional separation from my family for four more months is setting in and taking its toll on my stamina as well. The boys are coming to spend a week with me this coming Saturday, so I have set that as the next milestone, my next goal to look forward to, but after that, I will be too far north for anymore visits from family and friends. That will be when the Trail becomes its most challenging. I am not the only one struggling emotionally out here. The topic of conversation of late has been "how are you holding up?" amongst the hikers. Many are feeling like they don't want to do this anymore, just as I am. The novelty has worn off. The physical challenges have evened out. Food is routine now. Gear is a worn out topic. The Virginia blues is a new hurdle—a mental and emotional mountain to dash ourselves against.

J U N E 8

Dutch Haus Bed and Breakfast hosted a free hiker lunch. From the computer in the living room of this rustic home, I purchased a Father's Day gift online to be mailed directly to Dad's house. I chose the book *Mountains of the Heart* by Scott Weidensaul so I could share my own love of these mountains with my father more fully. Over lunch I met a few other hikers, including Rapunzel and 42 who were hiking with Dancer. Dancer's mother, Pokey, had gotten off the trail and gone back to New Jersey. Everyone was back on the trail by 1pm, and I walked with Brains and Brawn. I was glad to see them again and fill them in on the Railcar Inn surprise. So many faces merely come and go along the way, but gradually the sense of community, a hallmark of the trail experience, forms as more opportunities to develop continuity among the many trail relationships are presented.

Leaving Brains and Brawn behind on a particularly rocky uphill section of trail, I glanced up to see the towering, lanky white-haired figure of Melatonin coming toward me, carefully picking his way down the steep incline. He was southbound on a slack-pack, the second of two stints for him, using the B&B as a base. I originally met Melatonin in mid-May atop Chestnut Knob where we both stopped at a spring-fed pond to replenish our water supplies. His quiet, slow speech and mannerisms attested to the validity of his trail name, and I took an immediate liking to him for the stark contrast his sophistication offered to so many of the gung-ho, young men on the trail. Once I discovered that he is a retired scientist, his intelligent intrigue captured my imagination even more, and I was glad to have crossed paths with him once again. Perhaps we will see one another again along the way.

On the banks of Tye River I set up camp with Dancer, 42 and Rapunzel, continuing my latest trend of spending time with more female hikers. The campsite was on the north bank of the river, after crossing a long, beautiful suspension bridge. In a moment of girly silliness, it was decided we should hang our food bags from the suspension bridge since there seems to be a universal female disenchantment with the dubious task of hanging one's food bag from a tree. Rapunzel and I led the way and dangled our food bags from the middle of the bridge, laughing at the ridiculousness of our plan.

Rapunzel is from California. A childhood friend of mine had moved to North Carolina from northern California, and my friendship with her had broadened my horizons considerably in the eighth grade. Adam had spent his teenage years on the beaches of L.A., skipping school, surfing and playing volleyball, and his tales of hormone-embellished exploits inspired a short-lived desire to go there when we were in our twenties. The trip never seemed within reach to us financially, and so California's allure has remained with me to this day. The source of my intrigue, no doubt, lies in the fact that California's progressive politics appear to be the direct antithesis of the backwoods "get off my property" politics of North Carolina where I grew up. Rapunzel, like a ray of California sunshine, speaks my language—her interests lie in the psychology of relationships, responsible decision-making, and account-ability for one's actions. We seem to see the world through a very similar lens; thus, we have much to share about our perceptions of walking the trail, our relationships with friends and our families, and our own personal struggles to reach long-term goals. I am pleased to meet such a strong and intelligent young woman. A bond formed between us that evening as we lay on the bridge for a long time talking and enjoying the rising moon after hanging our food bags from the bridge. Muted evening light shone on gray rocks in the river making the view from the bridge otherworldly.

After dark, a carload of drunken teenagers screeched to a halt in the parking area on the south side of the river. I lay awake listening, knowing they were headed our way. We heard them on the bridge talking and laughing, and all four of us lay wondering what would happen to our food bags once they found them hanging from the bridge beneath them. Suddenly, there was a loud splash in the river below the bridge; surely they hadn't just cut our bags loose!? 42 yelled, "HEY!" and we all turned on our headlamps, climbed out of our tents and ran over toward the bridge. The startled intruders went running off the other end. Car doors slammed, and they peeled out. Upon further investigation, the splash was one of their beers they had spilled on the bridge and then dropped into the river. We all had a good laugh at just how the whole episode probably appeared from the teenagers' perspective. They had no idea we were camped there; they thought they had found a relatively secretive place to do their underage drinking, and suddenly a random shout of "HEY!" comes from the woods, and lots of bobbing lights begin advancing toward them.

As the only mother in the group, a bit jaded from

my own life experiences with drunken idiots, I lay awake worrying our visitors might return to even the score. The younger women, more trusting in their perceptions of the world around them, continued to giggle for a long time over our crazy victory over danger; their carefree acceptance punctuated for me just how much older I really am. I lay awake thoughtfully reviewing my stubborn pessimism, its sources and its weakness. I finally released my worries and fell asleep under the stars, watching the moon crawl across the sky.

Blackberry Milkshakes and 1000 Miles!

J U N E   9

The girls went on ahead, and I hiked into Waynes-boro at my own pace. I was moving faster than usual on the last few miles of good trail into town. Gentle downhills lend themselves to a sort of shuffle/jog kind of stepping that allows for keeping the knees slightly bent while the momentum of gravity pulls you down the hill. Every time I am clipping along quickly in this manner, I'm thinking, 'some day I'm going to trip doing this, and then maybe I wont do this anymore!' The long descents into the gaps where towns are usually nestled fade in severity behind excitement over anticipated amenities of civilization.

As I shuffle/jogged along, getting close to a road, I caught a faint whiff of flea powder. Sniffing the air, I looked up just in time to glimpse a house cat slinking off into the honeysuckle. What am I turning into? I must be hungry.

J U N E   1 0

It's Saturday morning at the Waynesboro library,

and I am waiting here to meet my boys. Adam brought them as far as Roanoke where they spent this past week visiting with Dad. Their pending arrival has created a huge shift in my focus. I have moved into mother-mode and am anticipating all the little things they will have forgotten to bring and will need.

At the motel, I collected and organized packages of food and plotted logistics for providing for their needs despite few resources. Outside the lobby was a huge hiker box of food. Hiker boxes are repositories of random items left behind by previous hikers or donated by the local community for use by hikers. My usual first thought of 'wonder what goodies might be in there for me?' was replaced with 'I could use this for packing up meals for the boys'. I scrounged all their snacks from this box. The boys will be excited with all the junk they get to eat to boost their calorie intake. Luckily, through the Shenandoah National Park there are camp stores, restaurants and tourist facilities. We won't be far from civilization during their time on the trail. That knowledge offers a little more security, just in case something unexpected were to happen. Watching this shift has offered new discoveries about my thinking as a woman and as a mother; it was inter-esting to see how quickly my priorities changed when my responsibilities included someone else's well-being.

On the phone last night, Adam and I discussed the possibility of Joseph hiking with me for the rest of the summer. Adam was supportive of the idea, since it would mean Joseph would be more closely supervised in an environment where he can grow and have good experiences. If Joseph were to stay home with Grayson this summer, chances are great that the overabundance of freedom would be too tempting for his teenage tendencies. Making good choices has become a challenge for him of late, so I see no need to provide opportunities for poor choices to dominate his summer. Grayson has been playing at a friend's house almost every day, and he will also be occupied with tennis camp. He seems quite content to spend his summer having Airsoft wars and riding bikes.

E V E N I N G —

Stress has returned. I was appalled as I watched myself obsess and worry over my sons on the trail. Despite Joseph's "juvie camp" with me in April, I still find this to be unfamiliar territory for the act of mothering. When Joseph was five, I attempted to take him backpacking and the experience was a disaster. My youngest had accompanied his father to visit grandparents; it was my intent to use this rare opportunity of relative freedom to regain some of my own joy of backpacking after being tethered to home and small children for years. I would introduce my oldest son to a world I had left behind and would instill in him the same love for the forests I had neglected in myself all that time, a noble idea that just didn't work out at all.

We packed up my Kelty external frame backpack with a dome family-size tent (heavy!), a down sleeping bag, a ThermaRest, a thinsulite pad for Joseph, food, butane stove, clothes and other various odds and ends for making camp. Joseph carried a daypack with his sleeping bag and his toothbrush. I was completely consumed by that wonderful feeling that permeates one's being when you revisit a skill you once knew like the back of your own hand; the feeling is a combination of mental and motor memory that births an indescribably deep

sense of satisfaction and a distinct sense of one's place on the continuum that is your life. The thought never once crossed my mind that this might not work; as far as I was concerned, I knew what I was doing.

The hike was one I had made many times alone up the spine of the Seven Sister's Ridge toward Greybeard Mountain. I knew there was a shelter on Greybeard, but I had never gone that far. I had the tent so we would not be bound to any particular plan of how far we would have to go. I was sure that somewhere along the ridge I would come to a place suitable for setting up camp. It was a late April day, warm in the sun, cold in the shade. The ridgeline rimmed the North Fork Reservoir in the cove below, and the soft, April afternoon breeze picked up enough force over the watery cove that as we climbed higher the temperature dropped quickly. The fading sun added to the chill. Blaze, our dog, trotted ahead. Walking briskly, I was warmed by my rapid circulation, but my comfort masked what was happening to little Joseph. Joseph was a chatty, happy child but like children will, he got colder than he should have been before he recognized his own discomfort enough to mention it.

Suddenly, our conversation went from how bloodroot sends its flower up before its leaves in the spring to the tingling numbness he was feeling in his hands. I stopped us immediately, afraid I had already waited too late, and he may be hypothermic before I could get him warm. Unfortunately, as soon as I stopped hiking, I too began to shiver in the cold wind. Blaze returned and circled us, eager to keep hiking. The vague sense of alarm I felt when he said his hands were tingling increased to a raging panic when he announced he wanted to go to sleep. I was already pulling my down bag out of the backpack and wrapping it around him as he sat on the leaves. All of our options were racing back and forth through my conscious thought, and I was struggling to get my mind to focus on any one of them long enough to take action. My own powers of reason were slowing as my internal temperature dropped—nothing like knowing you're approaching hypothermia and feeling unable to do what you know to do to save yourself and your son. Images of our gruesome demise, splashed across the evening news, preempted my thought process while I struggled to set up the tent quickly.

When Joseph's chatting fell silent, I felt my consciousness trying to surface as if from a long way away, knowing I had to keep him awake. I heard myself asking him to sing a song to me. He complained that he was sleepy and didn't want to sing; my mind wanted to accept this, since I didn't want to sing a song either. But, I tried again, heeding the far away voice of reason telling me I had to do this. Together we sang the alphabet song and climbed into the tent with the dog, while in my mind I debated the value of the tent without the rain fly on it to hold in our body heat. I decided against the time it would take to put on the fly and opted to continue with getting Joseph warm first. I put him on the thinsulite pad inside the tent and set him to the task of snuggling down into the down bag and zipping it up to occupy his body while he sang. I patted the ground to bring Blaze over to lay down beside Joseph and generate warmth. Only now did I stop to put on another layer of clothing myself.

I began to set up the stove just inside the door of the tent. My mind now raged against the tag on the side of the tent that warns against operating any type of cooking apparatus inside the flammable tent. Just as long as the dog lay still, we'd be alright. While I boiled water for hot chocolate, I pulled warning tags off pillows in my mind and sang the alphabet song with Joseph again. I stuffed a Ziploc baggie of potato chips down into the sleeping bag beside him and told him to eat them. He didn't want potato chips. To align him with my intentions, I began to explain the dangers of hypothermia; while my own body began shivering convulsions, I convinced him the carbs were necessary for his body to make the energy to stay warm.

"Are you cold, too?" he asked me. In his infinite childish wisdom, he admonished me and told me to use his sleeping bag and wrap up too, like him. More images flashed across the evening news. Mother dies, child survives. We ate potato chips together, and I wrapped his bag around me and hugged the dog.

The hot chocolate was the turning point for both of us. Getting the hot liquid in our bodies was the edge we needed to warm up the tent and the sleeping bags. We snuggled together once my mind had cleared and discussed our options. I had always parented by giving Joseph as much information as I could. I knew his childish brain would keep only what it needed and discard the rest as incomprehensible. Children are capable of understanding far more than most adults give them credit for; it is our own limitations as adults that stunt the expansion of our children's minds. Through a thorough debate of all possible ways out of this mess, we decided we did not have enough clothing to be comfortable in the windier than expected conditions. We opted for bailing out on the trip and getting home to warm up. We discussed the possibility of having to finish hiking in the dark, and we decided we could move faster without our gear. After warming up in our sleeping bags for about an hour and a half, we emerged from the tent in the fading light of day to repack what gear we would carry down the mountain. I took the daypack that Joseph had carried and put our water in it. Each of us wrapped a sleeping bag around our shoulders, and I put the rest of our gear in the tent. I left the dogfood and the food bag out of the tent so the bears could eat it without destroying everything, and we started off down the mountain.

Half a mile down the trail, we hit southern exposure under a leafless canopy. The gold of the setting spring sunshine colors my memory of that hike out to this day. Joseph chatted away endlessly in front of me on the trail, oblivious to the weight of guilt I lugged along with us. The dog foraged ahead, simply *happy to be back on the move. I wrestled my demons, silently and followed my son down the mountain.*

I drove to the local Pizza Hut where we ordered take out. Once at home, we sat in a hot bath eating pizza. Joseph hit me with another of his gems. "Mom, you don't make mistakes very often," he said, "but when you do, you make really big ones!"

Grayson walked behind me, but Joseph ranged so far ahead we could no longer hope to catch him. I lamented my worries to Grayson in litany format as we hiked. Grayson repeatedly assured me Joseph would figure out where to turn off for the shelter and would meet us there. My unfounded worries fed my growing anger over the change of my status from thru-hiker to trail mom. This week is going to suck.

J U N E   1 1

Calf Mountain Shelter: Joseph indeed found the turnoff for the shelter fine; it was Grayson and I who took a wrong turn and went an extra mile out of our way, because I was consumed with worry over Joseph's disappearance up the trail. Where is Dad when I need that thump on the head? By the time Grayson and I arrived at the shelter, there wasn't much room left—Rapunzel was there, Brains and Brawn, and some other hikers I didn't know. Tent camping not far from the shelter were two men and a five year old boy, Jenner. The banter between this man, his friend, and Jenner kept us all entertained far more thoroughly than any television show ever could have. Nothing could be more enjoyable than a precocious five-year-old learning to roast marshmallows for the first time and doling them out among a captive audience of adults. Jenner managed to sidle up next to me as bedtime drew near and slipped a sweaty, little arm around my neck for a hug before bed. I guess once a mom, always a mom. This tiny camper helped me make peace with this temporary change in my status. Oh, the power of that quantum universal web.

The shelters in Shenandoah National Park all supply campers with bear poles designed specifically for people to use as a means of protecting their food from being raided by bears. This system consists of "ridiculously tall, rusted metal poles with hooks sticking out in four directions. Another metal pole with a hook on top is used to lift your food bag to the top of the 20-foot tall contraption. Then, as the weight of your food bag swinging atop 15 feet of heavy metal pole knocks you repeatedly off balance, you're supposed to affix the elusive strap of your food bag to the top of this medieval torture device. No longer do we hikers need to rely on humor and creative camp cooking to entertain ourselves. We just all turn our headlamps onto whichever poor soul is attempting to hang their food up". This description is credited to thru-hiker 42; when she read this to me from her trail journal, I knew she had nailed it. Indeed, this very entertainment kept our whole shelter-full of campers laughing sporadically all evening at Calf Mountain shelter. Adding a five-year-old into the mix was the best laugh of all, as he followed the latest arrivals of unsuspecting hikers to the bear pole, chattering away at them about how to hang their food. Sweet little Jenner obligingly attempted to shine his Disney flashlight beam on the top of the pole for the hikers, to show them just where they were supposed to lodge their food bag, and encouraged them (relentlessly) while his beam of light danced all over the tops of the trees around the pole, following his distracted five-year-old line of vision. The hikers gave up, hung their food bags from a nearby tree like they had been for the last 850 miles of trail and went back to their tent leaving the rest of us snickering in the shelter.

J U N E 1 3

The first full day was an adjustment for Joseph and Grayson, with frequent stops, sore feet, bruised hipbones and some uncertainties. Both have earned trail names. Often trail names are dubbed when their owner does something less than intelligent. Despite his numerous reassurances to the contrary, Joseph forgot to bring some things he needed, among them long pants. He was reduced to wearing long underwear tights on the first night—which was quite chilly. With his mohawk shaven off and his black, skull cap on, he earned the name Ninja and carved a place for himself in everyone's memory as he paraded about camp in black Under Armour from head to toe.[†]

Grayson, insistent most days on leading the way up the trail to accommodate his uncanny ability to speed up on the uphills, rounded a curve in the trail this morning and found a bear standing on its hind legs to his right about 15 feet off the trail. In one smooth motion Grayson simply turned around and headed back the way he had come. His eyes were as big as saucers, and he exclaimed "holy crap, there's a really big bear!" By the time I rounded the curve with him again, the bear was making its way back into the bushes. I wrote a little blurb in the trail register that evening about the priceless look on Grayson's face, and so he was named Standing Bear by other thru-hikers that read about his experience.

I introduced the boys to Melatonin on a flat section of trail where we caught up with him when he stopped to study his maps for the best means of reaching Loft Mountain Wayside for lunch. Melatonin carries extra maps and detailed, descriptive books about the area, so he is a great source of information. We leap-frogged his pace all morning, intermittently hiking with him and then moving on ahead. Joseph, with whom I share so many traits, was also immediately enamored by the understated humor of Melatonin's slow, methodical speech patterns super-imposed over his obviously superior intelligence. Joseph jabbers incessantly, so this made the contrast between those two in full discussion even funnier.

Melatonin, Ninja, Standing Bear and I arrived at Loft Mountain Wayside with the famed Shenandoah National Park blackberry milkshakes on our minds and spread our gear out in the sunshine on the deck. We then trouped en masse into the restaurant to taste the long-acclaimed splendor of the modern dairy wonder. Alas! The woefully modern milkshake machine was on the fritz. No blackberry milkshakes for us.

JUNE 15

We arrived early in the evening at Bearfence Mountain Hut after a 12.4 mile day; the boys are toughening up much quicker than I did in the beginning. Grayson spent the evening playing in the fire. I was the only woman in the shelter last night, and I was grateful for my boys' presence to lighten the mood. I'm sure not everyone necessarily shared that sentiment. The men were silent and sullen like they always are. I turned in early, reading the last of *Da Vinci Code* so Joseph could take it home with him when he left. Grayson and I lay awake, side by side in the loft, long after dark listening to the cacophony of snores echoing around us off the log sides of the tiny shelter. We stifled gales of laughter, trying hard not to look at each other, but when particularly outrageous snorts would pierce the darkness, our heads would involuntarily jerk around to face each other, and we'd burst out laughing again, burying our faces in our sleeping bags.

At Big Meadows, Melatonin and my entourage collapsed in the shaded grass beneath a huge oak. Sun shining in fields of tall grass and wildflowers across the parkway was a welcome visual deviation from the deep-forested paths we'd been walking. Here, there was a restaurant and a phone, and they actually employed the services of a working milkshake machine. The boys and I got in line. Around us buzzed the deodorized, freshly showered, hair-styled, tourist activity. Other mothers stared past me unseeingly, their eyes glazed over so they would not have to address the disparity in our summer vacation style. Brains and Brawn relaxed at a booth by the window with their grown son and his girlfriend who had come to meet them for an afternoon visit. Outside, a deer walked into the picnic area, undaunted by the crowd, and wandered around watching the people out of the corner of its eye. Overweight fathers posed pictures of their overweight families with the deer. Finally, our number was called, and our food was ready. We took our burgers and milkshakes out into the shade to sit with the packs while Melatonin took his turn in the tourist trap. Yum, blackberry! Best four dollar milkshake I ever had.

There were numerous deer in Shenandoah, many

showing no fear of humans. This was the first time any of us had seen a buck in the woods or with antlers covered in velvet. Often we were only feet away from them on the trail, and they did not flinch. We saw a mother and her fawn. The fawn was mostly hidden by undergrowth, only the top of its tiny head and ears visible over the branches. But deer were just the beginning of wildlife in the park. One day, as Grayson passed by, a raccoon scrambled head first down a tree. I wasn't able to get Grayson's attention, so he kept walking on down the trail, oblivious. The raccoon scurried off through the forest with his back hunched, casting furtive glances over his shoulder every few steps. Moments later, a fox ran for cover way up ahead across the trail. He had heard us coming long before we neared him.

On our second day in the park we had the great fortune of watching a huge bear foraging in the woods about 25 yards off the trail. He ambled along turning over rocks and licking up bugs and worms he found beneath. He nosed under logs and into piles of leaves. Once, he walked straight toward the four of us that stood watching him from the trail; I had a split second of panic during which I simultaneously registered the size of this amazing creature, his proximity, and the level of insanity it took to be standing there watching him. Grayson told me later he had his hand on his pack buckle, ready to drop it and run. The bear was stunningly beautiful; I could see clearly the richly-colored tan fur on his nose and his shiny, thick black coat. He was busy though, ignoring us, and turned back to his rock investigation. We crept along beside him as long as the trail paralleled his movement; when the trail turned away, we took our last glimpses of his wild wonder and continued on our way, gasping in awe, relief, and amazement.

Grayson was disappointed we did not run across many snakes. The weather had cooled some though, and they didn't seem to be as active. The boys did find a pretty, silvery-colored worm snake living in the hearth around the fire pit at one of the shelters. Eventually, it returned underground as the stones grew hotter from the fire. On the next to the last day, Joseph was walking with Brawn ahead of us when Grayson and I came across a black and yellow striped snake that had obviously just eaten something; the lump in its belly was about halfway down its two foot long body. Grayson speculated it may have eaten a chipmunk. Half a mile later at the shelter, Brawn and Joseph asked if we had seen the snake and had it gotten the frog down its throat finally? They had seen the same snake in the process of eating the frog.[†]

While Grayson and I chased a mourning cloak butterfly, we found a zebra swallowtail—a spectacular giant black and white version of the tiger swallowtail—neither of us had seen before. We also got covered in burrs. Of course, there were the usual myriads of chipmunks. There were toads, newts, slugs, centipedes, millipedes galore, rabbits, and many birds we'd never seen or heard before. Their second night was the only time it rained, and we were warm and dry in Blackrock Hut. The weather was perfect the rest of the week.

My father whisked Joseph and Grayson back to civilization from Thornton Gap. He graciously brought sub sandwiches and soft drinks. I was able to eat with my family, call Adam from the pay phone, visit with Dad, and still put in the extra 1.5 to the shelter before dark. Both boys were appropriately filthy and immensely satisfied. Grayson is completely done with the backpacking vacation with Mom and ready to move on to the rest of his summer. Joseph has managed to maintain his enthrallment with the Trail and will be rejoining me in a few days for more thru-hiking torture.

Of course, I came across two, huge black snakes and a three-foot timber rattler within the last mile and a half of trail. I was disappointed Grayson missed the timber rattler. In all my years of hiking, this was my first encounter with a poisonous snake in the woods. I saw him long before I reached him as he was fully stretched along the side of the trail. While I examined his markings and counted 11 rattles, he moved across the trail and into the leaves on the other side. Obviously hunting, he moved slowly, raising his head a few inches off the ground every few feet to look around before advancing. I felt insignificant in his presence, at his mercy, and humbled by such a powerful creature. In his beauty was a glimpse of death, its intricate mystery manifested in the perfect geometry of his markings, the clarity and purpose of his colors, the stealth of his movements and the knowledge that the wrong move on my part could have me fighting for my life within moments. Truly awe inspiring.

J U N E   1 7

When you are tired and in pain after a long day's hike, it can be a challenge just to meet your own needs. Have I gotten enough water today? Have I eaten enough calories today? I have to stop now and rest my feet, etc. Mothering as a thru-hiker, I watched as dinner was accidentally dumped, my bandana caught on fire, shoes were duct-taped together, pack covers shredded, and the miles checked off, one by one. I was also glad to get up today with no children in tow, cook, eat, pack and hit the trail all within only one hour.

The song of a wood thrush eases the way for the coming twilight. The hollow drill of a woodpecker sounds. I am in my tent early, the last of the sunshine just touching the tops of the trees, with no tent fly separating me from the tree canopy. From down the hill floats up bits and pieces of conversation from the shelter, the cadence of voices rising and falling. I've chosen to tent tonight for the privacy one's own space offers. Every night for the last week I've stayed in shelters while Joseph and Grayson were with me.

I met Cuppa Joe when I caught him yogiing for a cookie from some weekenders. Yogiing is the thru-hiker art form of begging for food without actually asking for food, perfected after months of deprivation of the usual junk fare commonly available to us all in the real world. One casually mentions how long it's been since one had fruit, for example, when they see a camper consuming a banana. Cuppa Joe managed to score a cookie by offering a cup of coffee to a man who was eating a handful of cookies. I called Cuppa Joe on his ploy, and we had a good laugh. He then felt strangely compelled to share his spoils with me for being so brash as to point out his folly to his innocent victims. Yogiing the yogier...I accepted.

J U N E 2 0

Rain! Rain! On a summer's day! Rain felt so good in the heat of the day. Every uphill has steamed like a sweat lodge as the temps have been in the high 80s and every pore has poured sweat. The first storm cell moved in over Dick's Dome Shelter when I stopped for lunch. I sat in the dome with several weekenders, cooking frittatas and chatting about thru-hiking and camping. The rain stopped, and I moved on hoping to put in another five before tenting somewhere. I had gone about 2.5 more miles when thunder rumbled, and I heard the downpour approaching from the southwest like a freight train. I turned around and saw it pelting the treetops a few hundred yards away, and then watched as it overcame me, face uplifted; I simply laughed and laughed. We'd been without rain for so long, and it felt so good! I knew the trees were happy, and even the birds sang through the rain. Within a few more steps was the edge of a large meadow; as I headed into the open, the downpour stopped. I walked in wonder that the rain had come so suddenly and then stopped as I emerged from the protection of the thick canopy of trees. The meadow was bejeweled in sparkling droplets of water, grasses bent under the weight and the air clear and crisp from summer rain. Companies try to bottle that smell and sell it as shampoo, but they never get it right. It's priceless and cannot be captured.

This is Sky Meadows State Park and the sign says camping is forbidden. No choice but to hike in the rain through the park before setting up a tent. The park is beautiful; vast meadows of nodding grasses are punctuated with giant tulip poplars that have grown their whole lives in the open fields assuming their natural shape as gargantuan, mature trees. The natural, unfettered shape of the tulip poplar is incredibly graceful with branches that reach the ground. In the forest, these trees grow very straight with few lower branches, their lowest branches very thin and small. Not these; their branches are as big around as small trees themselves, and they begin only feet from the ground, filling out the full length of the trunk. The large meadows stretch for acres, interspersed with poplar groves and giant single trees.

As I entered the forest on the other side, a new storm cell arrived; the thunder was deafening. I saw a new type of tree I didn't recognize. The leaf configuration was like a nut tree but it had clumps of fragrant flowers, whose perfume filled my lungs on the moisture laden air. Behind me, the lightning suddenly struck the top of the hillside I had just descended, and the flash seared the air; thunder shook the ground where I walked. I moved on through a wall of pouring rain, marveling at the new trees, the sweet smell, and the freshness of the air. For the first time in days, I couldn't smell my own stench. A southbound hiker approached, offering advice on how to locate the trail after the next road crossing; we had to shout to be heard over the sound of the rain. Somehow, our shared experience of the downpour gave me a boost of cheer.

The newness of hiking in the pouring rain with no rain gear kept my mind off the miles. Before I knew it I had done another five, then six, then seven miles. I left Sky Meadows State Park, crossed the highway and was only one mile from the next shelter (nine miles from the last) when I found a suitable place to set up my tent. I was by a nice stream and alone after more than a week of the shelter scene. There was about a pound of water in each boot. Wet socks felt like gel inserts. I had stopped four times, taken my boots off, poured water out of them, wrung out my socks, put them back on, and kept going. Mercifully, the rain stopped just before I found the tent site, so I set up camp and cooked without getting further soaked. Everything under the pack cover stayed dry except a small portion of my sleeping bag stored on the very bottom of the pack. It was only damp and dried during the night. I was grateful for dry clothes and warm food.

This morning, I had to put on those same wet, stinky clothes that had not dried during the night. Eeeww! I waited until 10am to leave camp, so when I put them on, it was already quite warm outside. They were all dry within a couple of hours of hiking. Then, the day warmed up to sweltering again, and they were again soaked in sweat. I dried out the inside of my boots by putting on a dry, but dirty, pair of socks and letting them soak up the water in the boots, then putting on another dry, but dirty, pair of socks and letting them soak up the rest. I knew I would be doing laundry at the hostel tonight, so I could afford the luxury of having three pairs of wet socks. Luxury is all in one's perspective.

Bear's Den Hostel is in a stone lodge that looks like a castle. It was originally the home of Huron Lawson, a Washington physician and his opera singer wife, Francesca Kaspar, and was built in 1933. The property was purchased by the Appalachian Trail Conference and converted into a hostel for hikers and a retreat for nature lovers. Once again, as has been the case each time, I am filled with gratitude and amazement for the luxuries of clean clothes and a shower. Simple pleasures become pizza, soda and a pint of Ben & Jerry's ice cream.

By Friday, I will reach Harpers Ferry (known as the "psychological" halfway town), have my picture taken and sign the official thru-hiker register at the ATC (Appalachian Trail Conference) Headquarters. The latest plan is that Joseph will be joining me again in Smithsburg, Maryland. He will hike with me for the rest of summer. "Thank you", Brains and Brawn, for helping to sort through the pros and cons of this parental tactic and for all your wit and support during the Shenandoahs with the boys.

J U N E   2 1

Trail tradition compels the bravest of hikers to hike naked on Summer Solstice. Several hikers left Bear's Den in the afternoon, planning to make a stop for a free spaghetti dinner at the Blackburn Center later that day. Among us were Puffy Nipples and Cheeto. (Contrary to popular assumption, Puffy Nipples is male.) Melatonin and I sat on a log taking a break that afternoon. Voices caused both of us to look up just in time to see Puffy coming up the trail positioning a bandana from his pack waistbelt to cover his exposed self. "I have to see you people again!" was his rationale. Cheeto, the decidedly more intelligent of the duo, was fully clothed in normal hiker regalia. While they rested beside us on the log, they told us their naked hiker tales of passing a Boy Scout troop and of waving at cars at the last highway crossing. When Puffy rose to leave, tree bark left imprints on his butt. Off he went down the trail, glowing white in the summer sun. Where would we be without traditions?

After a wonderful spaghetti dinner on the screened porch of The Blackburn Center, Puffy, Cheeto, Rapunzel, and her visiting friend (dubbed White Trash for the white trash bag she used as a pack cover) and I opted for a few more miles to make it to the 1000 mile mark. There, in the middle of the trail stands a white pillar inscribed with "1000 MILES" down its length. On a side trail is the David Wesser Memorial Shelter. We had all dallied over our dinner so long we found ourselves pulling in to the shelter just as darkness enveloped the forest. Rapunzel had brought party para-phernalia—plastic gold medals, glow sticks, beads, necklaces, party hats and bubbles for our 1000-mile party. Her unwavering cheerfulness creates a bright spot in everyone's day and is usually contagious. Despite the darkness and our growing fatigue, we donned the beaded necklaces, spun our glow sticks and blew bubbles to dutifully mark our official transition to 1000-milers. Our "party" was quite low key. The peak of the excitement was the discovery of a giant wolf spider, at least 10 inches in diameter, that peered down on the happenings from the rafters while we all prepared our sleeping bags by flashlight. I lay awake for hours listening for the spider to creep down the wall beside me to play in my hair.

J U N E   2 3

Ed Garvey Shelter is fairly new, two stories high, with steps on the back and a balcony that looks down over the front. Hiker company included the area Ridgerunner, a couple of women hikers who remained tucked away quietly in the loft, Jambalaya, the female half of the thru-hiking newlyweds, Pepperoni and Jambalaya, (new trail names for Julia and Mark –who I had not seen since the Fontana Hilton in North Carolina) and Nomad, a recovering alcoholic, on the trail for its therapeutic ability to change lives. Pepperoni was off taking part in the four state challenge—a 42-mile stretch that carries the hiker across four state lines (VA, WV, MD and into PA) in 24 hours for those who have the stamina. Nomad had been on the trail, hiking southbound and alcohol-free since Penmar Park, at the Pennsylvania/Maryland border; he was hiking with his dog. Mudd had been rescued from the side of the road when a trucker had pitched the puppy out the window of his moving cab. Nomad carried a Walmart tent, an army Alice pack, and a nylon car-camping sleeping bag. He had no sleeping pad at all, but slept directly on the wooden shelter floor. His demeanor was one of positivism and acceptance, the casual certainty born of a lifetime of overcoming adversity. Late that evening, a huge electrical storm came up. Flashes of lightning could be seen long before it arrived. The storm moved quite slowly, so it hovered around the shelter for a long time. Everyone was awake but lying quietly in the dark as the downpour provided relief from the heaviness in the air, and thunder and lightning served as the evening entertainment. Nomad sat with his back up against the wall of the shelter most of the night, chain smoking his way through detox. I said a silent prayer for his courage.

Willow and Switch

What we claim as our identity has great power over us as individuals, and nothing is more foremost in the mind of a teenager than the question of personal identity. Joseph has returned to the Trail until August, and it seems his first concern coming back was to shed the trail name 'Ninja' that had been bestowed upon him in the Shenandoahs. "Ninja has a childish ring to it that doesn't cut it for me," he said. "I need something older." "How about Switch", I suggested, "like a willow switch, since you are traveling with Willow." The play on words was an immediate fit. We are alike in so many ways, finishing each others sentences, thinking the same thoughts at the same time, having the same hang-ups and expectations from life that it seemed immensely appropriate for his new 'older' trail name to be an extension of mine with a southern pun and the suggestion of trouble-maker. Joseph became Switch.

JUNE 26

We crossed out of Maryland after 10 miles of trail together. Welcome to Pennsylvania! I was very happy to be done with Maryland. For such a short mileage state, it was my least favorite. Much of the walking was easy, flat and good trail, but the rocky sections were so unpleasant they tainted the whole experience. There were no animals, and one stretch was devoid of even birdsong. South Mountain offered brief respite, boasting the first monument erected in honor of George Washington, a stone tower built in 1827, but infinitely more fascinating to both Switch and me was Gath's Tomb, in Gathland Park. This empty tomb was built by wealthy George Townsend, a war correspondent during the Civil War. It was his intent to be buried there, but by the time of his passing, in New York City, he was almost penniless and his burial wishes were never honored. A sentence on the historical marker reads: "Gath's empty tomb mutely symbolizes the uncertainties of Life, Fame and Fortune and the certainty of death."[†]

Most of the landmarks in Maryland were road crossings. As we emerged from the woods at a road, a car whizzed by; I looked both ways after it passed—no cars. I started across. Suddenly, from around the curve to my left came a car and from over the hill to my right came another. Too late; both Switch and I were already crossing. The car to our right slowed and waited. The car to our left barely slowed and blared their horn as they sped by. Yes! I am glad to be rid of Maryland. Wouldn't want to delay anyone by a millisecond on their way to the mall.

At PenMar Park, Pennsylvania, we stopped at a picnic pavilion to cook dinner sheltered from the sprinkling rain. A large group of Mennonites were having a covered dish dinner. All the men were dressed alike in hats and vests, and all the women were dressed alike in hair bonnets and long dresses. Switch was quite intrigued. I was much more intrigued by his attempts to cook his dinner on his new alcohol stove. The

Mennonite children stole peeks at the open flame adventures of his gallant attempts. I eventually had to let him finish cooking on my canister stove.

We found black raspberries for dessert another quarter mile up the trail, using precious fading daylight to stain our faces and hands, indulging in their unbelievably delectable sweetness. We dallied over a black snake, a toad, an orange newt, a conversation with some section hikers, and trail magic sodas in a cooler left by the side of the first road crossing in the state. There was still a mile to go to the shelter when darkness fell, and a light mist started. We stopped at a spring for water and got out our headlamps. I suspected the last mile would hold the illusion of taking forever. Sure enough, two tenths of a mile from the shelter it began to rain in earnest. I was getting quite testy at that point, knowing we should have beaten the rain. I can handle the rain, but I do not handle hiking in the dark in the rain very well. Unexpectedly, to our right, other headlamps appeared to help light the way. Puffy Nipples and Cheeto called out cheerfully. After starting at noon, we'd made it 15 miles.

The shelter system in Pennsylvania often has two smaller shelters next to one another instead of one large one. Both were almost full, but everyone made room, and we squeezed Switch in one and me in the other. As we set up our sleeping bags and cooked dinner, rain fell steadily.

J U N E   2 7

Rain, Rain, Rain, Rain. Pennsylvania continues to provide. We hiked in the rain since lunchtime. Lunch was sardines on saltines eaten while precariously balanced on wet logs on the side of the trail. Despite the discomforts, Switch remains his usual cheerful self, always ready with a ridiculous comment to cheer the moment. We dodged one heavy downpour by holing up at a shelter for a break, counting ourselves lucky, thinking we were missing the worst of it. Ah ha! Not so! About two tenths of a mile after the shelter, rain began again, a steady downpour that continued the rest of the day. We slogged and sloshed along, avoiding puddles for the first hour, and finally, when our boots became hopelessly waterlogged, walking straight through all puddles.

We caught up with thru-hikers Keystone, Giggles and Easily Distracted at Caledonia State Park at a picnic pavilion. Clotheslines were strung across the pavilion with wet gear hanging from one end to the other; everyone sat happily playing cards at a picnic table. They waved us over to their haven, and we joined them, stringing up our own line of dripping gear. We changed into dry clothes and cooked dinner. I drank hot tea; it all seemed rather surreal. The rain poured on.

At a break in the downpour, Switch and I packed up and donned wet clothes again, ready to head out. Rain began again, harder than before. Or, maybe it just seemed that way because there we stood in wet clothes, wet boots and wet packs. Everyone was incredulous that we were even considering it, but I figured we may as well. We're already soaked; we're fed. There was only 2.3 more miles to go to the shelter, and it was against state park rules to camp in the pavilion. So out we went into the sheets of rain only to find that the creek we had to ford had quadrupled in size, and we were now facing a serious water crossing. Switch behaved much like an ant whose scent trail has been wiped away; he walked in circles and back and forth raging, "Oh hell no!" I scanned the area for the easiest place to cross and headed out into the water. Soon, he followed suit. I cringed as the cold water reached my knees. We planted our hiking poles firmly against the strong current before taking each step. As we climbed out of the water on the other side, a cheer went up from the pavilion behind us. We cheered back and went a few yards farther only to find another, even deeper crossing, previously unseen from the pavilion. This one was thigh deep in the middle, but the current was not as strong. Each boot now weighed several pounds full of water. Luckily, after that crossing, the trail headed straight up a mountain, and we had no more water crossings of any consequence to contend with. Toads and little frogs scattered before us. A box turtle happily toiled up the hill in the rain, the yellow on his shell bright in the gloomy fading light.

Quarry Gap Shelter appeared like a haven. It is built like a Lincoln Log toy house with one long roof covering two small log enclosures on each end and in the center a covered porch with a picnic table. Potted impatiens hung on each end of the porch. Crushed, tan-colored gravel covered the ground around the area, so there was no mud. A cute, but overflowing, stream gurgled by the front of the shelter where a bench sat and more impatiens hung on plant hangers. Though we were expecting Puffy Nipples, and Cheeto to already be here, the place was empty. A quick check in the register revealed they had opted for more miles in the rain. We had this beautiful shelter to ourselves. We strung up our wet gear, changed into dry clothes, and curled up in our sleeping bags watching the rain and planning our miles for the next few days. A perfect ending to a challenging day. Life is good.[†]

J U N E   2 8

All day we slogged through three to six inches of water in the trail. After drying our boots all night, we tried our best to avoid the puddles this morning as we set out. The entire trail was waterlogged, however, and dodging puddles eventually became a frustration rather than a help. Switch, who had been hiking in trail sneakers all along, finally gave up and simply slogged through the water. I started out the morning in my Crocs with high hopes for keeping my boots relatively dry all day. In Crocs, I could wade right through the puddles, but they filled up with leaves and grit, which then ground away at the bottoms of my feet. I began to purposely wade through the deepest of the puddles to wash the scree out every few yards. This made for incredibly slow going. Still, the terrain was level, and most of the trail was old logging roads with many road crossings. We managed to put away 13.6 miles despite poor trail conditions.[†]

Lessons offered while hiking wet trails somehow take longer to register; the mind is soggy and cannot absorb another droplet. No matter how many times you tell yourself not to step on wet logs, when that slimy log disguises itself as the perfect surface available for avoiding sinking ankle deep in mud, your mind does an abbreviated calculation of the risks involved, and you find yourself making a mental note to call Gamblers Anonymous once you get to town, as you pick yourself up out of a puddle for the fourth time that day. Switch learned early on he had best not be too quick to laugh when he witnessed some of my spectacular launches, for inevitably, he would be next. With my knee troubles lurking in the background, my falls were always followed by a somber moment of silence while we both figured out if I was still alive. Once Switch detected movement devoid of groans and sailor's language, he would burst forth with giggles and encouraging euphemisms like "Sweeet! Good one!"

The rain continues.

J U N E   2 9

We took a short leisurely day and hung out in the sunshine at the Pine Grove Furnace general store for a long time. This is a much anticipated stop on the AT, known for the half-gallon-challenge, a ritual in which thru-hikers attempt to eat an entire half gallon carton of ice cream in one sitting. Their endeavors are timed and recorded in the ledger for all to read. Many others before us had done it, but making myself sick did not seem wise, and even Switch wasn't interested. We opted for burgers, ice cream cones and cherry cokes instead while drying out wet boots and socks in the sun.[†]

A pay phone call to Adam revealed that he and Grayson had made an impromptu stop at Kings Dominion in Richmond, Virginia before going home. They spent two days riding every ride in the park. Like father, like son; I know they had a blast. It warms my heart to think of them laughing and having fun together, just the two of them, especially since they are so alike—ha-ha, while Switch and I, who are so alike, struggle through flood conditions, wet gear, and lost rain jackets all in the name of fun. Yes; Switch left his rain jacket at the last shelter. I say: "Not my problem", like the guy in the Fed Ex commercial Dad likes so much. I think Switch is still in shock over the development, for he's been out here long enough that he knows how important such a piece of equipment can be. Not sure what he's going to do. The chances of it finding its way back to him are slim.

Flooding has been quite an issue in low lying areas for two days. Water has reached six inches deep along the trail in some places. Bridges are washed out. Fuller Lake (not my pun this time)[†] at Pine Grove Furnace completely overflowed its banks and wiped out an entire mile of bicycle trail, transporting several tons of gravel into the forest and depositing it like mulch two feet deep around the bases of the trees.[†] Caledonia Park went completely under water after we left there—it turned out it was a good thing we waded out when we did, because it only got worse that night. A ranger stopped us at a dirt road crossing this morning, asking us about trail conditions where we had come from. He told us of rescuing several hikers from Caledonia State Park—that would have been Keystone and his crowd ending up in town that night. The city of Duncannon, Pennsylvania, which is where we are headed, has been under a state of emergency and the Susquehanna River has risen 20 feet. We are fortunate to be safe in the forest, and I almost dread going into town. Switch and I have been alone in the shelters for the past two nights, which has been fun, but I recognize that if Switch weren't here with me, it would have been a lonely, wet, dreary experience. All things considered, we've weathered the storm quite well. We even had trail magic—homemade pizza, fresh salad and pink lemonade—for lunch at Birch Run Shelter yesterday from Stealth (GA-ME '05) and his sister, Beth. There's something about Switch's frequency that attracts good fortune. It always amazes me. (Of course, then he does things like lose his rain jacket—"Not my problem!" said the mother to the 16-year-old.)

J U N E 3 0

So...we meet this guy who does 25-mile days, started the trail in May in Georgia and has already caught up to us in Pennsylvania in less than two months. Seriously? Switch has now taken to randomly speeding up to pass me on the trail with his hiking poles flailing at crazy angles out to his sides. As he sails by me, he tosses out the flippant comment "passing on your left, started five days ago!" and we both dissolve in laughter.

We arrived in the town of Boiling Springs, Pennsylvania around 2pm. It was incredibly hot and muggy after all the rain. We had put in 12 miles to get there in hopes of picking up our mail drop and still having daylight left while we figured out where to stay, shower and eat. There didn't seem to be many options available to hikers in the town, which is an over-priced, upscale community listed on the National Historical Register. The 14 miles north of Boiling Springs are designated as a 'no camping' segment of trail which really throws a monkey wrench into things. Here we were in town with too few hours left in the day to hike another 14 miles, nowhere to stay, and no plan. After five days of camping and hiking in the rain, a little reprieve seemed in order, but how to get it was seemingly beyond what little reasoning capability I had left. The only means of making phone calls to explore options was a pay phone outside of the ATC Mid-Atlantic Regional Office. Each call gobbled up dollars on the phone card in pay phone fees. Even if we had been able to find a motel room, we would have to hitchhike to get there as the nearest motels were eight miles away.

Towns and their logistics have always caused me the most consternation during my time alone on the trail. Now I feel responsible for making Switch's time on the trail as enjoyable and memorable as possible, not wanting him to be miserable and end up hating backpacking. The 'no camping' ordinance infuriates me, and I wasted a good hour simply being pissed off and spinning in mental circles arguing the case to myself. I sat on the porch of the ATC office and watched as clean, nicely dressed families strolled by the lake on the sidewalk pushing baby carriages and holding hands, allowing culture shock to skew my reasoning beyond recognition. A ranger from the regional office began an excruciatingly long conversation with me about the ongoing differences between the goals of the ATC regulations and the campers and hikers expectations. His agenda made my head swim with the politics of society's rules, something I was out here to escape in the first place. Listening to him only confused me more and delayed my decision about where we were going to stay and what we were going to eat. By this time, I just wanted to cry.

After a brief meltdown into tears, I listened to Switch's quite reasonable suggestion; we ate some snack foods from the convenience store across the street and visited the Boiling Springs. Watching the water bubble up from beneath the ground served to clear my head somewhat, and I was able to settle on what to do. I called a phone number posted on the bulletin board at the ATC Office of a family offering to take in hikers that needed a place to stay.

Thankfully, I had reached trail angel, Greg, who drove from his home in Mechanicsburg; he had two other thru-hikers with him as well, Sun Crow and Sunshine Daydream. Greg brought the four of us to his place and made us feel like his home was our own. We did laundry, grilled hamburgers, made spaghetti, watched TV, took showers, and checked email. He even allowed me to use his computer to transfer my pictures from my camera memory card to CD. His generosity restored my faith in the trail that had flagged through the last week of rain and restored my faith in humanity that had fallen victim to the ranger's awful trail stories.

Greg took us to the post office first thing the next morning, and I mailed the CD of pictures home. We were back on trail by 11am. Melatonin was sitting outside the ATC Office in Boiling Springs. He didn't recognize Switch, who has changed so much from the last time Melatonin saw him in the Shenandoahs.

J U L Y   1

We've landed at Darlington Shelter where we can hear Fourth of July fireworks being launched in the valley. We attempted to night-hike back to an overlook to try to see them, but for some reason we got the heebie-jeebies and came scurrying back. Switch insists there was a bear following him. And now, a porcupine is chewing on the underside of the shelter making an awful racket.

D U N C A N N O N , P E N N S Y L V A N I A

We made it into Duncannon Sunday afternoon, procured room 26 on the fourth floor of the Doyle Hotel, and proceeded to be sucked in to the comforts of town. The Doyle[†],trail icon, was once a grand Anheiser-Busch hotel and bar, but has been privately owned for many years. It stands majestically rotting away on the main drag of Duncannon, Market Street, by the banks of the Susquehanna River—a faded, peeling tribute to the bustling life the town once knew. She is a splendid, old lady whose carefully patted face powder has become caked in the wrinkles of her skin and whose large-print flowered dress went out of style decades before. The walls are cracked and water-stained, filthy with hand prints and grime; the woodwork is dark and shiny with shellac. A single light bulb hangs from the ceiling in our room, an electrical cord dangling from the one socket in the light fixture down to the floor fan by the window. A long-silent bell for the porter is mounted on the wall, and a cast iron radiator with decorative scroll work would have once staved off the New England chill. The bar on the first floor is friendly and cheerful, filled with hikers coming and going with various requests. The bar serves food and has an internet terminal. Rooms for $20/night. Our view from the fourth floor window overlooks the swollen Susquehanna.[†]

Switch and I were at odds most of the day, hiking separately all morning and then silently after lunch. The trail itself was very rocky, difficult walking that required all of one's focus—no gazing about unless you wanted to suddenly take an unplanned trip to the ground. This area had a lot of disconcerting energy that was affecting us both. Several years ago, two hikers were killed in this very section of trail. The air was heavy. I had struggled emotionally with the trail since Boiling Springs, mired in non-motivation and a pervasive depression—quite disillusioned with the whole thing.

We arrived on the edge of town[†] after a hellacious descent across a boulder rock slide to be greeted by trail magic from Trailangelmary. She had a well-stocked cooler of Capri-Suns sitting by the trail. I came to the cooler and found Switch actually smiling. The ice in the cooler wasn't even melted—I took a few chunks of ice and rubbed them on my face and neck—wrapping them in my bandana and just holding the welcome coolness. A sign invited us to dinner that night at Mary's house. Wow! I felt a little better already.

We walked into Duncannon discussing what had gone wrong with our day, making our apologies, and sharing our excitement over being in town. When we checked in, five packages were waiting. No Pliers had found the rain jacket Switch had lost and, responding to Switch's plaintive pleas in the registers, had left it at the Doyle for him. We also had a message from Rapunzel, who was behind us now, that she had sent up the trail with another northbound hiker. Her cheerful, playful note made us feel loved and included in the greater community of hikers. It sure felt good to be in town.

We showered and did laundry first, then opened boxes of food and gifts. Our room disappeared under piles of Ziploc bags, food, clothes, towels, boots, poles, packs; you name it, it was spread out all over the place. At Trailangelmary's, dinner was roasted garlic soup, salad, corn on the cob, shrimp and potato stew, french bread, fruit and pie—oh, and beer. Just as we sat down to the first course, Melatonin staggered through the door. He had just arrived in town, trying desperately to get there in time for food. There were eight hikers including us: Melatonin, Sunshine Daydream, Sun Crow, Lone Wolf, Carnivore, and Sleep Walker. After dinner we watched Mary's home video of hikers being taken across the flood waters at PA 325 in the bucket of a front loader. The driver had helped Mary put up a safety line across the river for the hikers who arrived alone. Later, the waters rose too high, and no one could cross. The video made me even more thankful we had not been this far up the trail during the storms.

The decision to zero on Monday evolved after sleeping late then eating breakfast across the street at Goodies with Melatonin. We spent a glorious day doing mostly nothing. Switch listened to the radio upstairs in the room all day long with his feet propped up in the open window, watching the river and the trains go by. He seemed quite pleased with his perch.

I recently discovered that the tread on my boots was mostly gone after landing three hard falls during the rain a few days before. I called and ordered boots, requesting to have them shipped farther up the trail to me in Palmerton, PA. Asolo no longer makes this boot so they are sending me Stingers. The customer service rep says they are the next closest thing. I'm taking a chance the fit will work without trying them on. Makes me nervous, but I have little choice. There are no outfitters anywhere in Duncannon. Asolo gave me 15% off and free shipping. I'm not of the school of entitled hikers who believe a company should replace a worn-out product free of charge...1100 miles is a good life for a boot, but I greatly appreciated the discounts, as hiking boots are not cheap.

The next day dawned with plans for something new, a day of slack-packing 17 miles. There are as many variations of slack-packing as there are hikers. I had not slack-packed at all the entire trip. I have no real strong feelings for or against slacking, although the ever-present debate exists in the thru-hiker community as to whether this practice detracts from the classic, coveted thru-hiker status. I had simply never considered it seriously. This particular arrangement seemed like fun. Trailangelmary was shuttling a bunch of us, and before we left, she fed us all breakfast. She then provided dinner for everyone when we got back, and another shuttle to see the fireworks over Harrisburg that night, the Fourth of July.

So, we slack-packed from PA 325 back to Duncannon. It took Switch and me from 11am to 6:30pm to go the 17 miles. The first 6.5 we did at a 3.25mph pace, but after that, I began to slow down and only got slower as the day wore on. Even without a pack, 17 miles is a long day. My feet really hurt the last few miles.

We viewed the Harrisburg fireworks from a mountaintop neighborhood with a long distance view of the city. The display, reflecting off the water and silhouetted against the night sky, was surreal. Distance swallowed the sound, and the silent spray of colored-fire sparks seemed to belong to a world far away that I once knew but was no longer a part of. The effects sent homesickness like a wave through the crowd of hikers, and cell phones popped out of everywhere as hikers called home to wish loved ones holiday cheer. All the way back to Duncannon, Switch entertained the car full of women hikers with his adolescent anecdotes, then he accompanied them to the convenience store and downed a pint of ice cream for a snack. I snuck off to the pay phone and called Adam. The sound of his calm voice acted on my emotions like a reset button.

We awoke to more rain. Leaving Duncannon in the rain took every ounce of willpower. No one was ready to go; Trailangelmary wasn't even awake yet at 8am. Switch groaned and pulled the covers over his head, and our room was still a disaster. I ate breakfast in our room and left the Doyle at eight, going to Mary's house to wake her up; I started the coffee on her counter, folded brochures for the Billville event she was hosting in town the following weekend, went back to the Doyle to tell the other hikers the plan, and then met Melatonin across the street at Goodies for second breakfast. Steadily it rained. Melatonin was also experiencing a lot of foot pain and elected to zero another day to rest some more. I was sorry to be leaving him there, wishing I had the money and the sense to stay behind another day. Mary shuttled a van full of hikers, leaving us trailside with hugs and her well wishes.

The rain cleared after a few hours, but the pain in my feet only increased as the miles ticked by. I was finally reduced to tears by the side of the trail, a combination of wounded pride, dehydration, hunger and pain. All of the younger hikers had passed us and were miles ahead. Switch patiently reassured me he had come out here to be with me, and he was ok with all our friends hiking on without us. I had spent months being perfectly fine with always being left behind and having to make new friends every week or so, but suddenly my physical limitations were affecting my son, and I felt terribly guilty. If it weren't for my pace, he would have been miles ahead with all the 20-some-things, laughing and talking, walking together and taking breaks together. Instead, he was steadfast and loyal to his slow, old mother, patiently listening to my list of complaints and unwaveringly making me laugh at myself. Is this really MY offspring? How did this happen? From my perpetual, existential angst a happy, well-adjusted optimist spawned? I can only watch in amazement as he works magic everywhere he goes. 600 mg of ibuprofen later I made it to our campsite.

J U L Y   6

Starting the day by fording a rushing stream is the trail equivalent to that first cup of coffee in the morning. The climb up to the next ridgeline was another morning eye opener. Even hiking all day every day one forgets the intensity of an uphill until it's rising consistently before you. It seems that switchbacks are a "southern thang" for we've seen few since Virginia. Once the climb ended it would have been nice to have a great view as a small reward, but we were only treated to eight miles of rocks and poison ivy along the ridgeline. I'm not sure how people who are allergic to poison ivy survive on the AT. I've walked through miles of it; fortunately, neither Switch nor I am very sensitive to its oils and haven't had any yet. I've seen other hikers covered in its angry red welts.

Our excitement built as the day wore on, for we had plans to meet friends from our hometown at 5pm at the 501 road crossing. They are in Pennsylvania visiting relatives and had contacted us through Adam. As we neared the road toward the end of the day, every bend in the trail tantalized our taste buds. Our friends were bringing us a homemade dinner. We could hear the road above us, as the trail paralleled it for about a half a mile. Torture. Finally, we arrived. The 501 Shelter was just north of the road, so we took our packs there and came back to wait. What a treat to see a familiar car pull up and four familiar, friendly faces smiling. Monroe, Fern, Aaron and Sarah and their cousin Rebekah all gave us big hugs (a brave gesture considering our pungent thru-hiker cologne). We all carried food to the shelter, the perfect place for a gathering.

The 501 is no ordinary AT shelter. It is an enclosed house-like structure with bunks lining the walls, a counter, trash cans, a mirror, hand sanitizer, a huge octagonal skylight, and a long banquet-style table with vinyl upholstered chairs. There is a spigot outside for water, a solar shower and a port-a-potty. It's a regular

Holiday Inn compared to most shelters. Fern had cooked vegetarian, stuffed shells and fresh, silver queen corn on the cob. There was fresh salad, bread and butter, and ice cream. We all sat down to the feast, and even a few other hikers were able to get in on the food. 42 arrived in time for some stuffed shells, and Rapunzel and Samurai got some corn and salad. Getting to visit with friends from home, ever so briefly, was a highlight of the state of Pennsylvania, even with all its excitement. It was a treat that provided us with 'that little something' that enables you to carry on. As I said to them there that night, "'thank you' doesn't even begin to express the level of gratitude felt". Switch and I were so overwhelmed by the good company and the food, I'm afraid we said very little in their presence that made a bit of sense.

J U L Y   7

There's a certain liberation felt when breaking from the ranks and accomplishing the number of miles you want to hike instead of settling for the number of miles between established shelters. We tented last night for the first time since Switch joined me again. He is carrying his own solo-sized tent, borrowed from Adam's job. We did 16 miles to get here instead of the 11 to the shelter. A soft rain began about an hour after we settled inside our tents and continued well into the night. I do like the sound of rain on a tent. When I awoke to first light I felt free, in the privacy of my tent instead of a shelter.

J U L Y   8

We hiked into Port Clinton at 10am under pressure

to get there before the post office closed at 11:00. We grabbed a shower and a burger at the Port Clinton Hotel and were back into the woods by 1pm, successfully avoiding the town trap. Most of our friends hitched from Port Clinton back to Duncannon for a festival called the Billville Hiker Feed. We will keep plodding along. My slower hiking pace means any chance I have to add on a few miles helps me stay in the vicinity of hikers I already know.

The miles again today really, really hurt my feet. I'm beginning to fear there may be more at stake here than originally anticipated. Not sure if it's the boots, the miles, too much weight, or the Pennsylvania rocks. Process of elimination?

J U L Y   9

Two day hikers who are 2007 thru-hiker hopefuls were out with their two dogs on The Pinnacle for a picnic lunch. They offered to carry out our trash and took our pictures with Pennsylvania farmland painting the background as far as the eye could see. A large group of hikers, maybe an outing club, were there when we arrived. We were like a species of animal next to these well-groomed, deodorant-wearing people in tennis shoes.

Switch had an encounter with a buzzard just before The Pinnacle. He had climbed up on the rocks above the trail to entertain himself as we picked our way along this incredibly taxing section of trail. Two buzzards circled him. Suddenly, a loud hissing came from one of the rocks. I could even hear it from down below on the trail. Switch investigated and found a shallow cave formed by the pile of boulders; inside was a half-grown buzzard daring him to come any closer. Its parents hovered over Switch's head, circling menacingly.[†]

The trail opened up this afternoon and became a gravel access road that offered great consolation for my aching feet. The last few miles to Eckville Shelter eased by after days of limping along on rocky trail.

J U L Y   1 0

Rock Chalk let me borrow his foot book. It seems I have Achilles tendonitis and have for quite awhile. The stretches I do each morning are exactly what I should be doing for it—aside from discontinuing hiking. The balls of my feet have hurt so much over the last four days, I've had to cut our mileage back again. I fashioned a second metatarsal pad for my left foot out of toilet tissue and surgical tape. It has served its purpose well, and the pad plus less weight (as I eat the food) and fewer miles have all helped tremendously.

We've adopted a new approach to each day that is more relaxed and less stressful than when we were doing 15-17 miles a day. We've stopped to enjoy more views, taken our time over lunch, napped, taken more pictures and more breaks. It's helped Switch with his developing foot pain, too. The mail drops with eight days of food in them cannot continue. I've got to mail some of that ahead instead of carrying it. The money savings I anticipated by purchasing food beforehand has been absorbed in the cost of mailing bounce boxes and extra food all over the place. I want to take a lot of items out of my bounce box this time around too, and just donate them to a hiker box. I've paid more money in shipping than I would have just purchasing shampoo, razors and laundry soap in each town. Getting around in some towns is very difficult, so going to the PO and having everything you need arrive in one box is rather convenient. I don't think there are easy answers.

Shorter mileage has put us in camp earlier in the day. Tonight, because we are tenting at a huge hunters' campsite, we decided to have a fire to drive away the hordes of mosquitoes. It's a cozy addition to our evening despite the ensuing argument over how to start a fire. I retreated to my bug net tent and let Switch wrestle his own demons. After three attempts, he now is happily watching over his success.[†]

There's a Pennsylvania phenomenon that perplexes me. Switch and I have found four abandoned campsites in the last week. There will be a tarp or tent set up that has obviously been there for awhile. There's food, sometimes gear and clothing scattered about, and usually a lot of trash. Some of our hiking has been on state hunting lands, so it seems likely they could be hunters' campsites. It's kind of creepy though. Tripoli campsite, where we are tonight, has a lot of broken glass on the ground; down the hill we found another abandoned camp. I walked down to it, thinking back-packers were there but instead found an open tent with stuff sacks inside, bags of empty beer cans and a case of Capri Sun empties scattered about, confirming my suspicion these camps might be meth labs. A pillow was in the fire pit, a shirt, and various and sundry other garbage. We are both uneasy tonight.

JULY 12

We slept in the Palmerton jailhouse hostel last night. It's not really an old jail like everyone says but is the old courthouse building. The police officer that signed us in checked our IDs and wrote down our names. He eyed Switch warily when he heard my son's last name. He told us that around these parts, that name spelled trouble for the town police. I assured the officer we were from the South and that around our parts, the name spelled truant officer.

Thinking I was smart to walk to the post office while Switch slept late, I set out to walk the one mile early in the morning. Of course, I arrived before they opened and ended up sitting outside cursing my great idea and regretting the wasted time. My boots were due to arrive though and so was a mail drop box, so I waited. As I came away from the counter with my packages, I again cursed the folly of coming here without Joseph. I had received four boxes in the mail. Now I faced a one mile walk on the concrete sidewalk carrying this stack of loot. If only I could balance them on my head the way tribal African women do. Instead, I stumbled along resting my spoils against lampposts and trashcans every two tenths of a mile, nodding and smiling sheepishly at the elderly women out for their morning strolls.

E V E N I N G —

Our hitch out of Palmerton was with a man who told us he had always dreamed of hiking the AT. He was friendly and cheerful, chatting away as he drove us back to the trail crossing. When he stopped for us to get our packs out of the back of his Explorer, he fished in his wallet and pulled out a $20 bill. "Here, take this for coffee money," he said. "You might need coffee money."

On the north side of Palmerton, at Lehigh Gap, the AT makes a 1000 foot climb up Blue Mountain, a polluted, barren, Superfund cleanup site—a ghostland devoid of vegetation due to years of unregulated zinc mining. The climb is a jumble of boulders just barely shy of vertical. With a full pack, the climb loomed more formidable than anything we've encountered. Just before the top, I stood on one boulder to reach for the next. The vertical drop behind suddenly claimed my senses; I froze. Vertigo and panic rolled dice for my soul. Joseph scrambled up ahead of me and said, "come on, mom. you can do it!" I tried again, but the span was too far for me to pull body and pack weight up without sacrificing center of gravity and, consequently, my tenuous hold on the edge of this 1000 foot cliff. Panic won the roll of the dice, and I started to cry. I had never been so sure I was going to die. Joseph stood above me suggesting I hand him my pack, but I was so consumed by vertigo, if I moved to get the pack off, I would fall. He reached down and grabbed the top of my pack and started to pull; I unclipped my waistbelt and let him pull the pack off my shoulders over my head. With the weight of the pack off my back, I was able to make the reach and scramble up the rocks with no problem, the same way Joseph had moments before. We hugged and stood side by side in the boulder field on top of Lehigh Gap while I calmed down. A bird flew over; a giant dollop of bird poop splashed onto Joseph's shoulder, and my tears evaporated into laughter.

Our day ended with a side trip down a road in search of water and darkness overtaking us as rain began to pour. When I first found a small spot that might work for our tents, Switch argued for pushing farther; fortitude still weakened by my cliff-hanging experience, I resigned and followed him up the trail. When the rain began, we again argued briefly but back-tracked to the small, barely suitable clearing. Switch muttered apologies under his breath over and over while we both scrambled to get set up in the pouring rain. Our two tents are squeezed side by side, surrounded by thick pine forest. Glad that we weren't still hiking in the downpour, I lay in my tent marveling at the power of the trail to instill awareness. Switch was learning about consequences of decisions, and I could see him maturing before my very eyes. I listened to the rain and pondered the nature of fear and its relationship to physical strength.

J U L Y   1 3

Just as we approached a road crossing, two teenage boys passed us heading south. They stopped and said, "Were you with some other hikers?" We knew Rapunzel, 42, Samurai, and Rock Chalk were just ahead of us, but we didn't really consider we were "with" anyone, so we answered no. I puzzled over their question after they were gone. When we arrived at the road crossing, their meaning became clear. The teenagers had eaten the last of the trail magic hotdogs our friends ahead had left for us. Tonight, I am wrestling my indignation based on imaginary thru-hiker entitlement and wishing I could let things go as easily as my son.

J U L Y   1 6

A new menace to our sanity has appeared on the scene disguised as hungry mosquitoes. And, I don't mean your average backyard variety where a few red swollen bumps add to your summer cookout memories. I'm talking hordes of bloodthirsty varmints that swarm in clouds that could suck a small moose dry within half an hour. It is not uncommon to witness hikers running down the trail, arms and hiking poles flapping, screaming obscenities as they reach breaking point. The place at which this phenomenon claimed Switch and me was Wolf Rocks, an impossible place to actually run due to the deadly nature of the endless rock arrangements in the trail. So I'm hobbling, hopping, flailing, screaming down the "trail" and Switch is doing the same behind me, dousing my pack and the air in front of him with the questionable effects of Deet as he runs. I'm sure we were quite the sight. All I can think is, "I never have to go back to Pennsylvania again!" I was comforted by other hikers confessing similar defeats to one another in the Church of the Mountain hostel in Delaware Water Gap.

Pushing for the last few miles into the river town of Delaware Water Gap, Switch and I moved quickly down a long steep mountain coming off a ridgeline we'd been following for miles. At the bottom of this mountain, a small enclave of heaven folded around us, comforting, providing much needed water and spiritual renewal. Here the trail crossed a beautiful stream strewn with moss-covered rocks spilling from a mountainside draw lined with rhododendron. We had entered an isolated pocket, a micro-ecosystem that mirrored our sorely-missed southern Appalachian Mountains of home. A sense of peace descended upon us both. We gained reprieve from our weariness of the unfamiliar and the incessant miles of difficult terrain for those few moments as we rested on a mossy log and treated our water.

From the tiny town, we took a shuttle into Strouds-burg, Pennsylvania, a larger town, and landed in the mall, of all places. G-Man, Johnny K., Switch and I crept into the darkness of the mall theatre and settled into our seats to enjoy *Pirates of the Caribbean*, my first movie in five months. Such a simple diversion and such a profound effect. Mild angst released its death grip on my psyche—or maybe it was the fact that we were finally putting Pennsylvania behind us. Delaware Water Gap sits on the south bank of Delaware River; just north of the river is New Jersey.

J U L Y   1 8

We have taken shelter at the High Point Country Inn after two grueling days in the sweltering heat and hordes of mosquitoes. Yesterday, we attempted to take a break at Brink Road Shelter. We were out of water and had planned to eat lunch there, rest and fill up. Nothing doing. The onslaught of mosquitoes that had been pestering us relentlessly all day tripled as we approached this particular shelter. Clouds of mosquitoes in the air were so thick our skin became covered in the black bugs instantly. There was no escaping them. Needing desperately to eat and rest, our dwindling mental and physical reserves were simply unable to handle the added challenge of the nasty blood-suckers. We ran to the spring and filled our water bottles while gritting our teeth against their bites. If you stopped moving for just one fraction of a second, you could actually feel the clouds of them descending upon every centimeter of your skin. Sitting still, holding the water bottle as spring water trickled in slowly was pure torture. We ran back up the hill and threw up our tent shells, diving inside the mesh netting, dragging our lunches inside our tents. Hmmm, let's see...bears smelling our food inside our tents versus mosquitoes carting us off bodily—which shall it be? Switch napped while I fretted. What is his damn secret? How does he remain so maddeningly detached and calm all the time?

Hiking in the bugs presents its own very special

challenges. Kamikaze gnats dive-bomb your pupils periodically, creating a dangerous double-vision effect capable of sending even the most adept hiker sprawling. A small percentage of mosquitoes simply hover, and as long as you keep moving, they don't light on your skin but instead whine unceasingly, providing the macabre soundtrack to your slow demise. Plenty of death-defying hungry mosquitoes do land and munch away on any part of your body you cannot reach. The backs of my shoulders seem to be the favored fare, so I have adapted a technique that allows me to swat while still using my hiking poles for balance on the rocks. I carry both poles in one hand and a bandana in the other. The bandana I use the way a cow or a horse uses its tail, swishing it first over one shoulder, then over the other, fanning myself slightly in the process and effectively waving the mosquitoes back into the air so they can then cloud around Switch who is hiking behind me. We found that spraying Deet on several times a day makes us feel queasy and sick; we use it as sparingly as possible, saving it for times of dire bug stress, its dubious reprieve lasting usually one hour at best.

High Point State Park is also infested with gypsy moths. Caterpillars have eaten every last scrap of foliage from the trees, and the sun glared directly on us all day. I was nearing the semi-conscious state of heat exhaustion by the time the park offices came into sight. We collapsed in the air-conditioned lobby, and I listened as if hearing another language as the park ranger said I had no mail drop packages. "What? That can't be right. Could you check again?"

"I'm sorry," she said, "there ARE some packages here for you," and she handed two through the window. I breathed a sigh of relief, but my panic

returned after I opened the second package and realized neither one was our food box. What the hell are
we going to eat? I went back to the window and tried
to form a coherent sentence. The room swam. No more
packages. Come back tomorrow was the simple-
minded response.

Tomorrow? Shit. Even Switch's calm demeanor
seemed to wilt with this news. I knew he had no inkling
of what we should do. Unfortunately, I knew what we
would have to do, but the long hitch to town and the
ensuing motel and grocery store costs echoed the ring
of cash registers in my head. I was trapped in some
surrealistic cartoon where gypsy moths rule the world
and park rangers have the mental capacity of Elmer
Fudd.

After much deliberation, we called for the shuttle
from the High Point Country Inn. Here we sit, showered and resting in an air-conditioned room, watching
Johnny Depp in *The Secret Window* and cooking ramen
noodles on our stove at the bathroom sink. The owner
has promised to take us to town tomorrow for
groceries.[†]

J U L Y   1 9

More heat, more bugs, more trail, and we have
arrived at a shelter constructed on private land and
made available to hikers by its owner. Switch and I have
set up our sleeping spot in the loft of the small cabin,
turned on the electric fan, and closed the door on the
mosquitoes. Linc and Jeannie are tenting outside, as
well as Route Step. Two donkeys bray incessantly from
an adjoining field. The shelter has a hot shower, a sink,
electricity, a fan, and a scale for weighing packs. My
food bag weighs 9.2 pounds. Since our grocery trip, we

are carrying all sorts of heavy, luxury foods we wouldn't normally have, including four, single-serving boxes of ultra-pasteurized milk that doesn't have to be refrigerated and yogurt. I finally got service on Switch's cell phone and talked to Adam. He confessed that he mailed the High Point package via bulk mail despite my repeated warnings not to, which means it would have never arrived in time. It's a good thing he's as far from me as he is. All is well that ends well. The stop at the motel was probably wise anyway.

J U L Y 2 0

The new boots that arrived in Palmerton are a half size too small because my feet have changed size over the miles, but still they have relieved much of the intense pain I was experiencing. Our mileage has increased once again to roughly 13-15 miles a day, but the heat has become a new player in this game of "Kill the hikers!" With temperatures reaching almost 100 degrees and no canopy, thanks to the gypsy moth caterpillar infestation, I've discovered just how much a person can sweat. Hiking in the heat of the day has become almost impossible, so Switch and I have adopted a siesta lifestyle. We hike from eight to noon, stop from noon to three, and then hike again until seven or so.

Where Pennsylvania had run out of diversity and eventually offered nothing but rocks, heat and bugs, New Jersey has all that plus bears. Miles of ridgelines with young stands of trees offer a ground cover of huckleberry and blueberry bushes. We've seen mother bears shuffling their cubs along through the bushes on more than one occasion. Mama will stand on her hind legs and watch us as we pass and her babies' heads might just barely be visible over the tops of the low growing plants as they pluck the yummy berries. In the hiker box at DWG, I found two packets of pancake mix and a syrup packet. One morning, as the sun rose, I made blueberry pancakes, a wonderful treat with fresh-picked berries. Unfortunately, not much improves a 16-year-old's disposition at 7am. In the quiet of one sultry morning, we witnessed a bear taking a morning dip in a pond as we passed. Sun glinted off the water; the bear waded in first, then swam a small circle and waded back to shore, sending a spray of diamond droplets into the air when he shook. There are numerous lakes and ponds, as well as swamps, hence the mosquitoes. Truckloads of bats and frogs are needed here to balance things out a little.

Sunfish Pond is a glacially formed pond, really the size of a small lake. Its water is acidic, so nothing can live in it. Because nothing lives in the water, it is crystalline clear. G-Man, Johnny K., BLT, #2, Switch and I took a refreshing swim on a beautiful day. Two glider planes circled above on the thermal currents and G-man entertained us with stories of being a stunt parachutist. It was the kind of place that makes you distinctly aware life is good and you couldn't possibly have it any better than you do at that very moment.[†]

From the ridgelines you can see the path the great glaciers took across the land. The ridgelines are narrow and long between vast flat areas that once flowed with the slow-moving creaking ice that carved the lakes. From two abandoned fire towers, swaying in the breeze high above the ridge, we gazed out over where we've come and pondered where we've yet to go.

After Sunfish Pond, alongside the trail, a man sat with his back to a tree. I kept walking toward him. When I looked up, I recognized Woodstock, the section-hiker I had hiked with for a few days in Virginia. He lives in New Jersey and had guestimated my arrival from entries in my online trail journals and had come out to look for me on the trail. Woodstock took us out for ice cream at the next road crossing where he had left his car. It was a great surprise for a perfect day on the trail.[†]

JULY 22

"Death warmed over", one of my father's quips, comes to mind as a suitable description for how I felt as I staggered up to the trail magic picnic tables laden with food at Lake Tiorati Circle in Harriman State Park, New York. Several miles before, we had come to the top of an aptly named cliff called Agony Grind. It tumbled below us as a sheer drop of boulders, dirt and tree roots. Switch and I were exhausted from a day of climbing wet rocks and boulder scrambles, and we stood gazing over the edge of this impossible plunge as if we were glimpsing the impending disaster. I started down and suspended momentarily in the air as my boot caught behind me on a root. My body catapulted out into space as I pitched over the edge. The eternity of that split second stretched on and on as my mind fractured in hundreds of directions at once. The freeze frame ended with me upside down about a quarter of the way down the cliff, my knee raked out beside me at an unnatural angle, and all my pack weight resting on one elbow. Switch stood at the top with his mouth gaping open, immobilized with fear for what he might find. He called to me, then scrambled down sideways, holding the ground with one hand as he came. He fished the ibuprofen out of my pack without a word, and we sat there in silence pondering various forms of painful death.

J U L Y 2 5

Our campsite on Shenandoah Mountain, New York is high on a grassy knoll rimmed with huge boulders and dotted with young oaks and cedars. It is such an ideal spot that the grass is trampled in circular spots here and there where deer have used it to bed down. They will probably show up tonight and snort indignantly when they discover their beautiful room in the woods is occupied. To top it all, there is a perfect tree for hanging a bear bag—not some spindly, questionable thing, but an actual tree.

The bear bag hanging activity has caused many a spat between this mother and son. Bear bag hanging comes at a very inconvenient time if you are late arriving at a campsite. Cooking by headlamp is one thing; throwing a rope over a branch of a tree in the semi-darkness is quite another thing altogether. One night, while attempting to complete this dreaded task, we trampled all over a yellow jackets' nest in the ground. Switch got stung once, and we were so tired and stupid after hours of hiking that we stood there discussing his sting. Duh! So he got stung again, and we finally sprang to life and moved. That night, we ended up hanging the food bag right over the trail, as there were absolutely no other trees with suitable branches.

Not tonight though; there's even a good branch for hanging wet clothes on to dry in the breeze. We got here early enough to cook, dry our tents on a line (wet from dew from this morning), make our campsite, set up tents, hang our food and get in our tents all before dark settled upon us. It was so satisfying not to have to rush around racing lengthening shadows. Now, I lie in my tent, rain fly peeled halfway back so I can enjoy the breeze and the stars, listening to this great radio station out of Montauk, New York, enjoying myself immensely. The grassy place we picked is soft and comfortable. The radio station is the first "media" I've had access to in about 10 days. Usually the stations fade in and out as you go over mountains if you try to listen as you walk. It's nice to just lie here and listen.

We shared the New York City skyline as few people ever get to see it with Old School and his son, Young Blood, yesterday from the top of Black Mountain 34 miles west of the city just south of Palisades Parkway. The skyline stretched across a low spot on the horizon, blurred by haze, simmering in a pale golden fog of morning sunshine. It was our first glimpse of the city, and it set the tone for a great day. Our travels took us up Bear Mountain for lunch at the top, and down to the Trailside Museum and Zoo where we had second lunch at an overpriced concession window with Weatherman and No Pliers. We saw the caged animals (including bears) and exhibits, crossed a suspension bridge over the Hudson River, climbed Anthony's Nose and ended our day at the Graymoor Spiritual Life Center, at a pavilion on their grounds, where many of us ordered food delivered from a nearby restaurant.

J U L Y 2 6

Lunch on NY 52 was at a place called Mountaintop Market. I had a reuben on rye and a Haagen Dazs ice cream popsicle; Switch ate a loaded, turkey sandwich. We filled our water bottles from a hose on the side of the building and ate at a picnic table by the parking lot. The UPS delivery guy parked his truck by our table, and we chatted about the trail while he took his lunch break, too. I called ahead to reserve a room for us in

Pawling, but got an answering machine, so I left our names and asked to reserve a room for Thursday and Friday nights. We've formed a plan to get all our chores done in Pawling on Thursday, and take an early train into NYC on Friday to spend the day sightseeing.

We had a great night's sleep in our perfect campsite last night. The deer did come and snort and fuss at us sometime in the night, but nothing else bothered us. Two nights before, I slept soundly while Switch was up half the night watching a skunk circle our tents. Switch said the skunk came right up to the door of my tent. He was trying to wake me up without startling the skunk when the little guy then walked around to the other side of Switch's tent and began to dig in the dirt for bugs. He circled the tree where Weatherman's food bag hung, nosed around Weatherman's tent, then came back to a bag of garbage left at the William Brien Memorial Shelter by some thoughtless campers. He rummaged through the bag of garbage for the third time that night, and finally ambled off up the hill to bother No Pliers.

I have been sleeping better the past few nights, possibly because I've had access to more food during the days. At the "Fat Fest" hiker feed at Lake Tiorati, I ate two hamburgers on hoagie rolls and an ear of corn before they closed up the grill. The next morning, after camping there, I had a bagel with cream cheese and lox, two cups of coffee, a muffin and two nectarines. Lunch was a coke, hamburger, an avocado and grapes. Then, mid-afternoon snack was steak. Salmon for dinner. The following night at Graymoor, our dinner delivery was spaghetti and ice cream. I can't carry much more food than I am carrying or it becomes counter-productive. More food weighs more, more effort to carry it, more calories burned—need more food to carry more food. So, needless to say, I am grateful for restaurants when I can get to them...and a good night's sleep, instead of waking up hungry.

J U L Y 2 7

The day we arrived in Pawling, New York was filled with extremes. We awoke really excited about our plans to stay at a B&B and take the train into NYC. About half a mile from the Dover Oak—a huge tree that measures larger than the Keffer Oak back in Virginia—we ran into Ollie. She is a supervisor for volunteers who maintain the sections of trail in the Pawling area. We mentioned to her that we were considering slackpacking from Pawling to the Connecticut border once we got our motel room, and she kindly jumped right in and offered to take us. Little did she know what a mess she was getting herself into.

We drove to Pawling, stopping on the way to call the B&B again. Still no answer, just a machine. We stopped at the Chamber of Commerce to find out where the Sharadee B&B was located only to be told they were out of business. To top that, there were no motels in Pawling. We remembered seeing a sign on the trail advertising that some folks would let hikers tent in their yard, shower and do laundry, so Ollie drove us there. A young man answered the door, took one look at mom and teenager, looked at his feet, and said their hot water heater was broken, and they were not accepting any hikers. Then, Ollie drove us to the pavilion in the town park where hikers could stay for free. The pavilion was a mile and a half walk from the actual town and all its services. The shower was an open air shower with no stall next to a parking lot. There were bathrooms and a lake; my stress level was rising.

I was quite put out by the way our plans were falling apart. It had been 13 days since our last real shower with soap and hot water. If we were going into the city, we needed a safe place to leave our packs and a place to get cleaned up. The open-air shower just did not answer this for me, and neither did bathing in the lake as other hikers suggested. Somehow, the idea of getting on a subway in NYC with lots of people caused me to want to actually be clean, not just "hiker clean". With laundry a mile and a half away and nowhere to leave our packs, none of this was working out.

Ollie came through for us in a really big way. She remembered a motel on Hwy 22 near the Wingdale train station. Just what we were looking for! Away we went with Ollie to check out this new possibility. We reserved a room at the Duchess Motor Lodge, and then, of all things, Ollie took us out to lunch. We ate at an old metal diner, a northern relic Switch had never experienced. This one came complete with a sassy older waitress, colored hair piled atop her head. She was wearing a bright print dress and kept up a steady flow of banter with the regulars as she went about the business of running her counter. I kept expecting her to bust out a "Kiss my grits!" any minute. I enjoyed visiting with Ollie over our food; she was older than me, and her commitment to the trail was inspiring and made for interesting conversation. Ollie was on her way back to the Dover Oak to finish her trail maintenance, so we rode back with her and slacked the 9.5 miles to the Connecticut border. She had absolutely saved our whole day. We got everything we had planned, plus she fed us lunch. Thank you so much, Ollie, for being our Trail Angel. Your kindness and quick thinking gave us a day we'll never forget.

As we started our slack-pack, flies swarmed around Switch. I could see seven or eight haloing his head. He tried running from them. That didn't work. He tried wearing his shirt on his head; that didn't work. They buzzed around him relentlessly until he just sat on the side of the trail and cried—he had reached his breaking point, finally, after so many hardships. Our roller coaster of stress in Pawling had gotten the better of him, and the bugs and heat and sweat were the final straw. He had seen me break down four or five times in the last few weeks, and now it was his turn. I convinced him to continue up the trail to a stream where he doused his head and shoulders with cold water. This seemed to help, and soon the beautiful terrain and the easy walking cheered him right up. I theorized that without the packs jogging might actually be fun, so away we went up the trail at about four and a half miles an hour instead of our customary, plodding two. With only two miles to go, we came to some trail magic maintained by Mac & Cheese (thru-hikers from a previous year). There were chairs, a cooler of cold drinks, water, snacks, and all manner of miscellany a hiker might need like denatured alcohol, baby wipes, band-aids, etc. We plopped down and rested, marveling at how our day had gone from good to bad to good to bad to good. It was as if nothing was going to stop us from having a good time today and finishing New York. We crossed into Connecticut soon afterward and hitched back to our motel for our much anticipated hot showers. Time to celebrate with a trip to the Big Apple!

A more perfect New York hiker experience does not exist. We left Wingdale train station on the 5:28am for our hour & a half ride into the city. At 7:11am we arrived at Grand Central Station. I had told Switch he had seen it in movies before, but he couldn't place it. When we emerged into the middle of its grand hall, he immediately exclaimed "Oh, yeah!" I knew right away this was going to be so much fun.

We wandered aimlessly around inside the station before exiting onto bustling 42nd. I was surprisingly calm. I had sort of dreaded the stress of figuring out the train schedule, subways, and how to get where we wanted to go, but once I was actually in the city, there were no jitters, and I was ready for the day to just unfold—be that as it may. We hit the first Starbucks we saw, just a few doors down. The girls working there were happy and friendly. I guess they thought Switch was too cute because they gave him a Grande iced coffee for the price of a Tall. We gobbled pastries and tanked up on caffeine, planning our next move. The girls told us which way to go for the Empire State Building, and away we went. On the way, we stopped in a store that advertised internet access for $1.00, my first access to email since Palmerton.

From the top of the Empire State Building we oriented ourselves in the city. We studied the labeled diagrams of the buildings and matched them with the buildings below. For the first time, I began to understand the topography of New York City. Back on the street, we walked quite a few blocks before deciding to take the plunge to the subway. We found the World Trade Center subway stop and got there in no time.

Switch was quite pensive at Ground Zero. He had been 11 years old at the time the towers fell. We watched the workers for awhile, visited the memorial wall with everyone's names and read the displayed timeline of events. It was hard to believe this was where the attack took place; so much work has been done there in just a few short years. It seems like just yesterday in some ways.

We stopped for lunch at World Cafe where most of the customers were construction workers. I felt at home among the gossiping, blue collar men with their sunburned shoulders and broad smiles. New York was growing on me. There seemed to be a niche for everything. We walked through Washington Square Park, and there was a place for people with children, a place for people to poop their dogs, and a place for pets to socialize with other people's pets. There were bicyclists, runners, walkers, sitters, lovers, kids, dogs, businessmen and housewives. It was too cool—a smorgasbord of life.

We attempted to take the subway to Times Square. It took forever for us to find the subway again, and then we couldn't figure out which train. We had entered at an exit, and when we found the right place there was no attendant. There was a long line forming at the automated ticket machines since the attendant was absent. Three out of four people at the machines ahead of us had to ask others around them to help them understand the machine. Some of them were elderly; some didn't speak English very well. It was kind of sad watching this very human drama playing out, total strangers helping each other—one accepting another's confusion without judgment and stopping to help, the other trusting and helplessly handing over their money. So many people are cut off and left behind by technology, and yet such a situation creates the very opportunity for sharing so many lack in their lives. Ah, the beautiful dance...oh, it's my turn at the damn machine...stop daydreaming. Move along..

So anyway, I don't know what I did wrong, but

when we tried to use our tickets to get in the subway gates, Switch went right through and mine wouldn't work. So there he was on the other side of the metal bars, and I'm stuck on this side. So, I go tell a person at a window and they miraculously believe me (could it have been the stupid southern accent that gave me away?), and she buzzes me through a different gate. Great. I turn around, and now there are three sets of iron bars separating me from my son instead of one. Ooops. He has this look on his face that I know mirrors my own, sort of a "now what?" Then, he lights up and points down. We both find stairways and meet up by the subway tracks—duh! Ok, so it was comeuppance for my sassiness earlier about how easy riding the subway had been. I had been put in my proper place, country mouse visits the big city.

We couldn't figure out which direction we should be headed because in all the confusion I had lost my bearings. Switch asked someone, and soon we emerged from the tunnels into Times Square. He was delighted and in heaven. We visited Hard Rock Café, and he bought himself a skull cap as a souvenir and a Matchbox sports car for Grayson. We got drinks at Europa and then headed off—on foot—to Central Park.

The Park revived us. We flopped in the grass, set the alarm on the cell phone and Switch napped. I watched the horses and buggies and guys pedaling carts with people in them. Very odd. On our way out of the park, we passed a swampy pond area. Beside it was four acres that were fenced and off limits to people. This had been set aside as a nature preserve when the park was created to promote diversity in the ecosystems supported by the Park. Very cool. I was impressed and wished we had time to see more of the Park. But suddenly...we had a train to catch.

Our train was leaving Grand Central at 3:46pm. We needed that train because we had to be back by 5:30pm in order to get to the gear store before they closed at 6:00pm. I had purchased the wrong fuel the day before, and we had to exchange it before getting back on the trail. And so began the classic New York dash to catch our train.

We arrived at Grand Central Station with only six minutes left. I spoke loudly to Switch that we were going to **"Miss Our Train"**, so the guy in front of us in the ticket line would hurry. It worked, and he did, and I pressed buttons on the machine as fast as I ever did at work all those years. We got our tickets, ran to the track we'd come in on and...no train. Shit—which track? and how do you figure THAT out!? Switch tells me we have two minutes left. This was one of those miraculous moments where our similar genetics worked wonders for us; our minds worked in perfect tandem on separate parts of the issue. I said there would be a screen somewhere telling track numbers, Switch's digital age upbringing honed in immediately on the nearest screen, and he scanned the data; he said they don't list track 26. "No! no! the departure time is what you need," I said; he was on it, saying the track number and pushing me in the right direction all within one second. We ran and stumbled onto the train just as the departure whistle blew and the doors began to close...3:46 and laughing! As the train left the station, the sky opened, and the rain poured down.

J U L Y   3 1

The shelter was half a mile off the trail, straight down a rocky cliff, difficult to navigate even in daylight.

Long after dark, when I was just beginning to fall asleep, I heard the unmistakable sound of a hiker approaching. How could anyone come down that cliff in pitch darkness? They moved quickly and without any hesitation. I could see the glow of their headlamp creating a silhouette. It is Rael, who I have not seen in months of hiking. Rael is quite an unusual character, and he puts many people off with his intensity and his candor. He is not shy and will tell you, to your face, exactly what is on his mind, mincing no words. Mix this with his uncanny ability to assess subtle energy changes and to be the first to react to them verbally, and he can be quite a formidable conversationalist. He is short and muscular in build, and his movements are always quick and calculated. His mildly obsessive compulsive habits are distinct, and he's quite comfortable with acknowledging them. He hikes in the dark often and will stay up late cleaning and arranging his gear at the end of the day. Rael put up his tent and now sits cooking his dinner in the glow of his headlamp a few feet away.

We've camped with Model T and Ranger Dawg the last two nights, familiar faces from Tennessee. I talked over some of my fears of the Whites and Maine with Model T, he being the expert that he is on trail matters (author of several books and three time thru-hiker). Model T has his food down to a scientific method. He showed me some of his tricks, like having a hot cup of powdered tomato soup as an appetizer for each meal, using squeeze butter for extra fat, and smearing peanut butter on cinnamon bread for desert. He always sits with his back against a tree while he makes and eats his several course dinner. He and Ranger Dawg are both retired military men; they are early risers and are done with their day early in the evening leaving themselves plenty of daylight for their long, leisurely meals.

Ranger Dawg is a tall, handsome, silver-haired man. He keeps every inch of his skin covered due to a mosquito allergy, despite the heat. Ranger Dawg entertains us with crazy tales of his younger days, and Model T respectfully listens with a gleam in his eye though you know he's heard these same stories many times over.

Though my talk with Model T diminished some of my fears, it didn't change the very physical obstacle that has become my latest challenge to staying on the trail—simple starvation. The balance has been tipping dangerously in the wrong direction between getting enough calories and the added weight of additional food. It's been an insidious problem for the past week or longer because I have not been eating less food. We stop for a break every two to three miles, and each break I eat a snack. I also eat three meals a day. But, my high metabolism is taking its toll over four months of constant physical activity. I have been waking up hungry each night, lying awake cursing the bears that prevent me from keeping food in the tent. Sometimes I feel nauseous, or I'll feel hungry, full, and nauseous all at the same time. Others I've talked to are struggling with similar sensations. Old School, a thru-hiking father who is hiking with his wife and two sons (each of them taking turns as section hikers), told me that sometimes he has to force himself to eat, because he's so sick of the volumes of food.

During the night, in that weird half-awake-half-asleep state, I battle various terrible scenarios. It was during one of these macabre bouts of self-doubt a couple of nights ago when I decided I would have to leave the Trail. I wrestled with coming to terms with what quitting the Trail would mean and the reverberations that would resound through all areas of my life.

The following morning, I told Switch of my plan to leave with him when it came time for him to go home. He was shocked, and we discussed options for hours as we hiked. My nausea continued all through the morning, and I could barely drag myself up the hills. By our first break, we'd gone 2.3 miles, painfully slowly. In true trail magic fashion, mentors appeared to offer their gifts. Old School sat with us at our break spot. He and his son, Young Blood, never stay in shelters and rarely even tent near other hikers, so getting to visit with him usually means taking a break with him on the side of the trail while he smokes a cigarette. He told me of how badly he felt most days, but he had too much time and money and sweat invested to quit now; he pointed out there are only seven to eight more weeks left of this. His no-nonsense way of looking at it offered a clear and less emotional perspective on things. As Switch and I started up another mountain, a hiker named Gator approached southbound. He stopped, and without prompting, began to tell me of how he was doing a flip flop—hiking sections of the trail out of sequential order to make better use of resources, time, seasonal changes, etc—because he had taken two weeks off since his health was declining. He spoke of nausea, weakness, and exhaustion. He said it took him the full two weeks to get his strength back. He recommended one zero day per week, and he was gone.

Switch and I talked some more; our pace picked up. The day grew older, and before I knew it, we'd put away 10 miles at a pretty good clip. I felt 100% better and no longer had the same dire thoughts of needing to quit the Trail. We did 15.5 miles, met nice people, picked up a mail drop, took a cold shower (with our clothes on) by the side of the road, had a great lunch on the banks of the Housatonic River, and ate dinner with Model T, Ranger Dawg, and Sleep Ninja in camp. The latest theory is that perhaps I've had a virus that's made me feel sick, but I don't think that's it. I do think there's a serious issue with not getting enough to eat to match the level of energy output day after day. I am packing in the calories wherever there is opportunity, going into town to eat real food every chance I get, and just watching to see what happens with this. It's something that has the potential to end this journey if my health and strength become too compromised. For now, I am going to take it seriously and enjoy the pursuit of good food as much as possible. Tomorrow morning: breakfast in camp, second breakfast at a restaurant in Salisbury, Connecticut.

A U G U S T   2

Switch and I milled around outside the grocery store in Salisbury, making several trips into the air-conditioned building just to escape the 115 degree heat, while consuming individual pints of Ben & Jerry's ice cream. Model T's invaluable advice about how to pack the calories into any given day has already been put to use. Inside, I compared the calorie count and fat content of peanut butter to macadamia nut butter. Macadamia nut butter won out with 25 grams of fat per serving to peanut butter's modest 17 grams. I did not, however, adhere to his suggestion of drinking squeeze butter to increase my fat intake. Although I can appreciate where he is coming from on this point, I cannot even begin to consider this as a serious option. If I were stranded in the arctic in a life or death situation, that's one thing, but we're not there yet. I also adopted his idea of carrying a bag of cinnamon raisin bread to eat as snacks and appetizers for meals. This gives me something to look forward to that I've not had for months.

Figuring out exactly where to camp each night to make the mileage and the food work out just right is a constant topic for discussion. Of the three men we are hiking with, Model T and Rael have both hiked the trail more than once before. Model T and Ranger Dawg usually have specific plans for meeting friends at road crossings for town stays, and Rael has an internal battle he fights with himself about doing things the same way each year he hikes. I do not have either of these agendas, and I've hiked my own hike for so long I am not the least bit inclined to let other people's plans change my own. I have welcomed their knowledge of the terrain and of amenities available at certain road crossings though, and I've learned so much during my time hiking with these trail veterans. A certain authenticity of the experience has come from hearing their stories firsthand and hiking in their footsteps this time around.

Rael is camped beside Switch and I at the spring on Jug End Road. Model T and Ranger Dawg have gone into town with off-trail friends. Rael and Switch banter back and forth. Joseph is outspoken, so he and Rael butt heads. Rael jumps up and tackles Switch, wrestling with him on the ground; they are laughing. The world suddenly is a very large place.

AUGUST 3

We are stopped for a break beneath a shade tree on the edge of a hayfield just before heading up June Mountain in Massachusetts. We crossed into Massachusetts yesterday during a heat wave with a heat index reaching 115 degrees. We took a lot of breaks, swam in

Sages Ravine and Guilders Pond and hiked only 13.5 miles. Sages Ravine was cool and dark, a deep crevice filled with huge hemlocks, moss-covered boulders and a tumbling brook with beautiful swimming pools. The hot day sizzled above, the sun's rays coming down into the ravine as stray shafts of golden light shining on the moisture in the air, but we were nice and cool hanging out by the water. As we climbed out of the ravine, the temp rose by 30 degrees.

A U G U S T   4

Switch had met Linc and Jeanne once, and I wanted so much for him to be able to spend time with these kindred spirits. We caught up with them taking a break by the side of a gravel road this afternoon. We were all hungry and trying to figure out just how much farther we could go for the day. The choices of camping spots were not the best, and to stay together we needed enough room for at least three tents. At our next break, a fairly suitable campsite with no spring, Switch volunteered to jog up the trail a mile and investigate the next spring listed to see if there was enough room to camp there. No one could believe their ears. Sure! If you want to jog up the trail an additional mile, and then back, only to hike it again with your pack, I'll wait right here. We all plopped down and waited. In 18 minutes Switch was back with a positive assessment, and we all geared up and proceeded to the site. Youth is an amazing state unto itself that defies all reasonableness. I love that he is here in this place with me, living this adventure, hiking his own hike.

Rael crept into camp just as light began to fade.

A U G U S T   5

Rael and Switch and I are camped in the lush green backyard of a modest brick home. This is a blueberry farm known on the trail as the Cookie Lady's. Marilyn has baked and served chocolate chip cookies to hikers for years. During my conversation with her husband Roy, I discovered they were headed to the airport in Hartford, Connecticut in two more days. For days, Adam and I had fretted together during our brief phone conversations over how to get Joseph back home in time for school. Adam was broke and could not afford to drive all this way to Massachusetts to fetch him. I had talked to Dad, but the logistics of driving all this way to try to meet us somewhere at a road crossing in the middle of nowhere are daunting. I was frustrated that neither Adam nor Dad had been able to come up with a solution. Getting Joseph to a bus station or an airport seemed impossible from where I stood. This issue had contributed to my inclination to simply go home with Joseph when the time came; at least that way I would know he would get there. But now, for the hundredth time, the trail provided. Roy agreed to add Joseph to his entourage to Hartford airport. I was to see what I could do about procuring an airline ticket and let Roy and Marilyn know tomorrow. Joseph, who just days before had not wanted his summer on the AT to end, suddenly perked up at the prospect of flying alone—a grand finale, as he put it.

A U G U S T   6

A hint of autumn lingers on the gently blowing breeze. There are more leaves falling and a crispness to the mornings, now that the heat wave has passed.

The wistfulness that fall inspires in my soul is stirring. I am camped on Crystal Mountain while Switch spends the night in a hostel in Dalton at the foot of the mountain. Tomorrow, Roy and Marilyn will pick him up from the hostel and drive him to Hartford where he will catch a plane to North Carolina. I have mixed emotions. I am excited for him; this rite of passage—flying home alone—is the perfect grand finale, a good test of the skills we practiced every day out here while navigating our way from Maryland to Massachusetts. But, I am also very sad to lose my hiking partner. We always have worked well as a team, and this trip has been no exception. His company brightened some very dark days for me on the Trail, and his incessant chatter and wonderfully tireless sense of humor kept me laughing instead of crying for hundreds of painful, difficult miles.

Switch's grand total of 640 miles includes his stint in NC and TN, his time in the Shenandoahs with his brother, and his miles from Wolfsville Rd (Smithsburg), Maryland north to Dalton, Massachusetts. I will miss him terribly. I think back to the adjustment period I experienced when he first joined me, and I'm sure there will be another adjustment period now, in reverse, hence my wistful autumn awareness. Hiking up Crystal Mountain alone I realized I have only to worry about getting Willow to Katahdin now. I kept Switch's cell phone, a handy timepiece and a link to the outside world I want to hold onto.

A week has already passed since I was feeling so sick from not eating enough calories. Since then, I've eaten at least once, sometimes twice, in the middle of the night every night. I've added Flaxseed oil capsules to my diet for the fatty acids they contain, and I've added an additional snack during the day. I've also stopped in every town within five miles of the trail and eaten in restaurants. It's kind of fun—eating all the pure crap you can get your hands on.

42 left a surprise for me in the cooler at the hostel in Dalton. I'm walking down Depot Street and there's a sign: "WILLOW!" and an arrow pointing: "LOOK IN TOM'S COOLER!" So, I go to the cooler at the hostel, and there's this amazing round chocolate cake/cookie thing with gobs of cream filling between two round slices of cake—a whopping 780 calories packed into five little ounces. Oh Yeah! And the best part of all is that this caloric monstrosity is called (no less than) a Whoopie Pie. Thank you, 42!

A little mouse keeps running around on the outside of my tent fly. He thinks he's going to get my chocolate Whoopie Pie, but I just ate it all. The sun has sunk behind the mountain, and shadows are lengthening. I can hear Rael setting up his tent a few feet away in the darkness.

Grandma Gatewood Didn't Wear Wristbands

AUGUST 7

About 5:30am a soft rain began to fall. I lay in my tent thinking about autumn and about things that come to an end. The agenda is to climb Mount Greylock, the highest peak in Massachusetts, and to enter Vermont tomorrow. This journey is reaching its final stages. All the parts that I have feared are the parts that are left: the Whites, the fords in Maine, colder weather, and Katahdin. Circumstances continue to conspire to tempt me to end my journey. My low body weight is great cause for concern as the weather cools and the climbs get steeper. The renter from New Orleans, that I had been so eager to help start over and who signed a six-month lease for my condo, is now backing out of the agreement and moving back to New Orleans. I will have no income for the final two months of the trip. Switch has gone home, and I am left to hike alone again. The boys start back to school, Adam needs help with them and their busy schedules more than ever, and I miss home. Somehow, despite this pervasive sense of vague melancholy, I recognize a renewed sense of commitment in the back of my mind this past week. I strongly believe this will happen for me.

Adam has the last week of September off from work. Our tentative plan is to see if he can come hike to the summit of Katahdin with me and then bring me home.

E V E N I N G —

The trail was routed right past the post office in Cheshire, so I was able to easily send a few post cards home. While I was sitting outside writing, an elderly woman stopped to talk. She told me of a woman hiker she had picked up and taken to her house once. The inspiration this older woman received from her visit with the young female hiker was obvious, and her attempt to connect with me seemed to be a reification for her. It felt good to be a part of the revolution of women who are expanding our culture's vision of the female and pushing their own limits, creating change across generations.

I stopped at a convenience store at the last road crossing out of Cheshire and went in to use the bathroom and get some lunch. Lunch was a Slim Jim, a pack of nabs (it's a southern thang), a Dr. Pepper, and a pint of Ben & Jerry's ice cream. I sat by the pay phone in the parking lot and spread my tent out in the sunshine to dry while I ate and called my friend Cathy back home at work. Not a single person stared.

The climb out of Cheshire was not hard, but it was 6.8 miles. The forest was beautiful, old-growth red spruce. Logs snaked over a boggy area; a small, clear stream made its way through the dark green moss and over the rocks, creating a soft trickling sound. I sat on a rock by the stream and listened. I was aware of an energetic, spiritual connection to people on the other side of the world, quiet monks sitting by tinkling fountains in carefully tended gardens—artful praise for the very mountain stream I was visiting today. A bird splashed in a small pool off to my left, partially shielded by low hanging branches of spruce.

Bascom Lodge on top of Mount Greylock is a historic ski lodge—beautiful, rustic, and old. Built in the 1930s by the Civilian Conservation Corps, its architecture transports one to a simpler time. The dining area has long wooden tables, a huge, stone fireplace and hand-cut oak ceiling beams.[†] The shared bunk rooms open off a long narrow hallway on the second floor. Tiny closets on the opposite side of the hall contain individual shower rooms.

L A T E R —

A storm blew in this evening. After dinner was served, I went outside to explore the top of the mountain. The clouds raced and a mist began to settle around the stone lodge. Jagged spires of spruce pierced the horizon, black against gray fog. I walked up to the lighthouse tower that stands serenely atop Greylock. To my childish delight there was a door in the base. You could go inside! The heavy metal door banged loudly as the strong wind pushed it closed behind me; its echo resounded off the granite walls. Inside was a round room the diameter of the tower with a domed, mosaic tile ceiling. The lighthouse is a state memorial to fallen soldiers from Massachusetts, so the inscriptions carved in the walls honor their sacrifice. On the floor, an eight-pointed star was embedded with a raised seal in the center—a glowing torch and the letters "U.S.". Narrow shafts of light slanted through three tall, barred windows on the east, north and south sides of the circle. I sat quietly for a long time taking in the full effect of the memorial and pondering the inscriptions. As I rose to leave, I noticed a narrow passageway to the left of the door with an arched doorway; a faint yellow light glowed thru it. Could it be? More childish delight. 'Oh it's too good to be true! You can climb the lighthouse tower!' Around and around, I climbed the dizzying spiral staircase. From atop, I could see the gathering storm clouds racing by. The view of the valley was obscured. Far below, a ranger was approaching to lock the tower door for the night. I ran down the spiral staircase as fast as possible just because I could—stairs seem so easy after climbing up and down boulders. Oh, the fun things you weren't allowed to do as a child!

Outside again, I walked the paved paths around the tower and found the Thunderbolt Shelter, an old warming hut from the 1930s when Greylock was a premier ski mountain, before the days of ski lifts. Its intriguing history was briefly described on several metal plaques. I stood inside the hut imagining it as a bustling hub of warm activity on a snowy New England day. The storm overtook the top of the mountain as I walked back to Bascom Lodge. I stood under the eaves of the stone lodge conjuring images of Catherine and Heathcliff, of Emily Bronte's *Wuthering Heights*, until the rain blew into my little alcove and forced me from reverie. Inside, the dark, wooden stairs creaked when I climbed to my room. I lay in the bunk bed listening to the wind and rain against the glass window panes, the sound of Catherine's spirit tapping.

A U G U S T   1 0

I arrived at camp just as the sky darkened for a storm. It rained after everyone had already set up their tents for the night. I've been hiking in vicinity with

Model T, Ranger Dawg, Rael, Linc & Jeannie, and three Long Trail hikers, Mariachi, Eric and Melissa. We all gathered in the shelter to cook our dinners and catch up on everyone's news for the day, the evening ritual of tribal peoples across the globe for centuries.

Crossing into Vermont was a homecoming of sorts, for years ago I had left North Carolina as soon as I graduated college to travel in New England. I ended up in Vermont, working a tree farm, logging with draft horses and tapping maple sugar trees. It was here I learned to operate a chainsaw, drive a team of horses, snowshoe and cross country ski. I knew this state would seem like heaven after the more populated New England states to the south. The forests are beautiful; the air is clear with no humidity; the temperatures have been cool, and there are very few bugs. Entering Vermont has been a crucial mindset change. At the border, a hand-written sign on a piece of notebook paper taped to the The Long Trail sign read: "Welcome to Vermont! Quit yer bitchin' NOBO's!" (northbound hikers) I thought about the sign for several miles. All the thru-hikers have been complaining profusely since Pennsylvania. I'm done with complaining. Actually, the more I thought about it, the more I realized that everything was alright. No bugs, no heat, no rain, no pain. After doing 15 mile days for four weeks straight, now I'm doing 13s. My feet don't even hurt. And hey! My pack's not very heavy.

At Bennington, Rael, and I caught an easy hitch into town for resupply. We left our packs at the outfitters while we explored the town. We checked email at the library, grabbed greasy fried food at the Fish Fry and shopped at Henry's Market for deli goods—new foods to break the monotony of trail fare. I first met Rael in Tennessee. Some friendships develop purely from the common experience of shared trail. Updating one another on the progress of various people we had both hiked with at different times over the past four months added to our sense of trail community. I am still learning from Rael's way of doing things, most valuably the concept of frequent resupply stops to reduce the weight of food you carry—not to mention the luxury of eating more town food, since you're there for resupply anyway.

The first sign of moose was on Mount Greylock. Moose poop. An entry in the register said that someone had seen a moose crossing the road on top of the mountain. I've watched diligently for moose all this time, no moose. But, I spotted more moose poop today. Every time I come to a pond, I proceed slowly and quietly hoping to see one wading along the edges. No moose. Another register entry the first day into Vermont said one hiker was chased by a moose. I'll keep watching for one—I hope I see the moose before the moose sees me.

At Kid Gore Shelter, a chipmunk emerged from under the shelter floor and perched next to me while I was taking a break. The colors of his coat were brilliant; the brown on his back had a red sheen, and the black and white stripes on his back were distinct and intense. Obviously, this little guy had learned that hikers carry good food, so he was extremely tame and healthy. I fed him macadamia nuts from my bag of gorp. The pockets of his cheeks could hold seven macadamia nuts at once. Chipper scurried off and deposited the nuts in some safe hideaway for winter, then came back and checked out the other hikers' packs. I was glad I wasn't staying here for the night. Brazen chipmunk equals serious food bag damage, no doubt.

A U G U S T   1 1

Vermonters don't like a lot of blazes on the trail. You'll walk for a long time not seeing a single white blaze—something about it interfering with the 'wilderness experience'. How about the interference that mild panic holds? Sections of trail that follow roads have always caused a lot of confusion about exactly where the trail goes next, and now, with the infrequency of blazes the confusion lasts even longer, until you happen upon the next silent beacon on the side of a tree. Every hiker I asked at camp tonight had doubled back and walked the same section of trail twice today on a gravel road with no blazes.

Manchester Center is a town I have visited before when I lived in Vermont. All I remembered about the town was the Ben & Jerry's store on Highway 11 which, I was happy to see, is still alive and well. I didn't ever make it to the free showers on the far southwest side of town today, but I accomplished so many things that I had a great feeling of satisfaction about the day. I was alone, just wandering around town on my own all day. I hitched in early in the morning with Ranger Dawg and Model T. The woman who picked us up in the back of her pickup truck told us she would have never stopped for the two men if they had not had a woman with them. We all had a good laugh about the questionable characters of these two gray-haired and grizzled, retired military men.

At the post office, I made a phone call to my renter who is breaking lease and talked him into staying through the end of September. At the rate I am going, I am expecting to summit on September 28th or 29th. If he leaves by September 30th, I will not be out anything even though he was committed originally through the end of October. That is a huge weight off my mind, a negotiation I plotted for the last two hundred miles. I was glad to have pulled it off successfully.

My next stop was the bagelry for brunch. It was a crowded and claustrophobic cafe. The anxiety I usually have in such places was absent. I sat with my pack at my feet and ate a huge sandwich. I packed freshly-made cookies into my pack to take back to the trail and left to go next door to the photoshop. I transferred more pics onto disc to mail home and got fresh batteries for my camera.

One street over, I found an outfitter that carried Asolo boots, but the only pair they had in the half-size larger I needed were orange. Orange? Geez. For years in my twenties I had worn bright yellow Chuck Taylors, so I think I've outgrown the whole 'look at my footwear' phase. The salesman was calm and patient, but the saleswoman who came over and turned on the slick sales pitch was fast-talking and confusing. She wanted me to spend $30 on gaiters she insisted I needed, despite the fact that I'd come 1600 miles without them. I stared at her for a long time without saying anything, letting her go on and on, grateful I would soon be back out in the woods and away from the strange things people feel compelled to do for money. I told the salesman I needed some time to decide, and that I would let him know when I had made a decision. They both left me alone to walk up and down the ramp in the orange Asolos. Bright Eyes had bought bright red trail runners back in Virginia; I sat down and thought about her quiet, accepting and centered manner that had drawn me to her instantly, another female hiker out here hiking alone. I carried the box of shoes to the counter with my canister of stove fuel and addressed the box to Adam, sending my used size 7s home. Shew! Wouldn't want to open that box when it arrives.

I wandered down the street in my new, orange boots and stopped at the health food store. I bought an organic chocolate bar for Linc and Jeannie, since they never splurge on luxuries for themselves. I bought water buffalo milk yogurt and a fresh pear and sat outside the store and ate. Making a circle, I took a shortcut through some pine trees on the edge of a parking lot and ended up back on the main drag at the grocery store where other hikers sat with a week's worth of food spread out on a picnic table, packing and eating. Linc and Jeannie appeared, and I gave them the chocolate bar. Several other thru-hikers happened by, but I was done with town and feeling the pull to get back out in the woods. I caught a ride back to the trailhead with a man who was shuttling hikers back and forth and waved to Puffy and Cheeto who were just coming in.

A U G U S T 1 2

Bromley Mountain Shelter has wooden platforms for level tent setup on the hillside behind the shelter. My tent requires stakes to be set up properly so this arrangement leaves it rather floppy and shapeless. Rapunzel showed up this evening around dinner time. The last time I had seen her was at the "Fat Fest" at Lake Tiorati in New York which now seems like a lifetime ago. She's really been putting in some serious miles each day to catch up with friends after her last stint off the trail to attend a wedding. Her feet are bothering her a lot. We sat up late, chatting about her time off the trail and her big-mile days to get here. She came with news of the real world, airline schedules and family drama. It all seems so far away and removed from our peaceful life here in the woods. We worked our way through her culture shock. She showed me her bright orange tie-dye pajama pants her mother had sewn for her as camp clothes. Rapunzel changes clothes more than any other hiker I know. It's good to have someone to talk to again. We stayed up talking and giggling, long into the night.

A U G U S T   1 3

Annie's organic macaroni and cheese now comes in the shape of peace symbols. Oh, yeah! While my peace noodles cooked, I tore the rabbit off the noodle box and pasted him into the register with surgical tape.

Big Branch sports a fancy suspension bridge reminiscent of the one that spanned Tye River in Virginia. In memory of our Tye River adventure, and to celebrate our reunion, Rapunzel and I sat on the bridge and talked like we did that first night we camped together many miles ago. Before retiring to our tents, we hung our food bags from under the Big Branch suspension bridge and took pictures[†]. The vignette of our reunion on the bridge effected an awareness that all is well with this trail way of life; there is a distinct sense that we are in harmony with the world, and that all is as it should be.

Linc and Jeannie are known for their unfailing desire to go to bed with the chickens. Those who camp near them are sure to be admonished for any late night noise. Their old folks' curfew has created a long-standing trail joke the two of them call "having a geezer party". An open invitation to the geezer party, usually extended around 8:30pm, is their way of notifying all involved that they will not be held responsible for being sociable after 9pm—known as hiker midnight. My father's prankster legacy finally got the better of me and, coupled with my love for these two, spawned mischievous trouble. As the pair finished up dinner and began moving their things to their tent and hanging their bear bag for the night, I managed to convince everyone in camp—about 10 of us—to play a prank. We waited until Linc and Jeannie had turned in and were probably just starting to fall asleep. All 10 of us crept to their tent site and surrounded their tent as silently as possible. On cue, we all began a cacophony of exaggerated snoring sounds, punctuated with giggles, catcalls and whistles. As anticipated, Jeannie let out a squeal, "ok you guys, get lost!" Linc's quiet laughter could be heard as we all walked back to the fire.

A U G U S T   1 4

Rapunzel and I met up with Dirt Diva and Compass Rose while we were taking a break at Lula Tye Shelter. I had not encountered these young women yet, but had seen their crazy entries in the registers many times. Rapunzel knew them already because Rapunzel is one of those magical people that knows everyone, and everyone knows her. Dirt Diva and Compass Rose both wear black running shorts and orange-red short sleeve tops. They both have black, knee-high gaiters and terry cloth wrist bands and the healthy glow of women athletes. Dirt Diva proceeds to explain to Rapunzel and me about finding the wristbands in a Dollar General store in some town and purchasing them as a joke; one

wristband says 'Rock Star' and one says 'Hottie'. She
tells us that a man who picked them up hitch-hiking
told the girls the only reason he stopped for them was
because of their "team uniforms". So they had dubbed
themselves the Wonder Twins and did we want to be
inducted into their club? Rapunzel immediately
applied for acceptance. I, however, was leery of the
wristband thing and expressed my concerns. This
earned me an entry in the register from Dirt Diva telling
the world that Willow "has never really been into the
wristband thing." And so 'The Team' is born.

These young women are power hikers. They can
move out at four miles an hour all day long if so
inclined. They have just returned from a two week
'vacation' from the trail. We all make tentative plans to
meet at the Whistle Stop at the VT 103 road crossing
for dinner and ice cream, and the girls head out ahead
of us. Rapunzel and I figure we will probably never see
them again.

Later in the day, we come to the trail junction for
White Rocks Cliffs. There are Dirt Diva and Compass
Rose playing among a boulder field of rock sculptures,
posing and taking each other's pictures. Rapunzel and
I join in, and we all take lots of pictures of the hundreds
of precariously balanced rocks poised on logs and boulders among the larch. It is so good to laugh! Hiking has
gotten way too serious lately.[†]

The girls did meet up with us at the Whistle
Stop[†], and we had a wonderful meal and ate ice cream
with a southbound thru-hiker afterward. Sunlight was
fading by the time we got back on the trail. We're
staying in Clarendon Shelter tonight, each of us
making our plans for the next towns of Rutland,
Vermont and Hanover, New Hampshire.

AUGUST 15

Dr. Thunder, Mountain Lightning, and Sam's Cola floated in a net at the first stream crossing. Despite the morning chill still in the air, Rapunzel and I stopped to partake of the extra calories; Dirt Diva and Compass Rose were sitting by the stream reading the trail magic register. We read the entries of the hikers who are just ahead, looking for messages from people we know. Model T and Ranger Dawg are only one day ahead. Our teasing conversation about these two characters ended with the girls calling me 'Willer' in the spirit of Model T's Tennessee accent. I chastised them for their register entries about my wristband reluctance, saying a woman can't be too careful these days what she lets slip with these two around and pointing out there was a good reason their wristbands were only available at the Dollar General. I assured them they should accept my application for the club, and that my wristband should say "Kitty".

I broke ranks tonight, though, and am staying at The Inn at Long Trail. Rapunzel, Dirt Diva and Compass Rose went to a hostel in Rutland. I'm not sure where Linc and Jeannie and the rest of the crew ended up. The girls and I will try to meet up in the morning.

I have looked forward to staying at the Inn at Long Trail since I was at home in my own bed planning my hike a year ago. This inn is a rustic old lodge that has been a haven for hikers and skiers since 1939. Its charm is exactly as I anticipated. I sat on the couch in the lobby/living room for a long time looking at glossy pictures of Vermont farms and woodlands in their coffee table books. For dinner I ate Guinness stew in the pub with Lone Wolf and Eric, the Long Trail hiker.

A U G U S T   1 7

Yesterday, I pushed for an 18 mile day; I probably would have stopped sooner, but Lone Wolf caught up with me and convinced me to press on to the cabin at The Lookout. It was getting late in the day, and I'd not stopped yet to cook dinner; my strength had faded, and I could hardly put one foot in front of the other. Lone Wolf is a strong hiker; his ability to push up a mountain at breakneck speed pays tribute to his years of long-distance bicycling. I didn't think I could go farther, but my ego wanted to try just because someone else believed I could make it. I ate a Snickers bar while he meticulously listed all the reasons we should push on. I was glad he did. The Lookout is a tiny cabin situated just two tenths of a mile off the trail on private land whose owners have made it available as a shelter. We sat on the widow's walk and watched the sun set in a crystal clear evening sky, talking softly in the vastness.

Lone Wolf attempted to thru-hike the AT 10 years before but did not finish. Now, on his second attempt, he is determined to finish as a part of his commitment to change his life and has already passed where he previously left the trail. His exacting intelligence is more fitted for the halls of high finance than backwoods Vermont, and his professional background in atmospheric sciences causes him to randomly announce weather events. Darting blue eyes convey an angst that haunts him so fiercely, at times it is almost tangible. Under a million stars, we talked for hours about shattered dreams and new beginnings, concluding we are all the same, and yet, all so alone on this journey that is our lives.

Lone Wolf and I walked into a tiny town a mile off the trail called South Pomfret. The town consists of one general store with a lunch counter and a post office inside and a library across the street. We parked our packs on the pillared, front porch of the brick library and ate a deli sandwich in the general store. I wrote a postcard to Mom and mailed it from the post office window right there in the store. Way cool. It's little things that excite after months of logistical nightmares to meet the simplest of needs. We checked email at the library and headed back to the trail, a sweet and civilized break in our hot day of hiking. Too late, I realized that my mp3 player was missing. I blamed the teenagers I had seen in town and my own trusting naiveté for leaving my pack on the library porch. Even though I hadn't listened to it in over a week, suddenly listening to music was all I could think of because I couldn't have it.

Rapunzel, Dirt Diva and Compass Rose showed up at camp just before dark. Rapunzel said Linc had found my mp3 player a few miles back; he had guessed it was mine by the song listing on the screen even without headphones to listen to the music. I forgave the innocent teenagers. Poor teens; they always get a bad rap. I am tenting beside a father and his daughter and son who are all out for the weekend on a family adventure. I felt drawn to be near them as opposed to staying in the shelter with the other hikers.

Rael crept into camp late tonight under the cover of darkness. I could hear him long into the night cleaning, sorting and resorting his gear. The familiar sounds were vaguely comforting—this strange trail family of my own.

A U G U S T   1 9

The New Hampshire border marker is in the middle of the Connecticut River bridge on the edge of the town of Hanover. Rapunzel, Lone Wolf and I stood on the bridge lost in a surrealistic time/space warp as if starring in our own epic movie. This must be what it feels like to be successful, to realize a lifelong dream. We've come so far, yet it's hard to believe we are in New Hampshire.

In Hanover, hikers have the deck stacked against them when it comes to accomplishing even the simplest of chores. Despite the fact that it is a college town, there are no hostels and no readily available, easy to find, cheap resources for where to stay or what's available. Dirt Diva and Compass Rose and I set out with our laundry in tow to find a washing machine. We thought we would take the transit to the local laundromat. After waiting for half an hour for the bus to arrive, we read the sign. "No Transit on Weekends". If all else fails, read the instructions, right? We walked the mile out of town to wash our clothes and walked back. Not like we can't walk. During this ridiculous laundromat affair, the sad story came to light that the reason Dirt Diva and Compass Rose did not get cookies from the Cookie Lady in Connecticut was because the Cookie Lady was gone to Hartford to take Switch to the airport on the day they arrived at her blueberry farm. It was determined that I had effectively gypped them out of their rightful homemade cookies, and therefore I owed them. I was making no promises.[†]

Rapunzel and I dined at a Middle Eastern restaurant topping it off with another pint of Ben & Jerry's. I am finally relieved of the worry that I am not eating enough, for I was able to weigh myself on the scales at the Dartmouth College gymnasium where we took showers. I have gained back the weight I lost, and I now weigh the same as before leaving for the Trail. That number comes as a great relief and underscores the sense of settling in I've felt of late.

Trail history is intimately intertwined with the Mount Cube Sugarhouse. The family who owns this business has been instrumental in New Hampshire politics for generations. Mr. Thomson came out to the sugar house to make room for us to put out our sleeping bags. The sugar house is in the process of renovation, and he has been putting in long days to ready it for the upcoming season. He brought out a yellowed photograph of an elderly woman and a young boy standing by a picket fence with a farmhouse in the background. "Do you know who this is?" he asked. I took a wild stab, considering we were hikers even though I really had no idea. "That's Grandma Gatewood*," I said. "It sure is," he answered. "And who is that standing beside her?" My cleverness faded, and I couldn't answer him. "That's me!" he said with a gleam in his eye. "Grandma Gatewood showed up at our door that night. She said, 'Hello, there. I'm Grandma Gatewood, the first woman to hike the Appalachian Trail. What's for dinner?'" Mr. Thomson burst into laughter. This was obviously his favorite story to tell thru-hikers that came his way. He brought us a pint measuring cup full of warm maple syrup to sample and told us how the trail used to come right down the mountain behind his farm and across his land. The old house used to be a stop for hikers along the way, and his mother served famous, pancake breakfasts.†

* Emma Rowena Gatewood was the first female to thru-hike the Appalachian Trail solo, first in 1955 at the age of 67, again in 1960, and yet again in 1963 at the age of 75, this time in sections.

Getting to Mount Cube Sugarhouse was no picnic. The trail no longer comes down the mountain behind Mr. Thomson's farm but instead crosses the road two miles away. Rapunzel has still been experiencing a lot of pain in her feet and fell behind on the last long downhill to the road crossing. It was growing dark, and although we had planned to go to Mount Cube Sugarhouse, it was two miles west on the road. Puffy and Cheeto were long gone, and we didn't know if they had made it to the sugarhouse or not. Lone Wolf and Driftwood (a section hiker) set off on foot up the road, but Rapunzel and I couldn't walk another step. The road was deserted, and our chances of hitching a ride grew scarce as the sun went down. In disgust, we made a last ditch effort. We sketched out a sign on a piece of notebook paper: MT CUBE SUGARHOUSE. When a truck appeared on the horizon, Rapunzel danced about in the middle of the road waving her arms frantically and pointing to me, also in the middle of the road. I held the sign high, waving it above my head, shouting. The poor, bewildered truck driver pulled over and let us in his king cab. What choice did he have? On the way, we stopped and picked up Lone Wolf and Driftwood who had only made it about a mile; they climbed into the pickup bed. Puffy and Cheeto were at the Sugarhouse waiting.

AUGUST 22

I picked up several items of winter gear Adam shipped to Hanover. Even though I've become better at packing to minimize bulk, I was concerned about adding the weight of winter clothes back to my pack and wondering if I would need to switch back to carrying the Osprey just to handle the weight. I got rid of the stuff sack for the clothes; I put my socks and hat, long underwear and gloves in the stuff sack with the sleeping bag. The two capilene long sleeve shirts, the long pants and the fleece I stuff around the other items in the pack, filling in any air pockets. Rain jacket I keep rolled up on the outside of the pack. I've carried my 15 degree bag the whole time, so no weight change there.

I've sworn off carrying too much food, carrying four days max and stopping for resupply at every opportunity. I've asked that Adam divvy up larger mail-drops into fewer days' supply. If I end up with too much food, I leave it in the hiker box for someone else. I'll carry five days of food from Glencliff to Crawford Notch (my next maildrop): four days of breakfasts, two lunches, five dinners and five days of snacks. Two and a half days into it I'll be seven meals lighter, and I'll stop for the rest in North Woodstock. I'll eat lunch there in a restaurant, pick up one more breakfast and two more lunches and go on. See? The logistics are dizzying. I've stopped carrying more than a liter of water at a time unless I'm dry camping (camping with no water source nearby) for the night.

We are at the foot of the White Mountains. The Whites have been the most talked about part of the trail the whole trip north. They have acquired mythic proportions in the minds of the uninitiated NOBOs. For some reason though, a steady calm has descended over me ever since I crossed into Vermont. I've shed the fears I once entertained of the dizzying climbs and steep descents the stories promise. This doesn't mean I have replaced fear with some half-cocked egotistical indifference, merely that I have acquired an unwa-vering belief in the power of taking one step at a time. It is hard to argue with the amazing fact that I am now in New Hampshire where I once was in Georgia. Every day fellow hikers and I comment incredulously on our whereabouts. It seems like such a short time, and yet so long ago, that this journey began so far away. There is an attachment to the experience that is forming among all of us. No one really wants it to end; no one wants the real world to take over our little microcosmic society and scatter it back to reality. The looming Whites have brought us even closer, as smaller groups of hikers have now banded together, and we all move in one wave of purpose, our plans for each day made separately and yet ending up the same. We think alike, hike alike, suffer alike, laugh, cry and wonder all the same. Those who hiked fast in the beginning are either already finished or have burnt out, gotten injured or sick, or have chilled out and are now hiking slower. I've seen people I never thought I would see again, people who sailed by me months before, hurrying to Katahdin. And, to my amazement, I continue to meet new people as well. The only person I have seen lately from my earliest days in Georgia has been Banjoman. I lay in my sleeping bag last night on the tile floor of the Mt. Cube Sugarhouse store; by the glow of my headlamp, I relived the first four days on the trail by looking at the landmarks and mileage in my guidebook. The things that seem so easy now were not easy then. And, oh how life changes us so.

The questions I came out here to nurse are all still there. No answers have miraculously surfaced. I still have no idea what job I will have when I come off the trail. I do not know what I want to be when I grow up, and I don't know which crazy dream to pursue next. What I have learned, I've learned from following the Trail itself. Many times along the way, I would look up seeking the next white blaze, and it would be nowhere in sight. In the first few weeks, a sick feeling would take over as I would search for another blaze for assurance. There was a day, though, when I finally accepted that just following the trail beneath my feet would reveal the next blaze. I climbed a rocky section heading for a blaze up on a rock. I could not see where the trail went from there; it appeared to simply drop off into space over the edge of the mountain. When I emerged onto the top of the blazed rock, the trail snaked away beside me, hidden behind a boulder, there all along, silently revealing itself only when I was ready to walk it. I've gained an appreciation for this metaphor of life as the miles of trail have unfurled, day after day, state after state; nothing more need be said.

Bog Fever

"If you stay on [the path] long enough, you'll find it to be a vivid place, with its ups and downs, its challenges and comforts, its surprises, disappointments and unconditional joys. You'll take your share of bumps and bruises while traveling—bruises of the ego, as well as of the body, mind and spirit, but it might well turn out to be the most reliable thing in your life.... What is mastery? At the heart of it, mastery is practice. Mastery is staying on the path."—GEORGE LEONARD

AUGUST 23

After months of anticipation, Lone Wolf, Rapunzel, Sexy Monk and I entered the White Mountains. Yesterday, Ranger Dawg and Model T arrived at Glencliff hostel after hiking southbound from Kinsman's Notch to avoid having to descend the steep incline down into the Notch. By being dropped off at the Notch and hiking southbound, they were able to climb the steep trail, which is supposedly much easier and less dangerous than trying to get down it. The trail up Mount Moosilauke has an elevation gain of 3662 feet from Glencliff, most of which is in a distance of 1.8 miles. The climb is long, but reasonable—not too steep and good footing. The trail took us above tree line; the wind was so strong that walking across the summit was difficult. Cumulus clouds lined the horizon above the ridges in the distance. There was a steep descent to the shelter, but the view from our line of sleeping bags on the shelter floor is spectacular. We are looking out at Franconia Ridge about 20 trail miles away. Rapunzel fell just before arriving at the shelter, so we opted not to attempt the descent into Kinsman's Notch this afternoon but will try it in the morning when we are fresh and rested. A bad fall on such a steep descent really takes a psychological toll on your self-confidence. We are both on edge about tomorrow's descent.[†]

It's pretty chilly, and everyone's pulling on their long underwear and donning hats. The shelter filled early as nine of us opted for a short day. At least five that stayed at the hostel last night hiked farther. Banjoman is entertaining everyone with his back-packer's guitar and his endless repertoire of music. Some songs we listen to, and some we sing along. Lone Wolf surprised us with a solo of "Cat's in the Cradle". Camaraderie warms the chilly shelter.

A U G U S T 2 5

The steep descent from Beaver Brook Shelter down into Kinsman's Notch boasted rebar, wooden steps, loose gravel, boulder hopping and wet rocks—an 1820 foot drop in 1.4 miles beside a cascading waterfall. The sheer sections had 6x6s fitted into the rock with rebar holding them in place creating high steps of a sort. Most of the steep trail was rocks, mud and roots. A half a mile into the descent, I released the last of my fading apprehensions and really began to enjoy what I was doing. It took an hour and a half to reach the bottom; I was so excited that I used Switch's cell phone to call Adam from the side of the road. My call must have gotten through on the emergency signal because as soon as I hung up from my brief conversation, I had no more service. He, of course, had no idea what I was talking about and no scale at all from which to understand what I had just done; but, he made the appropriate supportive comments, and I was even happier to have shared my accomplishment.

When everyone made it down safely, we walked a half mile on the road to the Lost River campground snack bar, where I proceeded to eat $14 worth of junk food. I had a piece of cheese, a cup of yogurt, a package of M&Ms, a bag of potato chips, a hot dog, cranberry juice, a cup of coffee, and a Ben & Jerry's ice cream popsicle/bar thing. I added up the numbers on the wrappers—1300 calories! Climbing out of the Notch, all four of us laughed hysterically on sugar highs.

Coming over south and north Kinsman peaks the air was cool and sunshine appeared intermittently from behind great, fleecy clouds. Today marks five months on the Trail. The first few miles from Eliza Brook Shelter up South Kinsman were slow and rocky. Much to my surprise, I am finding the climbing fun. The boulder scrambles are challenging but doable. I have not felt like I was up against something I just couldn't handle. I was afraid there would be some sheer vertical climbs, but even the steepest climbs have plenty of hand holds and places for your feet. The trail demands total involvement; using every part of your body to climb, your mind remains engaged, choosing where to step next. It is the perfect union of mind/body—the true yoga of the trail. I have been happiest these last two days of bouldering.

The views are the incredible reward for scrambling over all this crazy stuff—roots, rocks, logs, bridges, mud holes, streams, blow downs, more rocks, climbs, boulders, more rocks. Suddenly you emerge above the trees and can see for miles. Franconia Ridge still dominates the horizon with its steep, sheer rock facets and the many folds and peaks of its ridgeline. We began its climb this afternoon, stealth camping by a stream at 3210 feet. We'll climb to the top first thing tomorrow morning and be above tree line most of the day tomorrow. Some of the peaks we'll be crossing were shrouded by clouds off and on most of the morning, so tomorrow most likely will be pretty cold and windy. At the post office in North Woodstock I picked up my primaloft vest Adam mailed. Perfect timing!

At lunchtime, we stopped at Lonesome Lake Hut, our first of the series of huts maintained in the Whites by the Appalachian Mountain Club. We had left Eliza Brook Shelter at 7:20am and arrived at the hut by noon, only 5.9 miles in four and a half weary hours. The AMC caretakers served tomato soup: $2 for all you could eat, $1 for lemonade, a snickers bar (which I ate first) for $1. I ate three bowls of soup; I could swear I could hear it sloshing around in my belly when I left. I was just full enough to make it to town where I gorged on chocolate and spicedrops while I shopped for two days worth of groceries for the next few miles to Crawford Notch. At this point, I had tired so of my maildrop fare that I asked Adam not to send any more. Lone Wolf, Sexy Monk, Rapunzel and I ate at the Landmark Restaurant before heading out of town. Lone Wolf ruminated algebraically all afternoon, weighing invisible, but vastly important, pros and cons and eventually elected to stay behind and check into a motel.

There are a lot of day hikers and weekend warriors on the trails in the Whites. If you want to stay in an AMC hut, one must dish out a whopping $80 per night. We met a southbound section hiker at the hut who told us exactly how to find the stealth site where we are camped tonight, so we wouldn't have to pay for a tent site at Liberty Spring. It worked out perfectly. That's real trail magic—gifts that come at just the right time, sort of like the toilet paper I found in the hiker box at the post office right when I needed a roll. Only thru-hikers get excited about such mundane items as toilet paper, I suppose.

The forest is evergreen: red spruce, hemlock, and fir. I'm sure there are others I do not recognize, as I never learned conifers well. The trees grow densely with rotting logs jumbled on the forest floor and many rocks and boulders scattered between them. Every surface is covered with thick, fluffy moss of all shades and varieties that muffles all sound. The resinous aroma of conifers permeates the air in this lumpily-carpeted emerald forest.

Moose were on the trail today—one hiker saw them, but I have yet to see any. I am hiking in a group of people, so I doubt we'll see any wildlife. Though I have thoroughly enjoyed hiking with other people, my experience has been that you see more critters when hiking alone. We have had some great laughs, shared some hard trail and seen amazing views, but I do feel a pull to return to my own pace and quieter times soon. There are three of us tonight. Although we are at a shelter, I chose to tent so I could have some space to just be quiet and write.

AUGUST 26

Franconia Ridge is a world unto itself. This exposed ridge is above treeline, and the trail is lined with rocks on both sides to mark the way. Here and there a cairn may be precariously stacked to indicate a turn in the trail. The world drops away on either side, and the mountain ranges extend forever. The ridge commands awe, and most hikers spoke in hushed tones if they spoke at all. Clouds of dense fog moved serenely around various summits, both near and distant.[†]

It was a very long day for Rapunzel and me and the last remnants of light were slipping quickly into shadows when I noticed a place on the side of the trail where others had walked into the underbrush. I pushed through the evergreen boughs and followed the faint indention in the forest floor up a hillside. I wasn't sure what I would find on the side of a hill, but I had a good feeling there may be a stealth site we could use. Sure enough there was one level spot, large enough for only one tent. I dumped my pack and scouted in the fading light while Rapunzel waited there. Nothing else to be found in the dense undergrowth—this was it. We opted to share Rapunzel's two person tent and set about to make camp and eat our late dinner by headlamp.

AUGUST 27

A very cold rain pours down. Rapunzel and I are warm, clean and dry in a tiny one room cabin at the Crawford Notch campground. The hiker bunkhouse only had one vacancy when we arrived, so the thoughtful lady in the camp store let us use this cabin. Lone Wolf showed up later and scored the last bunk in the bunkhouse. It feels wonderful to be out of the cold rain. I am even sitting in a chair at a table to write.

We stopped briefly at Galehead Hut first thing this morning, hoping for a breakfast we didn't get. There has been tension between the many thru-hikers that are trying to make it through the Whites this week, as there are limited free spaces to stay at the huts, and stealth camping is the only option left for those of us who don't find room. We are sandwiched in the middle of a huge group of about 20 hikers, all in the same 30-mile section of trail. Others who had found room at Galehead the night before had dibs on breakfast, and the caretakers seemed quite oblivious to helping anyone else. A paying camper came outside the hut as Rapunzel and I donned our packs to leave; despite the fact that we had just been turned away in our request to have the leftover breakfast food, he set down his plate of leftovers and fed the dogs right in front of the two of us. The key words there are "paying camper". Rael watched this occur, and I glimpsed a flicker of barely contained fury cross his face, but we turned and left before anything could be said. No worries, right? My mind worked its way around privilege versus injustice, concepts that pale when housed safely in the framework of rules. As Rapunzel and I climbed the next mountain in the morning chill, she listened patiently to my indignant rant.

We came to a less rocky section of trail after hiking seven more miles. The rain began just around noon. We had come over South Twin and Mount Guyot already, so the ridgeline was above us when it started to drizzle. A cold wind blew hard as we descended. I was grateful for our early start—we actually had visibility from the ridgeline and were able to enjoy being up there before the clouds locked down on us. We put on pack covers and rain jackets just past Zeacliff trail, and the rain grew steadily heavier and colder. We stopped to warm up and get some soup at Zealand Falls Hut. Although the hut was very crowded with day hikers taking shelter from the cold rain, there was soup being served for all. This time it was potato dill.

When we started out again around 1:20pm, we had about 7.5 more miles to go, and cold driving rain stung our faces. We put on rain pants and rain coats this time to help fend off the wind. Sexy Monk had arrived, furious for being turned away from Galehead this morning also; he was fighting a fever and needed a place to take shelter. He opted to keep moving with Rapunzel and me, so the three of us set out. Unfortunately, we were walking directly into the wind. This was the first time since April I was hiking in long pants, a rain jacket, fleece headband, and gloves. The trail out of the hut was miraculously flat with no rocks for 2.5 miles. We hit breakneck speed of about four mph, but then came to a section of bog bridges about a mile before Ethan Pond campsite.

The bog bridges were set too far apart to allow for stepping from one to the other. At the end of each log, you had to step down into the mud and back up two steps onto the next log. My knees were screaming, and my mood soured. I was exhausted from the cold, the pace, and nothing but potato dill soup to eat. I raged out loud at the AMC, the rain, and the bog logs, and Sexy Monk laughed to hear me finally succumb to my bad mood. We took a break, and sat by the trail eating snacks while Rapunzel went to sign the register at Ethan Pond campsite. Then, off we went. The rain stopped and Rapunzel and I picked up the pace again; Sexy Monk fell behind.

We chatted to stave off the foul weather and realized Rapunzel would be leaving the trail in a day or two to attend another wedding. She's then coming back to meet up with some other thru-hikers we know that are behind us. There is no way to know if we will see each other again. Suddenly I didn't know what to say.

AUGUST 29

I is early morning, and I am warm and cozy on a mattress on the floor of the attic of the Lakes of the Clouds Hut. At 5040 feet, the wind howls continuously, and the whir and shake of the wind turbine on the roof sounds an erratic rhythm. I arrived at the Mizpah Hut yesterday around 1:30pm after Lone Wolf and I climbed Webster Cliffs† in dense fog and mist. The trail up from Crawford Notch to Mizpah was serious business, with near vertical climbs and rock scrambles, but I am still enjoying the challenge. My pack had a liter of water, less as the morning went on, and four days of food. At the top of Webster Cliffs, we emerged from the mist into clear air above the clouds. The undercast spread out before us with just the peaks of Mount Jackson and Mount Clinton visible above the clouds. The cloud cover masqueraded as a vast, white ocean on whose rocky cliff shore we stood surveying the island mountaintops in the distance.†

Outside of Mizpah Hut, the wind was barely moving, and the temperature on the mountaintop in the sunshine was in the low 70s. After the rain the day and night before, the rocks were still wet in many places, but the trail had dried out enough to be navigable. I could easily see climbing up here in the rain would not have been a reasonable option.

The fragile alpine zone of these mountains is very beautiful in such a different way. Gardens of lichens and moss line the trail, their wild poignancy simultaneously complex and yet so simple. Red spruce, hemlocks and firs are all dwarfed by the severe cold winds, twisted into strange shapes around the boulders. Their scent purifies the air, resinous and festive. Bogs of deep, murky peat are traversed on boards stretched across for hikers; hiking poles do not reach the bottom.[†]

Mizpah Hut was super warm after strenuous hiking. As I sat eating soup, I looked up into the loft, and there stood Eliza who had hiked with Justin in North Carolina. She ran down and gave me a big hug and assured me of a place to stay the night at Lakes of the Clouds Hut, quite an unexpected treasure. She is working in the AMC huts for her second season and would be there that night. She caught me up on Justin's progress, telling me that he is going by the trail name Three Dollar, and he is about a week or so behind me. I was glad to hear he was doing well and was still on the trail. I stayed at Mizpah for an hour, eating soup and visiting with 'Liza and the group of thru-hikers that had come up that morning. I missed Rapunzel who had stayed behind to zero at Crawford Notch.

The hike from Mizpah to Lakes of the Clouds Hut took three hours. There was not as much actual climbing but a lot of rocky trail and elevation gain. On the way up Lone Wolf and I heard the eerie sound of the steam engine whistle as the train climbed Mount Washington's cog railway. The terrain looked as if we were on the moon, with giant boulders (quite wonderfully called 'glacial erratics') strewn about. Almost at the top of Mount Monroe, we took a break at a trail intersection. The silence now was so complete, our ears rang. A flicker of peace crossed Lone Wolf's countenance. For a brief moment, our individual demons abandoned each of us.[†]

As we rounded the peak of Mount Monroe, a section was blocked off with a sign stating that several species of endangered plants lived there. Then, from out of the fog, the silhouette of Lakes of the Clouds Hut appeared only a hundred feet away. We were there!

And so were 91 other people. Unbelievable! The place was booked solid with paying guests and an additional 17 thru hikers. It was a relative madhouse compared to the deafening silence we had just experienced. But, the crew of this hut had their act so very together that everything ran smoothly, and they made room for everyone. Eliza set me up in the attic and said I could bring a couple of people; I invited Dirt Diva and Compass Rose. Banjoman played his backpacker's guitar for the whole audience, and we all got food. The night was warm and cheery.

Around 4am the wind picked up. When I first awoke and crept downstairs to the restroom, I could see the summit from the attic window. Later, the wind brought in a cloud, and the hut was engulfed in white. Mount Washington's summit is only 1.4 miles away, the second highest mountain on the entire AT.

From the summit of Mount Washington[†], the undercast of white clouds made our views ethereal rather than far reaching but spectacular just the same. The summit house is an interesting piece of history; built of stone, it is the last of the original buildings from the 1800s. I could imagine what it would have been like to climb the mountain so many years ago and have the stone summit house be all there was on top. Originally a hotel called Tip Top House, the building now serves some other purpose, and we did not get to go in. There is a large modern facility there also, housing a small post office, two gift shops, a museum and a food bar.

A video called "Breakfast of Champions" plays in the main lobby. The Laurel and Hardy-like presentation is a couple of guys trying to set up a table and pour cereal and milk in 65mph winds on Mount Washington. They can barely stand up in the force of the wind; their table blows over, and then blows completely away. Their cereal blows away, as does the bowl and the box. The milk doesn't even begin to pour before it simply scatters on the wind. It was a pretty funny rendition of the quite sobering reality of this extreme region of the Whites.

On the wall is a long list of people who have died on Mount Washington with a blurb telling the circumstances of each of their deaths. Many had fallen to their deaths in Tuckerman's Ravine; many have frozen in freak snowstorms in every month of the year; hypothermia claimed many. The most recent death was August 4th of this very season.

Dirt Diva and Compass Rose and I hung out at the top for a couple of hours and then started the excruciating seven mile hike to Madison Spring Hut. The entire seven miles was navigation over huge boulders in and out of clouds.

The Cog Railway[†] chugs up and down the steep grade to the top, a single steam engine pushing one passenger car up ahead of it. Two trains go back and forth all day on a single track with a pullout part way down the mountain. One of the engineers came into the summit facility to take a short break; he was covered from head to toe in black soot from the smoke stack. We watched the trains maneuver past one another on the section of double track as we hiked down the ridge-line on our way out. We did not take part in the thru-hiker tradition of mooning the trains, but of course, we found out that Puffy did.

At Madison Spring Hut, we were served hot tomato soup. On the wall, a poster described a phenomenon

of the local ecosystem called fir waves. This phenomenon occurs only in the White Mountains of New
Hampshire and in northern Japan. Mature fir trees that
have grown tall shield younger, shorter firs from fierce
winds; the taller older trees take the brunt of the gale
force winds and collect the extreme rime ice year in
and year out. As a result of this constant abuse, these
trees die in 20-30 years; by then, the next generation
of trees has reached a height tall enough to protect the
younger row behind them. The waves are visible on
the mountainsides as bands of dead wood followed by
the dark green of the healthy trees, and lighter green
of the younger trees, then deadwood again. The waves
"travel" across the mountainsides every 20-30 years as
the cycle progresses.

From Madison Spring Hut, the trail ascended
straight up Mount Madison—again all boulders as far
as you could see (when the fog cleared periodically).
Every step involved picking your way over and around,
up and down. I was awed by the obvious power of the
long-vanished glacier and accompanying geological
forces that had created all of this eerie, grandiose
mess. Even-tually, we crept at one mph back down
below tree line, and our feet felt the wonder of the
spongy forest floor again, only to endure another
two miles of plunging downhill. My knees were
completely out of sorts by this point. I was never so
glad to see a tent site in my life.[†]

A U G U S T   3 0

I am pushing myself physically by attempting to
keep up with the younger women, who are much
stronger and faster than me, but the challenge calls to
my spirit. It did my soul much good to enjoy their

cheerful chatter during our breaks. The name Wildcat Ridge has spawned a whole new line of kitty jokes regarding my membership in the club and required wristband. "Meow! Meow!" has become our meaningless Wildcat Ridge motto.

Wildcat Ridge-Peaks E, D, C, B, and A are not to be taken lightly. This day kicked my butt. Straight up, climbing for hours—not hiking—hand-over-hand climbing. We stopped most of the way up peak E (the first one) and soaked up the sun on a huge rock. I was climbing with Lone Wolf, Driftwood, Compass Rose and Dirt Diva. Behind us, across Pinkham Notch, were the Presidentials in all their grandeur. We could see everything we'd hiked the day before, including the top of Mount Washington. By the time we reached Peak C, I was really tired. By the time we reached Peak A and peered over the edge to Carter Notch Hut, my legs felt like jello. There was the hut way, way below us, and a cliff rising up the other side of the Notch, which we knew was tomorrow's climb.

The trail then descended 1000 feet in eight tenths of a mile! Thankfully, there were boulder steps, unlike the ascent; my knees were buckling at random from weariness. I slipped and fell three times in one minute near the bottom and had to force myself to slow down and focus. Your mind is so intensely engaged for hours, and your body so totally encompassed in the task at hand, that by the end of the day, it is a struggle to keep it all together for the last exhausting mile. This day was the most total mind/body day of the trail.

We pitched our tents, all nine of them, in the Notch, stealthing rather than paying to use the hut. I think a few thru-hikers managed to get free spots inside. The wind blew torturously through our camp all night long as we were right in the saddle of the

Notch. Cold! Cold! Cold!

A U G U S T 3 1

13.4 miles in one day in the Whites! It's a miracle I am still alive. My legs are so tired, I could hardly move them the last few miles. Luckily, the last 2.6 miles were good, actual trail, rather than climbs and descents on rocks. We cruised into camp at about four mph. I fell behind the other hikers, even on the good section of trail. I can feel the toll the extra challenge is taking on my body. I've pushed too hard and compromised my own way of hiking too often in the last few days in favor of keeping up. Now, my body feels as if I have not taken in enough calories, evident also by the extra snacks still left in my food bag uneaten, and I feel a vague weakness setting in, as if I may have a low grade fever. I did a desperate hiker pirouette on the rocks, quite unintentionally, and almost fell in while crossing—a great save—and I was so glad I didn't end up with wet boots in the last two tenths mile of the day.

Rattle River Shelter is just outside of Gorham, New Hampshire. At least nine are tenting here. A few went on ahead into town. My plan at this time is to move through Gorham without staying tomorrow night to put some distance between myself and the mass of thru-hikers, hopefully find my own rhythm again and take better care of myself. Most of this group will stay in town and zero, most likely. When we crossed the river this evening, only 300 miles of trail were left. Maine is less than 20 miles away.

I picked up my package from the post office early in the morning. Linc and Jeannie were there, having hitched a ride into town from Pinkham Notch for supplies. Since they have not actually made it to Gorham via trail yet, they are heading back out to keep moving this way. Catskill Eagle and Joe Crow were also at the post office. I had not seen Catskill Eagle since eating ice cream with him in New York when Switch was still with me. He had let me use his Blackberry to call home from the Smokies a lifetime ago when I injured my knee. Rapunzel also hitched in from Pinkham Notch, so she can get to her friend's wedding. She's spending tonight with us at The Barn, a hostel here in town.

Between Rapunzel's arrival, Dirt Diva and Compass Rose's promise to accompany 'Willer' through Mahoosuc Notch, and my increasing fever, I have been persuaded to stay the night. I am wrestling with this decision, feeling compromised because of the constant contact I've had with people lately. This section of trail has been so different than the first few months when I spent most of my time alone. My body has betrayed me now, and I am truly sick. I need to rest and have physically accepted that I am staying here, but my mind has moved on up the trail and wants to be alone, away from the very human drama that has become my day to day. I am struggling to define personal boundaries within this group of people. Rapunzel and I seem to have that weakness in common, giving too much of ourselves to others, and then trying to find what it is we gave away again. I will miss her intelligence and our incredible conversations.

I called Adam from Driftwood's cell phone. Switch had transferred the service to his new phone at home, so the phone I carried stopped working miles back; I mailed it home today. The calm sound of Adam's voice grounded my scattered thoughts. He helped me make peace with my decision to stay here tonight. He validated the plan to abandon my agenda and endorsed going with what seems best at the moment. He's worried about me getting sicker and wants me to stay here longer if I have to. He also wants me to come home now, I know. It's strange to me that I just needed to connect with him and hear my own thoughts echoed back to me. We are both ready for this to be over.

S E P T E M B E R   2

Dirt Diva commented, "You have a hard time relaxing even when you're in town, don't you?" Out of my respect for her, I have given her observation much thought. Maybe it's time for me to abandon more than just my agenda. Maybe, I should silence my own mind-fuck and learn to just be. Not only did I stay here in Gorham last night, but I have elected to zero today as well.[†] Aside from walking to the grocery store a few miles outside of town with Lone Wolf, I've napped most of the day. Somewhere between the road walk in the heat of the afternoon sun and the local bus ride back, my fever may have broken.

E V E N I N G —

Compass Rose and Dirt Diva have revealed their true nature; as we prepared to raid the convenience store across the street for dinner fixin's, Compass Rose announced that she can't miss the Notre Dame football game that is coming on tonight. I stopped in mid-sentence and turned to her in mock revelation, "THAT's what it is about you two! You're jocks!" Her face got this confused look for a split second while she figured out that I was teasing her, and Dirt Diva fell out in the floor laughing. Compass Rose just shook her head and said, Oh, come on, Willer! Jocks?" but the term was now christened, and there was no going back. While I cooked spaghetti on the tiny kitchen stove in the barn, Sleepy the Arab lounged by the television watching a movie. "You're going to miss your show," I said to Compass Rose. "My show?" she looked at me in disbelief. "*Game*, Willer, game! It's a game, not a *show*! We're not watching *Days of Our Lives*, here!"

There were no terry cloth wristbands to be found in Gorham, much less ones that said "Kitty" on them.

S E P T E M B E R   3

Gentian Pond Shelter is housing 16 hikers. I managed to squeeze into a tiny spot next to Compass Rose. She and Dirt Diva made it here much earlier in the day than Lone Wolf, Driftwood and I, so she saved me a place. Both bunk platforms are full and people are using the middle of the floor also. Every inch of space is filled with wet gear, full clotheslines and people. Even with all these people in this shelter, not a single voice could be heard upon approach. Not until I stood in front of the open-sided shelter could the low murmur of the 10 or so thru-hikers inside be heard. Five months of being in the woods has blessed everyone with a soft-spoken awareness of the silence.

My fever has receded to category low-grade, but now I have a sore throat. We left Gorham this morning in a cold rain, compliments of Hurricane Ernesto. Cold winds on the summits of these mountains and the wet conditions are cementing my sickness in a way that will make it impossible to get over quickly, I fear. I hiked with rain pants and jacket and headband, even pulling my hood over my head on the summits in the raging wind.

The high mountain bogs make for quite interesting trail. The peat mud is very deep in some places. Bog bridges are usually logs or planks that have been nailed to cross-logs at either end. Some have rotted in places, and they crumble as you step on them. Some are just wide enough for one boot, and some are two, narrow logs side by side. Some are deathly slick, and some are scored with a chainsaw. Some logs are completely missing, and some of them are obviously brand new. But the best, the very best, are the floaters. On Cascade Mountain, Lone Wolf is in front and we're cruisin' down this long walkway of bog bridges. Black bog water glistens on both sides. Bog monsters moan and reach for us with their long hairy arms. Suddenly, the log he steps on next sinks completely under his weight, but it's too late! His forward momentum keeps him moving up the log, but it is sinking as he goes, and within two seconds, Lone Wolf is calf deep in bog water before he can get to the next log. I'm watching all of this from behind him, still standing safe on solid ground, stifling my laughter. He pulls himself free with a series of colorful expletives and continues up the trail. I skirted the trick log, and gingerly picked my way across moss and roots on the edges of the bog with the sound of Lone Wolf's cursing fading ahead on the trail.

"Ok, so which ones of you were hiking in front today and bit it on the sinking bog bridge?" I asked the shelter full of hikers. Dirt Diva laughed. "Ah, that would be me!" Several other groans came from various sleeping bags. Maybe following other hikers isn't so bad after all.

SEPTEMBER 4

I got mine today. I tripped while thinking 'don't step there' and plunged a boot deep into the peat mud bog, stumbling over myself trying to get onto the bog bridge before I sunk too deeply. I ended up in a backwards crab-crouch, sort of like that obnoxious 70s game of Twister, my butt precariously poised a mere three inches above the glistening muck—one foot on the bridge, the other sunk in over the top of the boot, one arm sunk in up to my elbow, the other hand still desperately clinging to a hiking pole. Grace. I had no witnesses.

At the Maine border, Lone Wolf, Driftwood and I posed by the sign for pictures. It's Lone Wolf's first real smile in days. This border crossing is especially sweet for him as his goal comes more clearly into focus after so long. The sign read: "Maine: the way life should be!" Can it really be true that we have walked to Maine?[†]

Full Goose Shelter is about as full as it can possibly be. Of the 21 hikers camped here tonight, 12 are in the shelter. Every inch of shelter space is packed, and every tent site is claimed. Cold rain and mist continues as Ernesto rages on. The storm and terrain have Lone Wolf perpetually grouchy and consistently proclaiming weather doom and gloom. I am bunked next to Dirt Diva and Compass Rose again, whispering like excited school girls about tomorrow's promise of the dreaded Mahoosuc Notch. It's reputed to be the most difficult mile of the entire AT, a boulder-filled crevice of gargantuan proportions. The three of us have looked forward to tackling its challenges as a Team now for a week, planning to laugh our way through the difficulty and take lots of pictures.

S E P T E M B E R   6

With Driftwood, Dirt Diva, Compass Rose, Trickster and What? the one mile of Mahoosuc Notch fell to another Team victory in two hours and 10 minutes. The depths of the shadowy crevice were one massive boulder scramble. Boulders the size of cars *are* the trail. You go over, under, and around them as best as you can, sometimes even resorting to taking off your pack to fit through narrow clefts. We laughed a lot, and everyone helped each other by passing packs through the crannies and pulling each other up the high boulders. Dirt Diva took pictures.[†]The long scramble was incredibly tiring, but so much fun. At the northern end of the Notch, Dirt Diva and Compass Rose said their goodbyes and took off up the trail. Their promise to accompany me through the most difficult mile of trail fulfilled, they were off to break new records and score more wins for The Team. We have plans to meet up again at Piazza Rock Lean-to in a few days.

Driftwood and I are in Bethel, a most charming Maine town that makes me want to live here. The hitch from the Grafton Notch trailhead took three hours last night at dusk—for a mere 17 miles. First we waited for a shuttle that never came, and then, we tried to hitch. We asked some day hikers and a ranger for a ride, which was futile. Finally, when a man did stop to pick us up at 7:30pm, three other thru-hikers showed up at the last second and crammed into the four-seater car with the two of us (plus gear). It was our misfortune and their gain that the driver took them to their destination in Andover before he drove us to Bethel. We didn't arrive at the Chapman Inn until 8:45pm. It was a long day, but we were both pleased with our decision to go to a less popular town.

I will be really glad to have the large group of hikers disperse a little. Finding space at the shelters the past couple of nights has been stressful for everyone. Hurricane Ernesto gave us two solid days of wind and rain going across the Mahoosucs. Summits were cold and extremely windy, with gusts that would knock you off balance as you tried to walk or climb, making me even sicker. I now have a full-fledged cold and generally feel like crap. I would love to zero again here in Bethel, but that would just throw everything off. As it stands now, there are still a few more 10-mile days due to terrain. Once past Bigelow Mountain, I should be able to pick up the miles and put in some more 15-mile days to shorten the time. My feet have benefited from the low mileage even though the terrain has been tough. Going back to bigger miles will be a shock. Driftwood and I have formed a plan to be in Rangeley by this coming Sunday, Stratton by the 14th, and Monson by the 20th. I am hoping Adam will be able to join me at Whites Landing to hike the last 50 miles and summit Katahdin with me. He has the time off from work already approved; now we just have to get him from North Carolina to Maine somehow. I am excited I may get to share that time hiking with him, and he will get to experience some of what the trail has been like for me. Projected summit date is Sept 28th, five days sooner than originally calculated from my warm bed at home a year ago.

Despite the late hour, the Sudbury Tavern was still serving food when we arrived in town, so we had a big burger and a beer. It gave me a chance to get to know Driftwood better. He's a quiet, tall, handsome young man. His manner is a visible blend of patience and independence. He is hiking the northern half of the AT this season and plans to hike the southern half next year. We stayed at The Chapman Inn, which is a B&B that offers a wonderful hiker hostel. I don't understand why more hikers choose to go to Andover instead. Andover is nothing but a general store and diner at a crossroads, whereas, Bethel is a cute town, with gift shops, a movie theater, grocery, diners, pubs, and B&Bs and an internet cafe all within a one mile walk. The Chapman Inn hiker hostel, used by skiers in the winter, can sleep at least 30 people in single and double beds, all made up with real sheets and pillowcases and blankets (a rarity at hostels). There is a rec room with a ping-pong table and a pool table, a sauna, four bathrooms, a full kitchen, living room, cable TV, and a kitchen eating bar and table. It's a comfortable, accommodating facility, all in a barn attached to the main B&B house.

L A T E R —

Driftwood and I left town about 2pm. It took two hitches to get back to the trailhead. The first guy that picked us up was on his way to Katahdin to complete a section hike. He offered to take us to Katahdin for a flip flop, and I must say I did seriously consider it for a fleeting moment. Funny how things just fall into your lap when you are in "the flow". We didn't get on the trail until about 3:30—this was after I ran in the corner mart and got a hot dog, which I ate while standing on the side of the road—and we had 5.8 miles to go to the second shelter. We tried to pick a shelter we thought no other thru-hikers would stop at, in an attempt to stagger our mileage schedule from that of the other 18 hikers. Racing for shelter space is no fun, and after our unwelcome hitchhiking detour yesterday, we were especially over the group thing.

The trail was fine on the uphill out of Grafton Notch, but when we hit the downhill from West Bald Pate our pace fell apart due to wet rocks and steep trail. The climb up to East Peak of Bald Pate was a solid granite face with just enough of a slope that you could walk upright on it. Nevertheless, as the slope rounded off nearer the top, I had to focus only on where I was walking and ignore the spans of void growing behind me, or vertigo would have claimed me, for sure. [†]

Yesterday, there was another climb scarier than this one near the top of Old Speck Mountain. The rock was a conglomerate type with a lot of large jagged crystals sticking out that formed squared off hand and footholds. The climbing, per se, was easy, but the face kept getting steeper and steeper. It was all I could do to stay on task and beat down the rising sense of panic that was trying to take over. If Driftwood and #2 had not been standing at the top waiting for me and enjoying the views, I might have succumbed to fear. As it was, I just kept finding a place for this hand, then a foot, then the other hand, then the other foot and not looking behind me at all until I got to the top. Once there, the views of the Andoscroggin River, the Mahoosucs and the Presidentials erased any residual anxiety.

Anyway, the point was that getting off the East Peak of Bald Pate turned out to be a little more than we had bargained for. By this time the sun was getting low in the sky, the wind blew cold up on top, and my muscles were locking up. I stopped and added an extra shirt layer, but stayed in shorts to save time. The descent was brutally long, slow and slippery. It grew darker and colder. We had eight tenths of a mile to go, and the trail got a little easier; by this time it was dark under the trees. We reached the shelter without headlamps with just barely enough light to see.

Bingo! No hikers. We had the shelter to ourselves. We could spread out all our stuff and not have to tiptoe over 12 other people, and shuffle around more people, for seven square inches of space to set up a stove. It was 7:30pm—it had taken us four hours to go 5.8 miles. Ugh! We might be out of the Whites, but it's not gotten any easier yet. What a long afternoon! I sure do wish I were in that soft bed back in Bethel.

S E P T E M B E R   7

An unexpected luxury presented itself at our planned lunch spot, Surplus Pond. From the trail, we could see a dock and a cabin. Turns out, the cabin was an empty rental with a privy, a deck, a picnic table, Adirondack chairs, a spring, a thermometer, a clock, and of course, a great view of Surplus Pond. We ate lunch on the deck in the warm sunshine—a perfect afternoon.†

Short day, easier terrain—we arrived at Hall Mountain Shelter at 4pm. That seems so early, but then, our only other choice was to do four more miles to South Arm Road campsite, and we really didn't want a repeat of last night coming into camp in the dark. The four miles in question are shown on the profile map as two steep up and two steep down—no go. Driftwood's pace and preference for solitude fits my style. It's been a good match, and we've enjoyed each other's company.

I've been sick now for seven days. First just feeling tired, then the low grade fever, then two days of generally feeling like crap while hiking through the hurricane with a sore throat, then the head congestion started, and now I've hiked for two days blowing my nose every half hour. Tonight, I still feel feverish and have started to cough. I took a Tylenol PM, so I'll actually sleep despite not being able to breathe, and despite the group of about 15 college kids noisily setting up camp behind the shelter.

250.5 miles to the summit of Katahdin. So close, and yet so far away! In the beginning, I didn't even make it 250 miles before my knee gave out. I've thought about those first 100 miles a lot lately; it seems like a lifetime ago, and I remember how difficult it was. And yet, it was the same thing I am doing now; it's still hard, but in such different ways. It's strange to think back on those first few weeks and remember the impressions and thoughts that occupied my mind then, and to recognize how much the anxiety and chatter has quieted now. I do not worry about anything; I've adopted such a carefree existence, I almost dread the harsh return to reality. How do I preserve this state of mind in the real world? I suppose that is what drives our economy—that question. Everyone seeks their Bliss Fix, regardless of what it costs or how temporary the effects. I feel a bit guilty, as a parent, that I am not worrying about my kids. But then, they are with their father, and they are intelligent boys; there should be no reason to worry just for the sake of worrying, like I think my parents did and so many other parents do. The efforts I have put into teaching my boys how to make good decisions, how to think critically, how to manage their personal relationships with integrity are investments that yield returns. They learned lessons before they were 12 that it took me until adulthood to figure out; that is my evolutionary legacy to them, I suppose. And so I hike, and enjoy the yoga of one step after another, my mind a blank slate upon which the universe paints a mural of its great secrets.

S E P T E M B E R   9

The past few days of hiking with Driftwood have been a relative heaven compared to the previous crowds in the Whites and Mahoosucs. His quiet kindness keeps me calm, and our few chats during the day are light-hearted. We've met only a few other hikers: a southbound artist, with a delightful smile, who is drawing sketches of places along the trail as he goes, two guys from Tennessee who are on the southbound leg of a flip flop thru-hike, and an older, very acrimonious man hiking alone. Within each encounter, there has been a certain psychological nourishment born of the shared goal of thru-hiking the AT. We are in a rare place that only a small percentage of people who attempt to hike the Trail ever reach, the final approach to Katahdin, the icing on the cake, magnum opus. The power of this mindset is unmistakable. We are changing before each other's eyes.

Driftwood and I had hoped to meet up with Compass Rose and Dirt Diva at the Piazza Rock Lean-to this evening, but when we arrived at the road crossing 1.8 miles before the shelter, there was only enough daylight left to make it to town for resupply. The cold rain of the last few miles left us both ripe for succumbing to the warmth and hospitality of town. We stood drenched on the side of the road and waited for cars. Our first chance was a flatbed truck with the cab full of construction workers heading home from work. I stood by the window of the cab and evaluated the grinning faces of the men inside. Driftwood hung back. "Come on, Driftwood! Let's do it! A ride is a ride." We climbed onto the back of the open bed truck and sat on our packs, entwining our fingers in the wire mesh between us and the cab window. I banged on the roof of the cab when we were ready, and the driver ground first gear. This was going to be one cold ride into town.

We stumbled into Sarge's Pub, frozen to the core. Several other thru-hikers were already eating there, and quite a few are now staying at the Gull Pond hostel. We are back in the middle of the crowd.

SEPTEMBER 10

I checked the register at Piazza Rock and saw that Compass Rose and Dirt Diva had stayed there last night with a few others. I am sad I missed them. I don't think I will be able to catch up with them now.

Driftwood and I had a hell of time getting out of Rangeley. I forgot my headband, and we both left our boot inserts there. Despite getting out of the hostel early, we ended up stuck at the grocery store waiting for the owner of the hostel. He agreed to bring our boot inserts to us when we called from Driftwood's cell phone. We waited on the curb drinking coffee and eating danishes.

Once back on the trail, we caught up with Lone Wolf. We hadn't seen him since Full Goose Shelter. The look of relief on his face when he saw us approaching was testimony to his fragile state. He woefully relayed his tale of exhaustion and trials. Driftwood and I both encouraged him not to give up now when he is so close to reaching the goal. We agreed to hike with him the rest of the way. We are all at Poplar Ridge Shelter tonight which only holds four hikers, so most are tenting. Knock-Knock arrived just before dark with my head band he had rescued from the hostel. E-Rock and Knock-Knock built a fire. The atmosphere among the hikers grows more pensive the closer to Katahdin we get.

S E P T E M B E R   1 1

Cirque: a bowl-shaped, steep-walled mountain basin carved by glaciation. Crocker Cirque campsite is on the north bank of the Carabassett River. At the bank of the river, I recognized it immediately from one of the pencil drawings the southbound artist had shown us. Ok well, at least it isn't a ford! A single board stretched from one boulder to another was the 'bridge'. It's easy to see if the water level were higher the crossing would be dangerous. I sat on the edge of the river and waited for Driftwood and Lone Wolf to arrive. A day hiking couple showed up, offering their leftover Gatorade while we chatted. I am at peace, enclosed within the rugged terrain of Maine, sitting at the bottom of this cirque. The mountains I crossed today were landmarks, mental giants that lay slain at my feet. I have less than 200 miles left of this journey, and I have finally found what I worked so hard to reach— this place of peace.

S E P T E M B E R   1 2

Driftwood and Lone Wolf and I are sharing a motel room in Stratton, Maine. This small logging town is but a spot in the road, but the food is good, the people are friendly, and the motel is clean. I've enjoyed a long hot bath, a shampoo, a steak dinner and blueberry pie. Our evening has been filled with phone calls to loved ones and plans for summit day. I specifically chose this motel because they have phones in the rooms. My tolerance for difficulty in meeting the most basic of needs is wearing thin. Standing outside at a pay phone just wasn't going to do it this time. After my phone conversation with Adam, I realize he is hesitant about the idea of coming to Maine for the last 50 miles. I must let go of any expectations I may have been entertaining.

S E P T E M B E R   1 3

Safford Notch is between Old Man's Head and Little Bigelow. Coming into the campsite, the trail wound between huge, round boulders, fallen from the cliffs above. It was difficult to be as amazed as we should have been, because by that time, we were racing darkness and rain to make camp. We were late coming off the ridge since the views were just spectacular. Knowing it was the last time we would be at such an elevation again until Katahdin, we were a bit reluctant to head down. The descent was easy compared to the heinous descents we've had in, and since, the Whites, but I tripped and fell anyway. I was going along on a pretty easy grade, doing that downhill thing that always makes me know that someday I am going to plant it, and I tripped. No big deal usually; just catch yourself with your hiking pole and keep going, but this time my number was up. I have no idea where my brain was, but it didn't react. It was one of those falls from childhood when you trip over an untied shoelace and vault yourself into space, breaking the fall with trusty scabbed knees while your mind floats off somewhere above your head and watches, disengaged, until the moment of impact jolts you back to reality. Yeah, so my right knee slammed against a rock and busted open a pretty gash from the impact, embedding lots of dirt and pebbles into it too, just like the good ol' days. I had to wiggle out of my pack before I could get up, and was quite dizzy for a minute or two. But, after my head cleared, I was able to put weight on it, miraculously, and away the three of us went with me leading at my best wounded pace. I guess the guys thought they'd better keep an eye on me from now on. I even tore a hole in my pants! Had I not just put on long pants on the windy ridge, my whole leg would have been shredded.

Rain pattered on the leaves as I set up my tent next to Chou Chou. I fell in the mud going to get water, and by this time I was sulky, low blood sugar and ready to cry. Rain held off, and Driftwood cooked the dinner we had agreed to share, trying something new, a New East angel hair pasta, boxed thing. I felt better after I ate, but then, couldn't find the trail out of their tent site back to mine in the dark. Lone Wolf brought his brighter headlamp and got me headed in the right direction. Finally, I am safe and warm and fed in my tent for the night where hopefully I can cause myself no more bodily harm for a few hours. I have cleaned my knee with the last of my antiseptic wipes and band-aged it. I'm going to be terribly sore in the morning. Rain pattered again softly on the leaves for a brief moment.

Per Lone Wolf, the forecast holds quite a bit of rain on into Friday. We've planned a short day tomorrow, so we can sit in a shelter and wait out the worst if we have to. No hurry now—we are a mere two weeks from Katahdin.

The last three weeks of trail has presented some of the most difficult walking I would have ever imagined. Almost every step has required fore-planning, a task force, and a committee to execute. You get so used to the trail being difficult, you look for the hardest way up a mountain, knowing that's where the trail will be. I will be relieved to be done with the mountains. A few days ago, in a boggy area, I got off the trail by mistake when it crossed an old logging road. I found myself walking on a wide, perfectly level trail with no rocks to trip over, no mud holes, just fallen leaves carpeting soft trail. My first thought was, 'this can't be right!' I turned around, found the last blaze and the turn I'd missed and sure enough, the actual AT paralleled this other, beautiful trail, but the AT was rocky and muddy, proudly sporting the usual incredibly difficult footing. All I could do was laugh. As Rael would say, it's all good.

I still have not seen a moose. I've been in Maine for 10 days and not seen a single moose. Everyone I'm hiking with has seen at least one moose, but I have seen none. Zip. Zero. Nada. No moose for Willow. I'll be the only thru-hiker ever to traverse Maine without seeing a moose. Perhaps, it's all just media hype, and moose don't really exist.

SEPTEMBER 14

With 165.2 miles left, we have passed the 2000 mile mark and are finally over the last big mountains of Bigelow Range. We rather collectively elected to keep going, as the rain was not that big of a deal, spattering off and on here and there. With a little bit of climbing and rock scrambling over Little Bigelow, after lunch at Little Bigelow Lean-to the trail opened up into simple walking. We put down 1.5 miles without even blinking. The rest of the day sailed by, and we were in camp by 3:30pm.

The trail led by the south finger of Flagstaff Lake nestled between two mountains with another mountain centered behind. A loon popped up from an underwater excursion. A few more miles of good trail brought us to West Cary pond, even more beautiful and serene. I set up my sleeping bag in the shelter, stood on my head to fetch water from deep in the box spring, and went down to the edge of the pond to absorb the silvery silence. The surface of the water was as smooth as glass. A loon floated in the middle, then disappeared with barely a ripple. The gray sky was a few shades lighter than the steel iridescence of the water, and the moisture in the air lent a fuzzy softness to the outlines of the trees on the hillsides around the pond. A few bright splashes of maple leaves stood out; the papery flit of a dragonfly's wings cut the silence. A few feet off the shore to the right was the orderly pile of sticks of a beaver lodge. Across the pond, through the trees, light reflected off the tin roof of a cabin. I wondered what it took in life to get to live in a place like this, quietly removed from civilization. I've lived in "a place like this" for six months now—I was moved to deep gratitude for my life and all its blessings.[†]

Driftwood built a fire. In the shelter is Lone Wolf, Driftwood, Chou Chou, Sleepy the Arab and I; BP is tenting. A weekender is also tented nearby. The weekender's exuberance and excited loud chatter ran counter to our pensiveness. His drinking stories didn't amuse any of us, and we all just wished he would shut up and go back to his tent. We dried our wet gear by the fire and talked about what we would miss about being out here, what we missed about home, what music we would listen to first, what goals we accomplished.

There Are No Moose in Maine

For a hiker the Kennebec River is deep, dangerous and wide. Where the Trail reaches its banks, a ferry takes hikers across. I've been excited about this river crossing since planning this hike over a year ago. The "ferry" across the 70-foot-wide Kennebec turned out to be a canoe that takes two hikers at a time and their packs. Steve Longley mans the ferry from 9-11am and from 2-4pm. The ferry is considered to be the official Trail;[†] there is even a white blaze in the bottom of his boat. I rose early to get a head start on the 14 miles to the Kennebec shore. Still hoping to see a moose, I went down to the edge of the water of East Cary Pond at 6am and sat for a little while. I saw the loons again, but no moose.

We arrived at the Kennebec at 2pm; somehow we had hiked 14 miles in only six hours, leaving at 7:10am and stopping for an hour lunch at Pierce Pond. On the way my knee began to give me some seriously sharp pains. The last 3.5 miles of trail was very uneven ground with many roots and not-so-choice footing; twisting and turning my feet to place my steps aggravated my already injured knee.

My maildrop had not yet been delivered to Rivers

and Trails camp store, but a letter from my friend, Sheri, had arrived along with a package of organic, chocolate-covered almonds and coffee beans from another UU family from home, Bette and Robert and Robin. These will be the perfect treat for the 100-mile wilderness!

The Rivers and Trails hostel was not in operation, only the camp store, so Driftwood, Lone Wolf, Chou Chou and I got a ride to the Northern Outdoors facility a few miles up the road and shared the cost of a room in their "logdominium". We ate huge amounts of real food in the restaurant. Driftwood ate an entire rack of ribs and every scrap of fixin's on his plate, plus banana cheesecake for desert—that was a sight to see! I hobbled around as little as possible, trying to give my knee a rest and turned in pretty early.

I did manage to make quite a few phone calls from Northern Outdoors. A courtesy phone that didn't eat up my phone card minutes in pay phone fees was located outside in the front parking lot. I sat in the dirt, leaning up against the building, while Izod-clad college kids came and went in their BMWs and SUVs. Knowing this may be the last time I could contact Adam before the 100-mile wilderness, I called him for the final word on whether or not he would be able to join me. But, Adam's grandmother has passed away in Mississippi, and he is heading south to be with his family. The trip to Mississippi will expend any money he'd saved for Maine, and he would not be able to make it after all. The news about Adam's grandmother was not unexpected, as she had been in failing health for quite some time; however, the reality of having no one from home to celebrate with in Maine is one I had not really considered seriously until this moment. Some part of my family has been with me for so many milestones of this journey, it is hard to believe I will experience the consummate climb alone. Adam soothed my disappointment with a promise to hike the final miles of the Great Smoky National Park with me upon my return. Hopefully, both he and the boys will be able to do a few days with me there, and we can celebrate in Hot Springs in October.

I touched base with Mom and my sister too, catching up with everyone in the family, so they would all know where I was; having access to the courtesy phone was a luxury I had not found anywhere else on the trail, and communication has been sporadic. Mom had bought herself a copy of the *Thru-Hiker's Guide to the Appalachian Trail* has been following along in the book since I was in Virginia so she could read about the places I was staying. "Keep on keepin' on!" she said.

I got up early this morning to call my father; if you don't call him before 7:30 you wont catch him at home. He too has been plotting my progress on his maps, guessing where I might camp each night and updating his timetable each time I check in. He noted where I was and told me he had figured me to be in the Caratunk area by this afternoon. He was pleased to hear I was ahead of schedule. When I was in Stratton, he had warned I'd better hurry, or I would be caught by winter weather at Katahdin. Then, he graciously informed me that he was depositing some money into my bank account to cushion my trip home. I guess I'll always be daddy's girl. The tremor of concern and pride in his voice left me with nothing I could say. This financial buffer erases the last of any worries I could have possibly dreamed up. It seems all I have left to tend to now is reaching my goal.

This morning my knee still feels bruised, sore, and weak. There was a hiker feed at Rivers and Trails camp store, though, so no one was going anywhere until we ate our free food. I took it easy on the knee all morning, and we caught a ride back down to the feed—chili and hot dogs and hamburgers and cakes and candy. My maildrop package arrived, so after a couple of burgers and sodas, I was ready for the two and a half days to Monson. Ranger Dawg and Model T, who were ahead on the trail, caught a ride back south for the feed, and I met Legs, a man who had signed the guest book on my online trail journal in April, wishing me well on my journey. No one had seen Rael. The magnitude of what I have accomplished by reaching Caratunk, Maine buoys me along on a completely empty feeling of no desire—could this be the great Emptiness of which the Buddha speaks?

Steve drove 11 of us back to the trail in his van at 2pm, and we headed off into the woods. We only did 6.5 miles over level ground; I went really slowly, doing only 1.8-2mph. My knee didn't give any sharp pains, but I didn't ask anything of it at all, taking every step carefully, attempting to save strength for the 13.3 planned for tomorrow.

Walking so slowly was actually a great relief. Everyone knew I was taking it easy, and they mercifully went on ahead, so I had time to enjoy the forest. It was an absolutely flawless day, very warm (in the 80s), and sunny skies. The trail led through deciduous forests which I've missed after being in alpine conditions for so long. Maples and birches are beginning to turn and the ground grows more colorful with fallen leaves every day. The red squirrels that live here are busily collecting spruce cones. The squirrels are quite bold; they are slightly larger than a chipmunk and have beautiful reddish gold fur. It took me awhile to figure out they were the source of the racket in the treetops—a long, loud chirrrrr.

Our large group camped at Pleasant Pond. Some stayed in the shelter and some set up tents along the edge of a dirt road that led to the pond. It was a beautiful evening, the air shimmering in the fading light of the day. Knock-Knock waded around in the water skipping stones, entertaining all of us with his stream of consciousness jabber. Some sat on the dock, some on the sandy beach. Evenings are quiet—we are soaking up as much of it as we can, knowing this will soon end.

SEPTEMBER 17

Another perfect day—Driftwood, Lone Wolf, Buzz (a new section hiker addition) and I stopped for lunch at Joe's Hole, an inlet of Moxie Pond. We lay on a small, dilapidated dock and napped in the sun. A couple in an outboard fishing boat came across the water with their springer spaniel perched on the front like a masthead. They waved.

A local guy came down the dirt road on a four-wheeler. He said he could show us Katahdin just up the road. I hopped on the back of the ATV and went with him. He said he was a lobster fisherman; we waved to his wife as we passed his house and waved to all his neighbors out cutting wood. The mountain he so proudly showed me made an impressive silhouette above the lake, but it was not Katahdin—though he seemed quite sure it was. He'd never hiked to the top of Moxie Bald even though he lived in its shadow. He told me the dirt road we were on used to be a railroad bed, and he showed me old telegraph wires still lying in the woods. He pointed out his favorite patch of thick moss and lichens—someone else attracted to such simple beauty. Catching a glimpse into this fisherman's unfettered, country life was an interesting connection with Maine—hopefully, we inspired him also.

Two long downhills were stressful, but most of the day my knee was fine with an ace elastic brace. We've decided to push on into Monson—17.9 miles—tomorrow. Town food is calling, and there's a bed with my name on it. Chou Chou called Monson from the Rivers & Trails camp store the other day and reserved a room for the two of us at a hotel. I am so over this sharing every minute of my day with men that I beseeched her to take pity on me. I even accompanied her to the post office in Caratunk for no other reason than to be with another female for a few precious moments. She gratefully admitted that she feels my pain as well, so we quite happily agreed to be roommates and carve out a little space for ourselves in Monson.

There have been gold colored wooly worms, orange slugs, yellow furry caterpillars, and even deer, but no moose! Deer walked very close to my tent last night. I could hear them snuffling the tent when they went by, at least three, maybe four. Hopefully, early morning by this pond will produce a moose.

I suppose the furry, white caterpillars with a black stripe down their middle have something to do with the black butterfly I saw with white bars on either side of its wing span. Woe unto she who messes with one of these little buggers. I became far too intimately acquainted with one of their kind tonight while I was sitting by the pond. Several caterpillars crawled on the rock where I sat. At first I was "saving" them, letting them crawl on my finger and performing an elevator service to get them back to a tree branch. But then, there were more on my leg; then, they were in my pants' legs. Then, they were in my shirt! Finally, I was forced to abandon my perch and retreat to the tent where I discovered two more hidden in my shirt. Their "fur" appears to have an irritant quality, and I now itch all over.

Once again, at dusk everyone gathered by the water, taking in the quiet beauty with little to say. There is an ambivalence among the hikers that appears to be universal; no one wants this perfect dream to end, and yet, everyone is so tired of walking, so ready for civilization's comforts. Monson is our last town. For that very reason, I will zero there on Tuesday. After Monson, there is only the 100-mile wilderness and Baxter State Park's crowning jewel, Mount Katahdin. I still have made no amazing discoveries, and have no earth-shattering plans for life after the AT. In fact, I'm still just as concerned, if not more so now, about what I will do to make ends meet after I get home. As Lone Wolf so aptly put it as we lay on the dock at Joe's Hole under the September noon, "how can I ever go back to lunch in the office break room again?" When I think of working again, I feel as if I am being dragged back to shackles and chains. I cannot imagine how to find a job that jives with my life, for every job I've ever had has been no more than a means of making a living. I fear the bills will come too fast for me to put much time into starting again. Don't wake me from this dream—not just yet.

S E P T E M B E R   1 8

The West and East Branches of the Piscataquis River were fords, but both turned out to be only ankle to mid-calf deep. Lone Wolf had obsessed over the danger of these fords for miles. His over-concern allowed me to not give them a single thought despite the fact that water crossings had once been high on my list of Maine's major obstacles to fear. He was worrying enough for all five of us. The East Branch had rocks to cross on, but I took my boots off anyway and crossed in my Crocs. One look at the placement of the rocks, and I knew I would fall in trying to stay dry; better to just wade in on purpose. Lone Wolf watched from the other side and just shook his head. Other crossings that were listed in the guidebook as being fords all have had logs or rocks, and the water level was just low enough to easily use these to get across. Finding that the first two fords were not too difficult[†] has been a huge confidence booster for me. I know there will be others in the next 100 miles, but I've been eased into it now, and I'll be fine, I'm sure. There may be nothing left to fear.

I want to spend some of my remaining time alone in the 100-mile wilderness. I've enjoyed (and learned a lot from) the group thing, but I would like to carve out some time for myself during these last nine days of hiking. I'm sure that sounds silly; but, when I think of the harried life I will be returning to in such a short time, these remaining days of silence in the Maine north woods are like drops of gold.

Monson is an old logging town of empty buildings and antique stores. The Lakeshore House is a hotel located above a Laundromat and a bar/restaurant. Our host, Jessica, is the best on the trail. She has agreed to drive us to a larger town tomorrow for a grocery run. I'm showered, laundered, fed, and in my bed. Everyone else is in the living room watching TV.

E V E N I N G —

Furry caterpillar wins this round. I have itched all day and am covered in little red bumps on my belly, hip and thigh where he was in my clothes. I figured out that the hairs came off of him and got into the fabric of my shirt and shorts. I've since washed my clothes at the Lakeshore House, but it seems the bumps are spreading—of course, my scratching isn't helping. Chou Chou said, "Willow, it's always something with you, isn't it?!" How very true, how very true.

SEPTEMBER 19

I haven't had a television in my home since 1992. Under the umbrella of trail kinship, I sat down with everyone else tonight and relaxed in front of the tube—eating. We watched *House* and *Grey's Anatomy*. I was actually entertained and welcomed the reprieve from the past month of thru-hiker drama. If I'm not careful, I could get addicted to this concept of no stress.

Relaxing in Monson seems like it is what I have been meant to do for all of my life. I have been so at peace with this day, with this place, with my hike. A calm has settled over me that would surprise Dirt Diva. No more town stress. No more stress. Period! Stress? What's stress? Speaking of The Team, I received a post card in Monson yesterday when I arrived in town. Those little devils mailed a post card to me in Monson, Maine from Gorham, New Hampshire on a day when I was WITH THEM in town! The front of the card says "Hello!" and is a wonderfully, tacky picture of two, sickeningly adorable kittens. On the back they wrote:

A Special Haiku for You!
Up, Up, Up we go
Many a mountain we climb
Katahdin we end!
Hope your hike is going great! We miss you! 2006 Hiker Reunion
with Twister and board games! Enjoy every last bit of your hike. It's
been outstanding!
The Wonder Twins (~Meow~hiss hiss!)

Their stunt makes me miss their silliness all the more. They are miles ahead now, probably only a few days from summiting. Damn jocks! I hope they have good weather on Katahdin; it's raining today.

Buzz is a section hiker from Texas who has been hiking in the vicinity of our group of thru-hikers quite by chance. He's a quiet soul, content to sit back and observe. It must be really strange to jump in the middle of a bunch of relatively cliquish hikers and attempt to figure out their language of trail jargon, mileage debates and inside jokes. He's staying at the Lakehouse with us, and I spent time with him in the kitchen, chatting and eating. He's a few years older than I, and engaging conversation was welcome. His calm, quiet demeanor must come from his profession. He tells me about his bee-keeping business and, as always, I am intrigued to meet someone who is happy with their life's work and who gleans a solid sense of success from their lives. On the wall behind us is a portrait of Bill Irwin, the blind thru-hiker, a testimony to the perseverance the trail so eloquently draws forth from each of us.

S E P T E M B E R   2 0

The 100-mile Wilderness—trail icon of solitude and symbol of the home stretch. At one time I had great reservations about crossing into its vast borders, but today it seems like just another day on the trail. I'm not quaking in my boots, still just walking. The sign at the entrance to the Wilderness scripted a formidable warning that one should carry 10 days of supplies. Within the first five miles I passed at least seven day hikers, some with no gear with them at all. So much for formidable warnings.

Big Wilson Stream ford was much more of the kind

of ford I had imagined them all to be like in Maine. The deepest water level reached my mid-thigh and lapped at the bottom of my pack. Thankfully, there was only one place in the very middle that deep; the current was strong. Chou Chou stood on the far bank snapping pictures of me as I crossed, in case I washed away and was never heard from again. Lone Wolf and Driftwood were already across as well. Another hiker came up behind me as I was crossing and passed me, in the deepest part of the river, a couple of feet downstream from where I stood immersed and uncertain. His legs were so long the deep water and the current didn't have much effect on his balance...but then, he is 19 and invincible. I appreciated the sense of responsibility for each other within our group and was glad I wasn't crossing this deep water alone.

S E P T E M B E R   2 1

The days grow obviously shorter. I didn't make it into camp tonight until almost dark. It was a long 15.6 miles that reduced me to tears in the last mile. Everyone's tired tonight and on edge. Who was it that said we were done with the mountains? Me? Don't listen to me. A mountain is a mountain no matter what its elevation.

I left my headlamp in my tent when I carried dinner preparations to the shelter, so I just cooked dinner in the dark. I re-hydrated a meal I had found in the hiker box in Monson, hoping for an inspirational change in fare, but I was so hungry, I couldn't wait long enough for it to cook all the way. I wolfed down the crunchy beans and rice and felt my way back to the tent for my head lamp and my TP.

Where's the damn TP? Probably back on the trail

where I last took a break, because it certainly isn't in my pack anymore! "Chou Chou?? Can I use some of your TP? What would I do without other people to help me out? It seems I can't even take care of myself these days!! First it's my knee, then it's caterpillars, now it's toilet paper! What's next? ...Don't answer that!"

I left a note in the shelter register lamenting the loss of my toilet paper, guessing I should at least entertain someone with this misfortune. Chou Chou followed my register entry with one listing her own ailments that ended with "...at least I have my TP!"

SEPTEMBER 22

I caught a first glimpse of Katahdin from Gulf Hagas Mountain—off in the distance, mythical in proportion. A hand-painted "K" and an arrow on a rock in the trail pointed to its profile just visible between some trees to the west.[†]

Sidney Tappan campsite[†] is a small, round, grassy area just off the summit of Gulf Hagas. As the sun went down, the chilly day turned cold; Driftwood started a fire soon after everyone arrived. I sat up late alone by the pile of orange, glowing, hot coals. The night settled. The tinkling of the coals told stories of fires long ago on the frontier of this cold north land, of cabins tucked away behind stacks of cord wood, sheltered for the winter. A breeze played in the tops of the nearby birches, rustling their remaining leaves then scurrying away across the mountain, turning to a soft whisper in the tops of the spruce on the next hillside. From the edge of the tall grass, soft squeaks of mice and rabbits sounded as they scurried about waiting, no doubt, for me to go to bed, so they could investigate closer. Above, the stars were countless, a night sky few people see anymore—jagged silhouette of spruce rimmed the view. One of my last nights in the north woods of Maine.

S E P T E M B E R   2 3

The first words out of Lone Wolf's mouth as he emerged from his tent this morning dressed from head to toe in full Mount Everest expedition gear were "I hate to say this, but it's supposed to rain all day today!" Never mind the fact that the cloud cover had raised the temperature greatly during the night making it quite comfortable, and that it was not currently raining. He took off up the trail before I ever even had my tent down. Chou Chou and I dilly dallied.

The rain didn't actually start until we were coming down the north side of White Cap Mountain, several miles into our day. The descent was a long staircase built of boulders positioned into the mountainside, a welcome and unexpected alternative to scrambling down a steep mountainside in the mud. We caught up with Lone Wolf at our first break at Logan Brook Lean-to; by this time the rain had let up briefly. The approach to the Lean-to on the trail afforded a back-side view of the log shelter fronted by a flowing creek and a steep mountainside all enshrouded in fog; it looked like a picture and didn't seem real.

Post Card arrived soon after; he cheerfully sang out that he had a present for me and produced my Ziploc bag of TP! He had found it on the trail the day before and had read our quips in the register. My dignity has been restored. His humor and smiling face was a welcome deviance from the sourness of our group of late. We've been together far too many miles. Post Card was one of the hikers that was miles ahead of me in the beginning, and would have summited a month ago, but he had suffered a broken wrist on a fall and was now back on the trail after his recovery. I had not met him before but had seen his entries in the registers most of the way. Strange to still be making new acquaintances after 2000 miles. He promised the next 20 miles would be flat and fast terrain, and then he loped off up the trail at his usual four mph pace. It was easy to see why I had never met him before.

Chou Chou and I arrived at Cooper Brook Falls Lean-to just before dark again, exhausted and wet. Lone Wolf and Driftwood had both elected to do more miles in the rain and were not there. Post Card had snagged the last spot in the small shelter with Buzz and Model T and Ranger Dawg. I visited with them after setting up my tent in the rain. Chuckbuster, a friend of Post Card's, tented next to Chou Chou and me, and just as dark was settling in Sleepy the Arab showed up and set up his tent also.

I lay in my tent and talked to Chuckbuster through the tent walls while he cooked his dinner. Something about the sound of his stove registered in the far reaches of my brain..."that wouldn't happen to be a Svea stove would it?" "Yep; I've had this stove for years; they're virtually indestructible," he replied. My friend Walter had used a Svea 22 years ago when I first began backpacking with him. I had one at home but had not considered it, because of its weight. I hadn't seen anyone use one on the trail at all. Turns out, I had met Chuckbuster in Pennsylvania; he recognized me, but I did not recognize him. He had been sitting by the trail eating his lunch when Switch and I had happened along. Once he told me, I remembered the day; we couldn't find where the trail picked up again after a campsite clearing. While we milled around looking for it, Chuckbuster had watched us silently. Nervous by his presence, I had not spoken to him, but now, here I was tenting next to him reliving our pasts and getting better acquainted.

Even though a cold drizzle came down most of the day, I hiked in just a long sleeve, capilene shirt. Moving generates enough body heat to evaporate the moisture as you hike. It sure beats sweating to death in a rain jacket.[†]

S E P T E M B E R   2 4

White House Landing[†] is a beautiful oasis, an old logging camp on the bank of the Nahmakanta Stream. Bring your wallet if you come, though, because the owners are keenly aware of their advantage, being that their camp is the only vestige of civilization for miles and miles of wilderness. Chou Chou and I elected to share a private cabin to pay homage to our impelling desire for space from the men. I showered by candle-light in the small wooden shower house, contented with this luxury no matter how rustic its presentation. The water dribbled from the shower head as if gravity fed, but it was warm and felt good.

To get to the Lodge and the cabins, which are across the water from the trail, one must give a blast on the air horn that hangs by a string from a tree by the dock. And then, per the instructions on the sign, you wait.[†]The sign specifically states you are to only blow the air horn one time, or else. Sleepy the Arab arrived later in the day; he was alone on the dock and could see all of us from across the water. He blew the horn. No one came for him. He waited. 10 minutes passed, and still he was waiting for the boat to come across to pick him up. Sleepy's patience wore thin, and he committed the sin of blowing the air horn a second time. This sealed his fate for another 15 minutes of waiting time, per the rules. He finally arrived on shore at the Lodge, chagrined by his "punishment", but smiling.

❀ ❀ ❀

Inside the Lodge, everyone packed newly purchased provisions into their packs, studied their receipts and settled their tabs. I heard someone calling, "Willow!! Get Willow!" Outside, Vegemite came scurrying up the hill from the lake. "Willow, come quick! There are moose across the lake!" Chou Chou stood on the lake shore. I accompanied Vegemite to her side and squinted into the late morning glare of sunshine on the water, trying to follow the direction of her point. Wayyy over on the other side of the lake, probably three quarters of a mile away, two moose meandered along the water's edge briefly before disappearing into the woods. Discerning their dark silhouettes against the equally dark forestline was difficult at best. Chou Chou and Vegemite and I debated whether such remote moving specks should actually count as me "seeing" a moose. At such a great distance, I argued they could be apparitions, mere tricks of the light. In the end, I had to concede to the sighting, anti-climactic as it was. I thanked the girls for looking out for my moose deficiencies as best they could.

S E P T E M B E R   2 6

I thought I was the last to arrive in camp last night, but as I visited with Driftwood over dinner by the door of my tent, Buzz came strolling in by headlamp just as darkness prevailed. Our tent city took up a large section of pine forest behind Rainbow Stream Lean-to. The lean-to was full also. The terrain was flat, but it was not fast. The trail wound around each lake, turning this way and that, carving an infuriatingly indirect path toward Katahdin. At times it headed south, then west, then north for a little way, then south again, then east. Rocks and roots dominated the trail and walking was impossibly challenging.

At the last shelter on the AT, we took a collective break. Everyone gathered around the Hurd Brook Lean-to trail register, entering their last ruminant or poetic remarks and messages to those still behind us. I felt an overpowering restlessness that would not allow me to just hang out and be sentimental. I jotted a brief message to Rael and one to Linc and Jeannie and headed out for Abol Bridge campground.[†]

At Abol Bridge, Katahdin looms on the near horizon, dominating the landscape. The camp store is abuzz with activity from local hunters. A pickup truck sits in front of the store loaded with the quartered body of a moose. This wasn't exactly the way I pictured encountering a moose either, but a moose it was, up close[†]and personal nonetheless. Maine's Moose Management must have requested a more graphic presentation since I had not been satisfied with spirit-moose on the lakeshore. There are sandwiches in the camp store, hot coffee, danishes and various trail foods. I purchased only enough food to get me through the next day—one day to reach The Birches (a thru-hiker only trail shelter at the base of Katahdin) and breakfast and snacks for summit day. If I am delayed due to weather, I guess I will be hungry.

We were in camp early enough to enjoy the rest of the afternoon, so I moseyed off to the pay showers with a prize pack towel Veggie let me borrow. A shower with a towel is always a good thing. Drying off with your dirty bandana loses its appeal after a few months. It took me several tries to wrestle water out of the ancient coin-operated shower stall. After two tries didn't take, I wondered if I would be getting a shower after all. I'm standing there butt-naked in 40 degree weather in a concrete bath house in Maine in September talking to a rusting mechanical box. 'Ok, is this age discrimination, or what? I know Veggie got this thing to work! Am I on candid camera?' I began to rationalize that I didn't really need a shower since I'd had one two days ago when the last spin on the dial registered somewhere deep in the bowels of the clanging mechanism, and hot water sprayed down.

When I emerged triumphant from the shower house and walked back across the campground, everyone was gathered around a fire Driftwood had built. A shout rang out, "Willer!" There in the midst of everyone was Dirt Diva and Compass Rose here to wish everyone a Happy Summit Day and to share pictures of their summit two days before. We hugged and danced around while they excitedly related their tales of the harrowing climb up Katahdin. "Tell me, how bad of a climb is it, really?" I asked Compass Rose. Her eyes glazed over, and she made a sour face. "That bad, huh?" I laughed. "Look!" she exclaimed, and she produced her camera. She had videotaped her approach to the infamous sign that stands atop the mountain marking the northern terminus of this epic trail. I watched the short movie of her final trail moments and felt a stabbing pain pass through my heart. Oh my god, this is going to be over day after tomorrow. Her trip has already ended, and here she stands before me talking about the trail in past tense. The weight of her accomplishment was starkly evident in the video of her walk to the sign. The camera had captured her reverence, her tears and her exultation—captured it all. I was delighted these two strong young women had been a part of my trail experience. Though I wished I could have shared their summit moment with them, I appreciated their thoughtfulness in coming back to Abol Bridge to wish us well. We would always have these memories to cement our friendships. They left with my promise to send them homemade cookies.

Driftwood disappeared into the darkness and reappeared with a long-dead Christmas tree in tow. The frenzied blaze leapt into the air and sparks rained around us. We each shared our given names, names that sounded hollow and meaningless after answering to trail names for the past six months. It was as if we were revealing secret identities as espionage agents or something, clues to our unknown lives far from this hallowed circle, far from this warped microcosmic reality. These were the names of strangers, vapid reminders of the inane world we had left behind. An air of hushed anticipation laced with a pervasive calm settled over everyone. It's a cold night.

Clearest Water

"The Appalachian Trail, eternal in its being, timeless in its lure, unfeeling in the experience it delivers, is not impressed by those who think they will conquer it. The AT is not something that exists to be conquered."

—LYNN SETZER

S E P T E M B E R   2 7

The sun is shining; fleecy white clouds float in an azure sky. The reflection of Katahdin shimmers in first Oxbow Lake, then Daicey Pond, Elbow Pond, Tracy Pond—landmarks on the final approach to the base of the looming mountain.[†]

I left Abol Bridge a little after 9am. The trail was flat and easy footing, following Nesowadnehunk Stream most of the way into Baxter State Park with many beautiful pools and waterfalls that beckoned for us to stop and picnic or swim or just sit and do nothing. I found myself daydreaming of my family being here, and that Adam and I were watching the boys play in the waterfalls and pools and ride inner-tubes in the shallow rapids. This last 10 miles inside Baxter was such fine hiking it seemed as if it were set up this way as a sort of victory lap. The walking was pleasant and my pack light with only one day's worth of food. I arrived at The Birches a little after 1pm with Chou Chou, Brownie and Soulman. Though the sun is shining, I have chosen to rest in the shelter for awhile, basking in the quiet of a little time away from the group.

Words do not do justice to the emotion of a thru-hiker at Katahdin. We've all come so far and it has taken so long, no one can really believe we are here. At first, a few weeks back, we would randomly look at one another and say, "We're in Maine!!" Now, it's "We're at Katahdin!" But now, Compass Rose and Dirt Diva are on their way home; the finale is almost eclipsed by the gravity of life after the trail; it is so joyous and so monumentally sad all at the same time. Tomorrow, I will summit, and my hike will be over. This crazy, 21-year-old dream will be just a memory.

As I walked the first few miles into the park this morning, I pondered the white blaze and how it has guided me on this whole amazing journey. Although there will not be any white blazes when I return home, I trust the way will somehow reveal itself once I reach the right place on the path as it has all these long months on the trail. Descending Chairback Mountain in the 100-mile wilderness on the first day of fall, I looked ahead down a jumble of rocks for the next white blaze. The descent was steep and nothing but a pile of boulders at all angles; the blazes had been painted directly onto the rocks on the summit, but now I did not see any. I gained a decent place to balance for a moment and stood still, looking for a blaze before I chose which rock to move to next. Slowly, a small, intentional pile of rocks became distinguishable among the random array. No blaze, but a cairn. I smiled as I continued picking my way down the mountain, realizing it isn't always going to be what we expect to see that points the way down the trail; the path may unfold in ways we don't anticipate at the time. I must hold this in mind for the days after I finish—faith that what comes next will be revealed all in good time.[†]

SEPTEMBER 28

I summited Katahdin at 11:15am, starting my climb at 7:30 in the morning. The weather was cloudy and cool. On top was a cold condensation and a bitter wind. I was so psyched to be climbing Katahdin that the climb seemed easy compared to my expectations. Maybe I thought it was going to be like climbing Mount Everest or something. I took my time, letting almost everyone leave camp ahead of me. As the incline increased and more boulders presented themselves in the path, I became more relaxed. Recalling the Whites and the exhilaration that had inspired, I was thrilled that Katahdin's climbing was similar. Apprehension melted.

I passed a few people, then stopped to add layers of clothing as the air got colder and the wind kicked up. Visibility was only about 50 feet. In places I could sense the open spans that stretched out below on a few open face climbs. I was enveloped in a dense cloud. Vertigo probably would have changed my perspective of the climb had I been able to see just how much of a drop there was. Moisture beaded on my clothes and hair.

The closer to the top, the more the wind blew. At the Tableland, no more gargantuan boulders blocked the wind, and the temperature dropped tremendously. The Tableland is a huge wasteland of small boulders the path winds its way over; the incline here is insignificant, and you are mostly walking and boulder hopping. There were boulder stairs close to the top, and the incline picked back up for the last half mile. Visibility was only a few yards.

I saw people gathered around the sign before I saw

the sign itself. I was surprised that I was already at the top. The climb up seemed so short, so easy, so already over? I heard Chou Chou yell out "WILLER!" over the dull roar of the wind. She had kept the spirit of Compass Rose and Dirt Diva alive like a true team recruit.

Fierce wind made the peak incredibly cold. I put on two extra layers. Driftwood snapped my summit photo right away, and then I found a spot behind a boulder and huddled there out of the wind. For some reason I wasn't into having 20 photos of myself taken at the sign. I had him take the one picture and hoped it came out well—an obscure form of denial maybe? I ate the sandwich I had carried up, a protein bar, a Slim Jim, a fudge round, m&ms, and a granola bar. A bunch of us hunkered by the boulder to get out of the wind. There was a flurry of picture-taking, then huddling out of the wind to warm up again, then another flurry of picture-taking. I crawled out from behind the rock to take a few pictures of some of my friends on the sign, and then huddled again. My hands were so cold I could hardly work the cameras people handed me; I had left my gloves at the ranger station with the rest of my gear. Driftwood loaned me his glove liners, and he wore his glove shells. That saved my hands, but the rest of me had gotten so cold I was losing the ability to move nimbly at all. My time was up, and I would have to start down soon or freeze to death.[†]

As I walked down, I felt astounded. Nothing seemed real. I passed other hikers, all working their way toward the top, and congratulated them since I wouldn't be with them at their summit. Most were hikers I had hiked with at various times along the way; some I'd not seen for a month or more. My words sounded like a script I was hearing someone else read.

I walked alone for awhile, then Driftwood caught up, and we made the climb down together which was a really nice ending. I had so enjoyed hiking with Driftwood those few days out of Grafton Notch, and this would be our last chance to reconnect before parting ways. We had fun with our descent, finding new ways to climb down rather than reversing the same techniques used to climb up, chatting all the way about our families and our hike, thoughts gradually turning toward home.

Sleepy the Arab was resting on the trail about a mile below tree line, and we stopped and sat with him, sheltered and below the cloud cover. From here we could look out over the mountains and see patches of sunshine moving over the distant hillsides and bright splotches of color in places where the leaves had already changed. We snacked and talked. Lone Wolf paused with us. Everyone that passed our resting spot was pensive and quiet.

Driftwood, Lone Wolf, Sleepy and I descended farther and stood on the bridge at Katahdin Stream; the water was sparkling and crystal clear. The enormity of the idea that one must remove oneself from society for months at a time to achieve this sense of calm, this feeling of peace and oneness with the earth was contained somehow in the water's crystalline shimmer. Will I ever feel this "at peace" again in my life? Consciously, I cherished this moment of accomplishment and personal satisfaction, for already it was receding somewhat under the weight of responsibilities hulking just outside the gates of Baxter. "Isn't that the clearest water we've seen on the trail?" My companions' silence conveyed a shared longing, as each of us stared wistfully into the water's depth.

S E P T E M B E R   2 9

Fleeting notions that something is amiss surface here and there unexpectedly. The first to jostle its way into conscious thought occurred in the backseat of Sleepy the Arab's father's sports car as we sped away from Baxter State Park. I turned to look at the sunset through the back window, and suddenly was keenly aware of leaving something behind, some very important piece of my life was fading with the sun in the distance. I refused to honor this sentiment as my eyes filled with tears; instead, I turned back to rejoin the conversation in the claustrophobic interior of the small speeding car, wondering if I would get carsick on the winding roads, marveling at how fast everything was going by.

The Appalachian Trail Inn is housed in a huge farmhouse built in 1901 on the main street of the small paper mill town of Millinocket, Maine. Three stories of narrow staircases and a maze of rooms and hallways creak invitingly of decades of weary lumbermen, clandestine trysts, frazzled families, and worldly boarders. Faded, flower print wallpaper and dark wood lend a sultry, overly familiar warmth to the interior. Buzz and I secured an attic room with Sleepy the Arab, dumped out our gear and had a beer at the Blue Ox while our laundry washed next door at the laundromat. It is good to shower, do laundry and eat, as it always is in town, but the exceptionality of these luxuries was left behind in the boreal hush of the north woods. Gone is the feeling of voracious satisfaction that comes from knowing this meal is one of only two you may have in a week's time; there is no feeling of novelty to the hot shower since most likely there will be more showers more often now, and there is no desperation to get into clean clothes as clean clothes are once again an everyday expectation.

Eventually, a number of people we'd hiked with over the past few weeks gathered in the back of the bar around the pool tables. I found myself strangely aware of my age difference and more self-conscious in this crowded, loud, social setting. A giant, carved, wooden, cartoon moose stood on its hind legs behind our table, grinning at his own contribution to my pseudo-moose sightings. Ghosts from various bar rooms over the course of a lifetime whispered in my ear, but that young woman was far from this older one I have become. When E-Rock handed me a pool cue, it was as if I'd never held one before; I missed the cue ball altogether, successfully sealing myself out of the game and defining for myself that somehow things are different. Veggie and I whispered about the cute young men, men that seem even younger to me now. Somehow along the way, I've crossed an invisible threshold. 'So this is 40?' Veggie's surprise at my age only echoed my own surprise at finding myself there, at a bar in Millinocket, Maine. In the ladies room, the absurdity of the evening was punctuated by the oddity of tandem toilets with no dividing wall and a bathroom door that opened wide into the main room of the bar. Veggie and I had a good laugh; she returned to the pool table and I to the rambling, old, boarding house on the corner.

BackBone

Celebration is not in order until I actually hike the final miles of the Trail skipped in March after my knee injury. I am singularly focused on this goal, despite the excitement of visiting with family and friends. I will not accept the title of thru-hiker without having finished, and after hiking for so many months, I cannot put down my expectation of completion. Little did I realize just how complicated being immersed in home life was going to make this last section.

The idea that Adam and the boys would hike with me was immediately hedged by the inevitability of school for the boys. To accommodate the school's lack of willingness to view the hike as a learning experience, our plan was amended to include them on the weekend for the last section of trail walking into Hot Springs. Celebrating my "summit" in this quintessential trail town will be almost as appropriate as celebrating in Millinocket, Maine, especially since it is so close to home.

Adam and I packed separately. I offered to do a "shakedown" of his pack to help with his final pack weight. Although he was interested in my input, his years of hiking experience working for a juvenile wilderness camp gave him a wealth of knowledge that dwarfed my six months of trail experience. My own routine was streamlined after months of prepping in strange towns and accepting limited resources as par for the course. After several delays, by the time Adam was ready to go the sun was high. In the woods, this would translate into setting up the tent and cooking in the dark. My impatience was barely contained by a brain in full throes of endorphin withdrawal. Since coming off the routine of hiking for 8-10 hours a day my muscles had been cramping and burning, screaming for the abuse. At times I had to go for a run just to quell the jitters. The shakedown of Adam's pack was forgone in favor of getting on the road.

At the Cades Cove entrance to Great Smokies Park, we pulled into the camp parking lot after dark only to be greeted almost immediately by a park ranger who pulled up in a pickup truck. She explained that I am no longer considered a thru-hiker, as the park definition of thru-hiker is someone who approaches the park on foot for a distance of 100 miles or more and leaves the park on foot. This lack of distinction meant I did not have the status needed to be allowed to stay at trail shelters without a reservation. She explained we would need to exit the park, drive 20 miles away to a pay campground and stay there; then, in the morning, we would be required to register for the shelters where we intended to camp during our hike through the Smokies. She drove off. I stood by the car in disbelief, reeling from culture shock. The sound of her truck approaching again lured me back to my senses. She pulled alongside and offered a piece of paper and a pen to register our shelters with her tonight, saying she would turn the paper in for us in the morning. I had not planned which shelters we would be at, since I had no way to gauge how many miles Adam would be able to hike; we quickly pulled out the map of the park and jotted down shelters for the next five nights. She warned some might be full already, in which case, we would be in violation; yet, she had no way to tell us which ones were already full. The compounding complexity was made even more macabre by the late hour; it was almost midnight. We drove to the campground to pay to camp, the only time I paid to camp the entire 2000 miles of the Trail.

We left a restless night behind in a misty, mountain dawn and drove back to Cades Cove parking lot. A rabbit darted out from lush greenery on the right of the road and met an untimely death beneath the wheels of the car. I pulled over and cried. Nothing was going right. In comparison to the beauty and flowing peacefulness of Mount Katahdin, this final section of trail in these sacred Cherokee mountains was haunted with turmoil and doubt. I had to force myself to continue with the plan.

Parked at Cades Cove, I questioned whether the rangers would investigate once the car had been there for a few days; I was angered by the criminalization of camping on federal land. A bear meandered through the campground, making morning rounds of garbage cans. Adam's excitement over seeing the bear accentuated my own relative indifference. I'd seen so many bears during the last six months, their presence was expected. If anything, its appearance was a constant that reassured me all was not lost.

As the incline increased, Adam lost momentum. Matching one's pace to another's can be a challenge. Hikers that hiked 'together' didn't actually walk together often; hikers navigated sections of trail at their own individual pace, reconvening at shelters or nice break spots along the way, like a spring or a shelter. Even couples like Linc and Jeanne were often a quarter mile apart on trail. But, Adam's experience as a juvenile camp counselor dictated everyone stay together. Seeing me hike away up the mountain without him was unexpected for him. His pack was obviously overloaded by thru-hiker standards, for Adam had to be a much stronger hiker than he was displaying. I was intensely frustrated by his insistence that I wait for him, and I was somehow unable to communicate six months worth of hiking etiquette. Instead of climbing to a plateau for a breather, Adam stopped mid-incline, declaring he was taking a break. He opened his pack and proceeded to remove numerous items, searching for something. I leaned on my hiking poles studying the wastefulness of his actions, ticking off precious daylight hiking minutes lost, thinking of the 15 miles to go before we reached the shelter where the rangers expected us to camp legally. For some reason, the urgency of the mileage required was not making an impression on Adam, and I simply could not understand why. Underway again, my attempts to explain trail culture and time management fell short of instilling any thru-hiker motivation. The importance of what I was trying to convey was out of context for Adam. Our perspectives on hiking were worlds apart, each born from different hiking cultures. He had no thru-hiker agenda, no mileage timelines, no goal; he was a backpacker not a thru-hiker, and to him this was a camping trip.[†]

On Thunderhead Mountain he turned back, declaring he was not doing this if it was not going to be fun. I raged that had he bothered to read my trail journals online for the last six months he would know that hiking 10 hours a day was not all fun and games.

Survival at 6000 feet in the Smokies in the fall was prominently on my mind. Adam carried the stove and our two person tent. I did not have my tent with me. The additional weight of the larger tent would be too much for my ultra-lite pack, plus food, water and stove. There was no choice other than us both turning back or both of us continuing. If he was coming, he would have to kick it up a notch, or we would not make it 93 miles in a week to Hot Springs to meet the boys. Or...I would have to let go of my expectation of finishing this week. Our raised voices were swallowed by the vastness of Thunderhead. The reality of dwindling daylight hours versus giant mountains between us and the car convinced him that the 4.5 more miles to shelter was wisest. Once at Derrick Knob Shelter, the presence of other campers diffused our mini-drama, removing its immediacy and bearing us into the next day.

Clingman's Dome is the highest mountain on the Appalachian Trail, an impressive 6643 feet, the third highest peak east of the Mississippi. Much of its elevation is matched by the ridges and mountains that surround it, and the climb up from Cades Cove boasts 2461 feet of this gain. This "first" day's hike had been no joke at 4.8 miles from the parking lot to Russell Field Shelter and 9.2 trail miles with 1167 feet of elevation gain up to Thunderhead. The Whites of New Hampshire had represented a great unknown for me in the first few months of hiking, and I feared them; once experienced, however, their mystery infused me with energy and enthusiasm, feeding the rest of my journey north. These peaks of the Great Smoky Mountains have stalwartly stood in defiance of my feeble human attempts to embrace their challenge, first sending me home with injury and now threatening my second attempt with failure as well. Therein lies the mysterious power of this ancient land. The Cherokee people knew of this power and held these mountains sacred, only climbing their peaks for matters of the spirit. Bring your strength; bring courage. Leave all desire, all attachment. This is no place for will. This is not shelter. These are the mountains I have summoned. This path is harsh; its lessons painful. Its rewards come only through offerings of sweat and tears, and quite often when stripped bare, we are left facing the ugly truth about ourselves. Our civilized lives are all about comfort and ease; we avoid challenges and difficulty; we want things to be free, to be easy. Even my 10 hour days of hiking had lulled me into a place of unconventional comfort. This mountain was rising before me now, beckoning, commanding of me a higher self, pushing me to my knees, to humility.

Over the course of this journey that had begun in a plane over Hickory Nut Gorge, my inner strength had developed in more ways than I even knew at the time. Self-reliance had replaced co-dependency. The definition of difficult had narrowed and tolerance for pain broadened. Everyday necessities in any other context had become mere luxuries to be sacrificed in favor of reaching this singular goal. In short, the caliber of faith in myself that I carried far outstripped any semblance of the person Adam had known for so many years. Now, the respect I had sought from him in my endeavors was present, and it was my turn to concede. We struggled with the blending of old and new, stale and fresh, learned and wished for. Walking became the mantra once again, as it had for 2000 miles. I silenced my agenda.

Our second day spawned a tentative exploration of this new way of being together. We hiked 9.6 miles, some together, some separately. Less than a mile from Clingman's Dome on the second night, Adam and I stealth camped with plans to catch the sunrise from its peak. In the pre-dawn chill on the tower round, we stood together silently. A burnished autumn sunrise crept across the Blue Ridge horizon, a deep midnight blue with the red-gold glow of the great orb slicing the darkness open.[†]

Somewhere between our drama on Thunderhead and sunrise on Clingman's Dome the plan was completely rewritten. Blisters Adam developed on the first day had slowed him further, and we were already short of the miles necessary to finish by the weekend. At Newfound Gap on our third day, where highway 441 crosses the trail, we hitched a ride back to the car. We left the park behind and drove to Standing Bear Farm, a trail hostel just to the north of the Smokies where Adam could regroup. The mileage and the climbs had offered him a clearer understanding of my entreaties regarding pack weight and time management. A thorough pack shakedown changed his whole attitude. He dropped pounds from his pack, and I was shocked at what he had been carrying—everything from a battery-powered electric razor to several books to five full changes of clothes. At Standing Bear Farm, we slept in a cabin[†], cooked pizza in their hiker kitchen, showered, bandaged Adam's feet, and visited with other hikers. Back on the trail the next morning and freed from his burden, Adam moved at the pace I had originally anticipated. Two short days and one 15.5 mile day brought us into Hot Springs.

Engraved plaques embedded in the sidewalk mark the AT as it enters the southern edge of this remote, mountain town. I cried when I saw them. Attachment is a tenacious beast. This road walk was supposed to be a family victory lap, with a dual celebration at the Paddler's Pub of Grayson's birthday and my trail finale. Instead, the boys are not here, and Adam and I are going home. The end of this hike eludes me still. Along the Great Smoky ridges, 33.7 unfinished miles whisper like the memory of something left behind that needs to be retrieved. Adam did not grasp the scope of my disenchantment. Tears abated into silence.

OCTOBER 16

GREAT SMOKY MOUNTAINS
NATIONAL PARK, NEWFOUND GAP

It took four miles for the noise in my head to cease. Once my thoughts settled into a rhythm, I opened up and really started to move. Mostly, the quiet in my mind is what I am seeking. I don't know if it's the flow of endorphins that makes me feel so peacefully content or if it's the meditative monotony of walking the trail. But I'm certain that I feel so very different out here now than I have for this past week of being back in the real world. All of the issues of being home have fallen away and seem so distant; out here it is so easy to understand that all things arrive in their own time.

I am strangely fed by the unexplained, wild energy that courses through the ley lines of the earth here. Walking the backbone of these mountains calls to mind that this ancient ravaged place is a fold in the earth's surface, a fold created when geological pressures crushed the continental plates together millennia ago. A fold. A place of great change. Fierce winds accompany me along this mountain apex of potential—wind, omnipotent agent of change. Acceptance and peace wash over me. Quietly, I walk.

TRI CORNER KNOB SHELTER

The day was overcast and windy but not very cold. As I neared the shelter, a spitting rain began to fall. I arrived at 4:50pm doing 15.6 miles in six hours and 20 minutes with a few sight-seeing stops along the way. Satisfied.

OCTOBER 17

Intense wind raged all night. When I left the shelter at 8:20am, the other vacationing hikers that spent the night were still in their sleeping bags with no plans to go anywhere anytime soon. Wind howled and rain pelted the roof and sides of the shelter intermittently. Being on the leeward side of the ridge, I knew as soon as the trail traversed to the other side the wind and rain would be less severe. The trail had crossed the ridgeline many times yesterday, so I was counting on today being more of the same.

The wind was frighteningly fierce racing up the southeastern side of the ridge and slamming over the ridgeline. Still high in the clouds, rain pelted my face so sharply, I was forced to turn my head slightly sideways in order to see. Despite all this, I was hiking fast and was not cold. I wore full rain gear, seldom needed on the entire hike.

Once below the clouds, the rest of the day was dry and warm with a beautiful, overcast, gray sky painted richly in layers of clouds. I struggled to get my mind around the concept that this long journey was going to end. At Davenport Shelter, I stopped just to be stopping at the last shelter...for the last time. I sat there, alone at this rundown, older shelter for quite awhile, recognizing this quiet end for what it was and nothing more. Suddenly, I was ready for it to be over. I accepted it and was not sad, only ready. I lifted my pack onto my back one last time and left.

The last of the miles ended at 5:30pm where the trail crosses Green Corner Road, 200 yards from Standing Bear Farm. The same silence I'd hiked in all day enveloped me. No one cheered. I took no picture.

My warm house is like a womb. I am numb.

O C T O B E R   2 0

A cool, autumn breeze rustles the curtain at the living room window; outside, burnished leaves float to the ground. The color on the mountainsides, a full three weeks after my summit, is now reaching the level of color in Maine during the end of September. My mind is in full resistance to processing the completion of the hike. I still feel as if somehow it will continue, that there are still miles to go, that there's another state, or that I'm just taking a few zero days. Though I am at home and becoming more settled each day in my space and more comfortable with off trail demands on my mind and time, my comfort zone still lies on the AT. Only when I find myself daydreaming of things that happened, or steadily walking the trail in my mind, do I feel a sense of peace. It descends over me sound-lessly, effortlessly and completely then, and I can feel my new stressors slink away to hide in shadows of uncertainty. Unconsciously, my body posture changes; I hold my head higher, my back straighter and my shoulders relax. Briefly, I am filled with joy; but then, confused sadness creeps in, for I fear I have lost my way. The blazes no longer lead north; indeed, the blazes are not there at all. In their places lurk deadlines, appointments, red lights, and busy signals. Gone are the hours of contemplation, the single goal, and the silence. I find my mind racing, wheels spinning, seeking, seeking: what have I forgotten? Where should I be? What needs to be done next?

Yoga Sutra 2.10 states, "In their subtle form, these causes of suffering are subdued by seeing where they come from." Being home has reinstated the old patterns of feeling as if every minute of every day I must be busily accomplishing something. But, my trail-conditioned single-mind has been slow to make that adjustment. Instead of embracing my new multi-tasking handicap, I've been condemning myself for not being able to jump back in the game and pick up right where I left off. Therein, I'm sure, lies the source of my sadness.

This misplaced energy brings to mind the misfortune of the little mouse who got into my things in the storage unit while I was away. There was a sheaf of wheat that had lain in a basket in my living room as a decoration; it was packed away in a box along with the basket. This industrious mouse had diligently removed every grain of wheat from the chaff and moved them one by one, unfortunately, not to his own home for safekeeping, but to yet another box in said storage unit. We both lose.

The surface of the water glassy, the black lines on the bottom almost standing still—warm water closes over my head. My body has cried out for release of stifled energy, screamed for the endorphin high for weeks since my return home. Arms beneath the water stroke tentatively, almost lovingly, through the warm water; my body follows; legs last to engage motion, push off from the side, kicking easily into rhythm. Mind falls silent. I reach the far side of the pool fully submerged in the ecstasy of physical motion. Turn; push off. Still there is nothing. Silent mind. Arms together and forward; stroke out. The black blaze dances on the bottom of the pool. Arms together and forward; stroke out. Can this be all there is to peace, this space of mind/body union? The White Mountains of

New Hampshire shimmer on the bottom of the pool. Wall; turn. Freestyle. The sound of 100,000 gallons of water envelopes my senses as I hold my breath for one, two, three strokes and turn my head to breathe in, first on the left; then, one, two, three strokes, then on the right. No mind. Here I have found peace, immersed in the pale blue water.

ABOUT THE AUTHOR

Amy Allen holds a B.A. in Interdisciplinary Studies from Appalachian State University with a concentration in Anthropology and an English minor. She has over 28 years experience backpacking and hiking. This is her first book. She lives in Western North Carolina with her husband, Karl Allen, and Pachinko, the cat. Amy continues long-distance hiking and has completed the Foothills Trail, the Black Mountain Crest Trail and parts of the Benton MacKaye Trail.

CPSIA information can be obtained at www.ICGtesting.com
Printed in the USA
LVOW10s1917200515

439244LV00004B/161/P